The Absurdity Principle

Common Nonsense in Modern Society

Book One
of the
Screwball Trilogy

by Gary Gentile

Bellerophon Bookworks

Bellerophon Bookworks
3 Lehigh Gorge Drive
Jim Thorpe, PA 18229

Additional copies of this book may be purchased from the same address by sending a check or money order in the amount of $20 U.S. for each copy (plus $4 postage per order, not per book, in the U.S. Inquire for shipping cost to foreign countries). Alternatively, copies may be purchased from the author's website, and paid by credit card:

http://www.ggentile.com

The front cover photograph was taken by the author.

International Standard Book Numbers (ISBN)
1-883056-43-8
978-1-883056-43-8

First Edition

Printed in U.S.A.

CONTENTS

PREAMBLE
Preposterous Poses and Postures

A Rose by Any Other Name . . .

Various dictionaries define the adjective "absurd" in a number of ways: "contrary to common sense or sound judgment," "logically impossible," "utterly opposed to truth or reason," "ridiculously unreasonable, unsound, or incongruous," "having no rational or orderly relationship to human life," "laughably foolish or false," "utterly or obviously senseless, illogical, or untrue."

Absurdity is the quality of being absurd. I define modern absurdity as "any human action that transcends the bounds of logic or reason," "any condition in which logic and rational thought yield to preposterous incongruity," "any situation in which an incidental cause leads to an irrational effect," "any resolution in which reason and logic are not the sole determinants."

I could go on, but you get the point.

In today's society, absurdity is alive, well, and growing by leaps and bounds.

Worse than that, people routinely accept absurdities without comment, or without making any attempt to correct them. I will go as far as to state that many people cannot even recognize absurdities: they accept absurd circumstances the way they accept the law of gravity, as something that exists beyond their comprehension and beyond their ability to control.

. . . Would Smell Like Heresy

It is wrong to permit absurdities to persist.

Most people can be made to acknowledge absurdities when they are pointed out to them. Yet people generally shrug them off because it is easier to ignore them than it is to confront them. Correcting wrongs and abolishing absurdities require the expenditure of mental energy that many people lack. They go with the flow of short-term avoidance rather than put up a fight for long-term reform.

This attitude of laziness enables absurdities to multiply. Because absurdities thrive on apathy they are proliferating wildly: malignancies that are gradually debilitating society the way that cancer slowly kills individuals. Treatment is available but rarely implemented. Once entrenched, absurdities tend to metastasize until they overwhelm traditional wisdom.

I submit that absurdities in modern society can be corrected – *should* be corrected – if only people would appreciate them for what they are, refuse to acquiesce to them, and lobby their Congressional representatives to rectify them.

In one way or another, I have been fighting absurdities all my life.

The earliest encounter that I recall occurred during my grade school years. My cousin Frankie Testa took a nickel from me. This was at a time and an age when five cents represented monumental wealth to a child. We got into a loud argument over confiscation of my money, but no matter how much I cried and tried to get my nickel back, Frankie would not give it up. He was older and bigger than I was, so I could not take it back by force.

The screaming brought my mother into the fracas. When I stopped my tears long enough to explain what the fight was about, instead of confronting Frankie and seeking justice, she callously offered to give me a nickel in order to shut me up. I refused to accept it. She was never able to understand that I didn't want *her* nickel; I wanted *my* nickel. And I did *not* want Frankie to have it.

My next recollection of absurd injustice happened in junior high school. As I was walking along the corridor between classes, an exuberant boy rushed past me and pushed me out of the way. I teetered sideways and bumped against a classroom's open door. An angry teacher charged out of the room, wanting to know why I banged against his door. I explained the situation, and pointed to the overactive boy who had pushed me. As punishment, the teacher gave detention slips to both of us. We both had to stay after school: he for pushing me, and I for being pushed.

I was apoplectic. I was the innocent victim, yet the teacher acted irrationally and saw fit to victimize me again. Little did I know at the time that this was a common occurrence not only in established society, but in the so-called justice system.

In my early 20's, I stopped at a local 7-Eleven on my way home from work. After I placed my items on the checkout counter next to the cash register, the clerk rang up my purchases. I watched carefully. I called his attention to the mistake he made when he charged me 15 cents for a 10-cent Hershey bar. I showed him the price that was clearly printed on the wrapper. He told me that 7-Eleven's price for 10-cent Hershey bars was 15 cents. Take it or leave it – that was the cost of convenience shopping.

I left all the items on the counter and walked out of the store empty-handed. Not only did I never return to that particular 7-Eleven, but I never shopped again at *any* 7-Eleven – *ever*, for the rest of my life. For the sake of 5 cents, 7-Eleven lost my patronage for more than 40 years.

By now my readers might be thinking that I have a hang-up about losing nickels. Not so. I have a hang-up about being overcharged, cheated, fleeced, swindled, ripped off, and screwed in the nonsexual sense. The amount is not as important as the principle involved.

Forty years might seem like a long time to hold a grudge, but I looked at the situation differently. If I continued to do business with 7-Eleven, I would be condoning and actively supporting 7-Eleven's policy of overcharging its customers; and worse, at my own expense.

Instead, I chose to register a silent protest against an unfair business practice. If everyone in the country followed my example, 7-Eleven would soon have been forced to change its excessive-charge policy – or go out of business. But so many customers were willing to let themselves be hustled without an argument that 7-Eleven has prospered.

In Perspective
Throughout this book I will use comparisons to emphasize points that might otherwise seem trivial or less than absurd. For example, in the scenario that is presented above, the issue of overcharging by half a dime might seem unworthy of discussion. But compared with the base price of the particular product, a 5-cent surcharge represented a 50% increase in the suggested retail price.

If 7-Eleven charged half again as much for all its other products, then (in relation to modern-day prices) a 2-dollar quart of milk would cost 3 dollars; a 4-dollar package of hotdogs would cost 6 dollars; a 6-dollar tub of ice cream would cost 9 dollars; a 10-dollar bag of charcoal would cost 15 dollars. If 7-Eleven sold automobiles, a $30,000 car would cost $45,000; and you would have to pay sales tax on the extra $15,000.

Keep these perspectives in mind when you determine relative values.

Complaint or Compliant?

If you encounter something that is wrong, the chances are that nothing will be done to correct that wrong unless you call attention to it. You can talk to yourself until doomsday but the complaint will never be heard.

Throughout my life I have heard numerous complaints. People complain to their family, to their friends, to their neighbors, to complete strangers – to anyone who will take the time to listen to their complaints, and even to those who don't want to hear their complaints because they have complaints of their own that they want to declare.

It may pay to complain, but complaint exchangers are wasting their breath because they complain to everyone except to those who are in a position to resolve the issue under complaint.

If you buy an item that is defective or that is in some way substandard, then lodge a complaint with the manufacturer or with the store where you purchased the item. If you receive poor service, complain to the individual who provided the service, or to the individual's boss or manager. If you have a complaint about government performance, complain directly to the worker who performed poorly, complain to the worker's supervisor, complain to relevant politicians, complain to elected representatives, or complain to all of the above.

If you can't complain in person, write a letter. Letters achieve a sense of permanence; they are saved and filed for future reference even if no action is taken. Yet instead of taking ten minutes to write a letter and send it to an address where it might do some good, people will complain for hours to people who can't do anything more than nod their heads in commiseration. This is not only absurd; it is stupid.

These suggested methods will not guarantee a resolution to your complaint, but they have a greater possibility of achieving success than gossiping over the backyard fence. You must take a proactive stance where it will do the most good. And you must keep plugging away if your initial effort fails.

The Pampered Pet Syndrome

Many people go through life like pets or farm animals. When you switch off the lights in a room at night, a pet does not respond or acknowledge any change in illumination. A cat continues to lick its paws in the dark; a dog scratches fleas with the same frenetic vigor. They act this way because they have no control over the lights; because they have *never* had control of the lights. They think no more about sudden darkness than a human being thinks about the setting sun.

If you switch off the lights in a room full of people – without announcement and without good cause – they react instantly. They don't *want* to be in the dark. They demand that the lights be switched on again, or they locate the switch and flip it on in protest. Unlike pets, people are used to being in control of artificial lights, and most will take what action is necessary to exercise that control.

All too often, people act like pets with regard to circumstances that they believe are beyond their control, or that they have grown to ignore, or that they have been trained by society to accept: things like government rip-offs, political shenanigans, official corruption, unfair laws, and the gradual erosion of freedom.

These are the people who moo and mill like cattle, but who will not search for the switch themselves. They wait for someone else to do it – or not do it. They complain to people around them – and that is all they do. They feed at the trough when the trough is full, and complain when the trough is empty. This attitude of meek submission is ingrained in some people and conditioned in others. Their only reaction is an apathetic shrug, or perhaps a mild bleat: "What can *I* do about it?"

These people are led to the slaughter block to serve without protest as fodder for political power mongers.

A Passion for Justice

Cheryl Novak once told me that I have a passion for justice. I never thought of myself in that light, but I knew as soon as she said it that she had hit the proverbial nail on the head with a metaphorical sledge hammer.

I have always been motivated by a sense of justice. The corollary to a passion for justice is an abhorrence of *in*justice. I have always reacted strongly to any kind of injustice, especially when I was the prejudiced victim.

The Absurdity Principle is the result of a lifetime of wide-eyed observation, stern interaction, and vigorous disputation. There is great deal to learn from reading this book – for those who are willing to listen and to follow my example, and who wish to make the world of the future a better place for their children.

It's not your fault that the world is the way it is, but it *is* your fault that you're not willing to help change it.

You *can* make a difference – but only if you try.

The Fax of Life

It is not necessary to embark upon a full-scale crusade against absurdities. It is necessary only to object to those absurdities that you encounter personally. Some – perhaps most – of your objections will be overruled, especially if you stand as a lone objector.

It is a well-known adage that the squeaky wheel gets the oil, but I am forced to admit that in the majority of cases, one person acting alone cannot make a loud enough squeak to effect an overall change in policy – although at the very least his personal situation may be resolved to his satisfaction. Let me cite three examples of positive change.

I travel a great deal, and am often on the road or at sea for weeks at a time. I always returned from extended absences to a mountain of mail and a stack of faxes. Most of both were junk advertisements. The worst part about fax ads was that they used my paper and carbon cartridges. It was costing me money to receive announcements and promotional schemes in which I had no interest. Yet I needed fax capability for my business.

Fax ads had toll-free return phone or fax numbers. I always called to have my number removed from the sender's database – but there were hundreds of other senders to take their place. I finally devised two methods to deal with the problem.

I habitually called a toll-free phone number before retiring for the night. After the connection was made and I heard the recorded message, I put down the phone, went to bed, and tied up the advertiser's phone line for the night – or until the sender's automatic system timed out and disconnected the call. The sender had to pay for every minute that the returned call line was open.

I devised another system for toll-free fax numbers. I stacked all the fax ads on a shelf next to my desk. I placed the entire stack of received faxes in my fax machine, and sent them to the latest sender. The sender received not only the ad that he sent to me, but scores of other ads from other senders.

Then I got truly creative. I taped three fax ads together, inserted the first sheet into my fax machine, called the toll-free number, let the first sheet go through my machine, then taped the leading edge of the first sheet to the tail edge of the last sheet. This created an endless loop that transmitted continuously until the recipient realized what was happening. If I started the transmission at night, the trick wasn't discovered until morning. By that time it used up hundreds of sheets of the recipient's paper and decimated his carbon cartridge. These fax ad senders got the message fast, and deleted my number from their database.

The Wheel that Squeaked

A guy in my neighborhood bragged about how he took advantage of the handicapped parking law. Pennsylvania offered a special license plate to disabled veterans. The plate was sold at a reduced price, and it permitted the driver to park in handicapped parking spots. This guy had developed an ulcer during peacetime service, and was discharged with a 10% disability pension.

I was incensed. Handicapped parking spots were designated for people who found walking difficult or painful, not for military malingerers who could walk as well as anyone else. He liked the convenience of being able to park close to the door. In doing so, his vehicle occupied a spot that a truly handicapped person could not use.

I wrote a long letter of complaint to my State representative. Lo and behold, a couple of months later the State rescinded the parking permit unless the veteran obtained proof of a walking disability from the Veterans Administration. Otherwise, the veteran got only the reduced price for the license plate.

I won't kid you. It wasn't my sole complaint that instigated the modification to the law. My letter was only one of a number of complaints that the State received from outraged constituents about unworthy veterans who were misusing the special license plate. The State wasted no time in plugging the loophole.

A similar situation arose when Americans were annoyed by the telephone advertising blitz. I remember all too well when more than half the phone calls that I received were from telemarketers. The situation escalated until Congress was prompted to adopt the Do-Not-Call system.

Complaints are like votes. No single vote elects a nominee to office, and no single complaint effects a change in the status quo. People should lodge complaints with the same enthusiasm that they take with them to the polls.

The Plain Truth

Thomas Paine was an avid supporter of the American Revolution. In 1776, he wrote a pamphlet that was published and distributed under the title *Common Sense*: a philosophical treatise whose doctrine advocated secession of the colonies from the rule of England.

Paine's working title for the pamphlet was *Plain Truth*. This title reflected the writing style that he chose for his revolutionary thesis: plain and simple language that the commoner could readily understand, whether he read it for himself or, if he was uneducated and illiterate, had it read to him. Paine disdained the highfalutin jargon of academia. He wanted to reach the great unwashed masses, not the minority of intellectuals.

I have written *The Absurdity Principle* in much the same vein: in familiar or colloquial lingo without pretense and legalese; with more of a spoken vocabulary than a written vocabulary. There is also a certain amount of tongue in cheek, especially when I am poking fun at absurdities that are so overtly, well, absurd.

Grammatical Constructions

In writing this book and its screwball sequels, I have followed certain rules that should be understood at the outset. Mostly these rules concern the use of pronouns. A pronoun is a word that substitutes for a noun. Pronouns are generally used to achieve scanning brevity and to avoid repetition of a noun or an unwieldy group of nouns.

The problem with pronouns is that they can be imprecise and lead to confusion. Partly this is due to the fact that people misuse pronouns, or misinterpret their use, and partly because of deficiencies in the English language.

The most commonly misused personal pronoun is "they," the plural form of "he," "she," and "it." Consider this example of tense confusion: "I don't believe a State Trooper should go faster than the speed limit unless they are in uniform." Many people speak this way without realizing that "a State Trooper" is singular while "they" is plural. Most people would hear this sentence without noticing anything wrong with it.

There is a good reason for this, and it is not necessarily the fault of the speaker or hearer or the American educational system. It is because a State Trooper is a person who is either male or female, but the English language has no singular personal pronoun that leaves the gender unspecified. Thus people default to the plural personal pronoun "they" instead of using the awkward phrase "he or she."

This is only one of many absurdities in the English language. In English grammar, an absurdity is euphemistically called an "exception to the rule," which everyone acknowledges as acceptable usage because they were taught to allow it. (In linguistics, "everyone" is a collective noun that is singular in usage, but to most ears the word "they" probably sounded correct.)

In literary circles there has been a movement to use "(s)he" as a substitute for "he or she." This form is awkward in print and unpronounceable in conversation.

It is not my purpose to give a course in semantics. In this book I will use the pronoun "he" when the gender is either male or unknown, and the pronoun "she" when the gender is known to be female. If you have a hang-up about this usage, get over it now.

Against my personal opinion, I will use the pronoun "they" or "their" whenever the noun that I am replacing refers to a collective entity, such as a group or a company or a government agency. Thus I could have written the sentence above as, "If I continued to do business with 7-Eleven, I would be actively condoning their [7-Eleven's] policy of overcharging its customers."

I prefer that the standard usage be changed to "it" instead of "they," because a company is singular and has no gender, but I don't think such a change will ever happen. I suppose I will just have to "get over it."

While I am on the subject of "they," years ago I read a sociologist's opinion that when people said "they did this" or "they did that," these people were showing evidence of paranoia; that these people – dare I use the pronoun "they" – believe that there is a conspiracy against them, and that the mysterious unknown "they" are responsible for all their woes.

I heartily disagree. While it is true that paranoiacs inhabit the world, they are in the minority, while use of the pronoun "they" is nearly universal. It is more a manner of speech than a measure of unreasonable distrust.

I have listened intently to the usage of "they" in general conversation. People generally employ the pronoun simply as a matter of convenience, when they are uncertain or don't know the name of the group or organization in question. Take for example, "They are talking about raising taxes."

A superficial reading of this sentence might lead a true paranoiac to believe that the speaker was obsessed with suspicion about a covert organization that wielded power and ruled the government behind the backs of the President and elected representatives; whereas in reality the speaker just doesn't know who "they" are. "They" could refer to tax reformers, designated officials, minor bureaucrats, or some or all of the above.

On the other hand, the speaker may well know who "they" are, and assume that his listeners know just as well, in which case the pronoun achieves the purpose for which pronouns exist: for the sake of simplicity.

In the following text, I will use the pronoun "they" in its most customary and commonly accepted sense. For the sake of simplicity, I will sometimes address the reader as "you."

Section One
The Foundling Fathers
or Babes in the Woods

The Outset of Absurdity

The Declaration of Independence is one of the greatest single documents ever written: a sublime testament to the advocacy of freedom and human rights, and one that is practically without equal in the world. The language and literacy are so beautifully composed that the text reads more like poetry than prose. The concepts that are embraced by this magnum opus nobly surmount all previous attempts to define the role of government in the conduct of human affairs.

I have the utmost respect for the brilliant and farsighted individual who framed this monument to diplomacy, and for the brave men who had the courage to append their signatures at great personal risk. Had the revolution failed, the British would have hunted down every signatory and hung them all.

Thomas Jefferson drafted the Declaration in such a succinct and splendid manner that it communicated superlatively the grand scope of America's position and philosophy to the distant sovereign authority without reservation. Jefferson was firm if not defiant in his denunciation of the King of England, complete with accusation and intimidation, and leaving no doubt about open rebellion.

Although the grandeur of the Declaration is not without grandiloquence, its framer and signatories were not without prejudice and inconsistencies of character.

The Declaration is fraught with incongruities which are open to interpretation (or misinterpretation). It contains concepts which were relevant to the times during which it was created, but which have become outmoded and which are no longer held valid in light of modern ideals, enlightened moral principles, and technological advances.

Notwithstanding its obsoleteness, Americans cling to this static document as if it represented the immutable laws of nature instead of the transient laws of mankind.

If these sentiments sound like heresy, so be it.

Man or Mankind?

Jefferson declared in no uncertain terms: "We hold these truths to be self-evident, that all men are created equal, that they are endowed by their Creator with certain unalienable Rights, that among these are Life, Liberty, and the pursuit of Happiness."

In *Animal Farm*, George Orwell lampooned this most basic tenet of the Declaration by adding, "But some are more equal than others."

I would like to believe that by "men," Jefferson meant "mankind": all human beings, male and female, young and old, black and white, rich and poor, believers and nonbelievers. However, against my ardent leaning, I must in good conscience admit that Orwell's satirical observation was more descriptive of the truth.

Congress has been interpreting and re-interpreting Jefferson's definition of "men" for more than two centuries. The interpretation keeps changing – perhaps not as often as the weather, but at least as often as political expedience permits. What modern day Americans *want* "men" to mean differs greatly from what the framers intended it to mean.

History has confirmed that the signatories meant wealthy white males, or perhaps landed Caucasian masculine gentry, but clearly not blacks, women, or children, with young black girls occupying the bottom of the totem pole on all three counts. In other words, they used the word "men" in an oligarchical sense. (For readers who have forgotten their high school history, an oligarchy is a form of government in which power is held by a minority. This differs from a democracy, in which the minority of rulers is elected by the majority of voters to represent them.)

To enumerate, black men, women, and children had no rights whatsoever. White women had limited rights, but not the right to vote. White children had no rights but were not persecuted the way blacks were persecuted; even today, children's rights are severely restricted until they reach the magical moment of adulthood: a moment that differs depending upon the rights in question, and which varies from State to State.

Jefferson was in good company with nearly half the co-signers who owned slaves. Clearly, these prosperous Caucasian males did not consider uneducated African natives to be their equal. Nor did they believe (despite their Declaration) that slaves should possess the same "unalienable Rights" that was granted to "men" in the very same sentence. Yet this obvious absurdity was pronounced and accepted without question. The bastion of black slavery persevered for four score and seven years after the Declaration was submitted to the King of England.

Jefferson and his fellow slave-owners were guilty of arrogance at the very least. Had these men deluded themselves into believing their own propaganda? Were they not as reprehensible as the King of England for ignoring the rights of their fellow men (and women)? By what irrational way of thinking did they differentiate between white men and black men, between men and women?

The Less Equal

Lest there be any doubt about how the U.S. government interpreted "men" in the Declaration, consider the stance on slavery that the Supreme Court took in 1857. Eighty-one years after the Continental Congress declared that all men were created equal, and were endowed with the unalienable right of liberty, slave Dred Scott sued for freedom from his owner, John Emerson.

At that time, slavery was legal in some States and territories, but illegal in others. Emerson took his slaves with him when he moved to States and territories in which slavery was illegal. The basis of Scott's claim was that he could not be a slave if he lived in a State in which slavery was illegal.

Nonetheless, the Supreme Court ruled that freeing Scott from slavery would deprive his owner of his legal property. Furthermore, the Court ruled that no person of African descent could claim citizenship in the United States. This meant that free blacks in Northern States, in which slavery was illegal, did not have the rights of citizenship. Free blacks were not just lower-class citizens – they were not classed as citizens at all.

The Preamble of the Constitution of the United States secured "the Blessings of Liberty to ourselves and our Posterity." Absurdly, the pronoun "ourselves" did not apply to blacks whether they were free or not. Neither did it apply to Amerindians. All these people were essentially classless.

Thus the Supreme Court issued a ruling that contradicted the intent of both the Declaration and the Constitution, in order to conform to the accepted norm that existed in antebellum times. I submit that even today, Supreme Court rulings are not always based on the Articles of and Amendments to the Constitution, or on other codified laws, but in conformance to the current political stance.

After hundreds of thousands of human lives were lost in the War of the Rebellion, the fourteenth Amendment to the Constitution was ratified, in 1868. It stated: "All persons born or naturalized in the United States, and subject to the jurisdiction thereof, are citizens of the United States and of the State wherein they reside."

It is interesting to note that while this Amendment included persons of African descent, it excluded Amerindians, who had lived for thousands of years on the land that the United States then occupied and governed. Amerindians sometimes had their lives, but did not have their liberty or the right to pursue their happiness.

Slavery by Any Other Name . . .

President Abraham Lincoln freed the black Southern slaves, but he did not end slavery. Nor did his Emancipation Proclamation grant the status of equality to everyone in the country. Slavery and inequality have persisted well into the twentieth century, although in different forms and under different guises.

In his Gettysburg Address, Lincoln declared his hope "that government of the people, by the people, for the people, shall not perish from the earth." I think he would have been sadly disabused to learn that by the twentieth century, his concept had perished, and that the government of the people was controlled by only some of the people for the enrichment of those very same controlling people.

In Perspective

Consider this true personal story. I left my place of employment to take my pregnant wife to the hospital because she was about to give birth. My employer denied permission for me to leave, but I left anyway. My employer notified law enforcement agencies of my departure. I was soon hounded by police and the FBI, who came after me with guns.

In order to avoid detection, I had to wear a disguise and sneak into the hospital by claiming to be a relative other than the husband of my wife. After she gave birth, and I was assured that the baby was healthy and safe, I avoided law enforcement officers and returned to my place of employment. I was promptly arrested, locked in jail, tried in court without a jury of my peers, and sentenced to three months at hard labor. I was incarcerated with people who were in prison for murder, rape, theft, forgery, and a host of other violent and nonviolent crimes.

I was denied the right of appeal.

. . . Is Still Slavery

Impossible, you say, in modern-day America? Not by a long shot. Violation of human rights is more common today than most people are led to believe or are willing to accept. I was only one of hundreds of thousands of natural-born American citizens who was caged like an animal, and who suffered total loss of freedom at the behest of a Big Brother government gone awry.

The most frightening book that I ever read was *1984*, by George Orwell. It was not on my high school reading list; I read it on my own. The book is a dystopian novel about totalitarian control of the people and the complete loss of freedom and individuality. These were concepts that terrified me.

Imagine my horror when I later learned that some of Orwell's dire extrapolations already existed in America, and that rights that were guaranteed by the Constitution could be abrogated so easily by bureaucratic fiat.

History is replete with many forms of human bondage. Slavery was a way of life in ancient Roman times. Soldiers, sailors, gladiators, and domestics performed tasks for an effete aristocracy, and often paid for their servitude with their lives. Warships were rowed by men who were chained to their seats; they were called galley slaves.

In the seventeenth century, the British navy established press gangs to waylay suitable men, knock them unconscious by a blow to the head, bind them, and haul them onto warships to serve in menial capacities. These warships were already far at sea by the time the men regained consciousness or were unbound. They were then impressed into involuntary service for as long as they were needed. Some of them were literally worked to death.

This British form of slavery was called "impressment."

One of the reasons that the United States waged war against England in 1812 was the British impressment of American citizens. It is ironic then that the United States government adopted the same policy of impressment when the politicians in power found it expedient to do so. Granted, suitable men were not knocked unconscious or bound with rope when they were impressed into service. In a manner that was only marginally more civilized, they (and I) were threatened with imprisonment for a term of five-years for avoiding impressment.

Certain classes of citizens were absolved from the form of slavery in which I was ensnared: all females, children under the age of eighteen, males over the age of twenty-six, males with physical defects or mental deficiencies, and males who were married. In other words, the government targeted unmarried males who were physically and mentally fit, and who were between the ages of eighteen and twenty-six.

Because of the unsavory connotation of impressment, the U.S. government changed the name to conscription, or draft, or compulsory enrollment in military service. The employment of euphemistic synonyms did not alter the meaning.

Congress ratified the thirteenth Amendment in 1865. It stated in clear and certain terms, "Neither slavery nor involuntary servitude, except as a punishment for crime whereof the party shall have been duly convicted, shall exist within the United States, or any place subject to their jurisdiction."

I had committed no crime, yet my constitutional rights were taken from me, and I was condemned to two years of involuntary servitude in the U.S. Army. Once indentured, I was beaten, tortured, humiliated, deprived of freedom, deprived of due process, and forced to do things that were against my nature. I had my life, but I did not have liberty or the freedom to pursue happiness.

Military Service, or Servitude

As long as we're in the Army, I will segue to military training inanities as if the term were not an oxymoron. Some readers might think that I am being childish by drawing attention to Army behavior that is generally well known and documented, and therefore not worthy of consideration.

It is precisely *because* Army behavior is so well known and documented that people tend to disregard its absurdity. They have come to *accept* this behavior as ordinary and reasonable instead of seeing it for what it is. As you read the following examples, keep in mind that all these absurdities are cumulative, and add up to a totality that is vastly more absurd than the sum of its absurd parts.

Here is one admittedly minor case in point that everyone takes for granted: spit-shined boots. Numerous books and movies have focused on this senseless activity as if it were a military virtue. Appearances are important in certain situations: applying for a job, appearing in public, attending a corporate conference, hitchhiking, and so on.

Keep in mind that the primary purpose of military training is to engage the enemy in mortal combat. Appearances are irrelevant in a firefight. Vietnam regulars and Vietcong guerillas would shoot an American soldier no matter how well he was dressed.

A mirrorlike gloss on boot leather does not make a person any better of a soldier. In Vietnam, I had to scuff my boots until every vestige of polish was eradicated; the reflection of light off a highly buffed surface was literally a dead giveaway to the wearer's position.

Yet in basic training, I often stayed up late at night to shine my boots in order to pass morning inspection. If you think I am quibbling about a triviality, try working a physically demanding sixteen hour day, then spend several hours polishing boots and shining brass instead of getting some much-needed sleep, and see how you feel about it.

To make matters worse, the first thing we did after morning inspection was to low-crawl over dirt and sand. This process immediately scraped the polish off the boots and scratched the leather. That night I had to spit-shine my boots again so as to be prepared for the next morning's inspection and subsequent low-crawl.

The same goes for tarnished brass. Every night I had to polish my belt buckle to a fine luster that outshone gold. And every morning the low-crawl scraped and scratched the finish off the surface. In Vietnam, we intentionally rubbed course sand over the buckle so it didn't reflect the faintest glimmer of light and attract the enemy's attention and lead.

This might make you wonder what we were training for – a Boy Scout parade or a combat mission.

In Perspective

For real juvenility, think about saluting. Every time an enlisted man spots an officer, he is supposed to salute or suffer the consequences. Picture a civilian job in which you had to demonstrate subservience to your boss by getting down on your knees. How would you like it if your boss docked your pay because you failed to genuflect?

The requirement of submissive behavior is unacceptable in the workplace. An employee who was forced to kowtow to his boss would run for the shop steward, or complain to the union, or lodge a grievance with the Department of Social Services, or file a lawsuit for sexual harassment.

Yet this kind of behavior is demanded *by the Army.*

The Army Way

As my training sergeant used to say in all seriousness, "There are three ways of doing things: the right way, the wrong way, and the Army way."

I inferred this to mean that the Army way was neither right nor wrong, but different to the point of absurdity. With that said, I will continue to describe some of the most ludicrous incidents that I experienced personally or saw firsthand during my term of servitude. Readers who were never in the Army might find these events so bizarre as to seem unbelievable. I have no need to fabricate or exaggerate any stories. The truth is stranger than anything I could ever have imagined.

In basic training, trainees were court-martialed for such minor rule bending or forgetfulness as walking away from the firing range with a spent and empty rifle cartridge in hand or a pocket.

Trainees were given so short a time for meals that many could not finish eating before they were thrown out of the mess hall. Anyone caught taking uneaten scraps outside was fined one-quarter of his monthly pay.

If a trainee got sunburned in the hot Georgia sun, and went to the hospital for treatment, he was court-martialed for destruction of government property. This says it all about the status of a draftee. The government considered a soldier to be "property," the same as Dred Scott.

Remember that "G.I." stands for "government issue."

I knew of a soldier who was caught removing discarded items from a trashcan. He was court-martialed for theft of government property – that is, for taking something that the Army had already thrown away.

Both in basic training and in jungle warfare school, trainees were periodically assigned to KP duty. (KP stands for kitchen police). KP started at 4 a.m. and ended at 10 p.m. Trainees on KP missed the courses that were scheduled for that day. There were no makeup classes. You just didn't receive that particular coursework, whether it was in the field or in the classroom, even if it was weapons training. As a result, some soldiers were sent into the battlefield with weapons that they didn't know how to use, or vacant of priceless knowledge in how to stay alive.

Every minute infraction of the rules was treated as a major offense. An order to which a trainee did not respond fast enough in the mind of the person giving the order was also treated as a major offense.

The mildest form of punishment for such infractions was humiliation: for example, running in circles until you were dizzy, standing with your nose against a tree and repeating inane sayings, or lying on the ground with your face in the dirt and addressing a cigarette butt.

Less mild forms of punishment consisted of physical abuse, such as doing pushups, or standing at attention in the hot sun for hours, or working on a non-com's or an officer's personal projects.

The punishment that was intermediate between humiliation and deduction in pay was additional KP. This meant that a soldier so punished was even less qualified in the battlefield than his fellows.

It's pure cop-out to shrug off these unwarranted

punishments by saying, "Sure, but that's the way it is in the Army." These punishments must be put into perspective with other jobs: in the office, on construction sites, in tollbooths, in restaurants, in schools, in utility companies, in manufacturing plants, on assembly lines, in government bureaus, and so on. The only place of employment in which these extreme measures of punishment are conducted, and are accepted as the norm, is in military service.

Your boss is not allowed to make you talk to trees, or stand at attention in the sun, or lie with your face in the dirt. No civilized country should approve or permit these forms of gross misconduct – especially at the whim of an individual who is beholden to no higher authority.

What makes these punishments even more unjustifiable is that once you're in the Army, you're not allowed to quit. You must serve your entire sentence.

The Army is not sacrosanct. It should not be held above the law.

In Perspective

Remember the hullabaloo about the alleged mistreatment of Iraqi soldiers who were held in detention at Guantanamo Bay, Cuba? If these prisoners of war had been treated the way I had been treated, the outcry would have become an international incident. Members of the press and the United Nations would have made a stink that would have been smelled from the Moon.

Why must prisoners of war be treated better than the soldiers who were being trained to capture them?

More "Armway"

If a trainee returning from a weekend pass was late in signing the register by as little as sixty seconds, he was fined one-quarter of his monthly pay. He would also be assigned to extra duty, such as scrubbing toilet bowls with a toothbrush. This would never be allowed in a civilian workplace.

The pay scale was less than the minimum hourly wage. For this tiny emolument a soldier faced the strong possibility of serious injury or death.

The punishment for arguing with an officer was a fine of one-quarter of the soldier's monthly pay, even if the soldier was right and the officer was wrong. This is equivalent to being dunned a week's salary for getting into a quarrel with a fellow employee whose pay grade was higher than yours. Labor laws do not apply to Army personnel.

Trainees had to perform tricks before being permitted to enter the mess hall. Those who could not perform these tricks were not allowed to eat. Tricks included pushups, sit-ups, running in place, and traveling hand-over-hand along overhead horizontal bars.

A daily morning duty consisted of raking the sand around the barracks into even lines, like the straight rows in a farm field. Afterward, trainees were ordered to race around the building, thus obliterating the lines. How senseless.

In jungle warfare school, tropical combat patrols were simulated by wearing the clothes and carrying the arms and equipment that would be issued in Vietnam. During a week-long training maneuver that was held in November, the days were cold and the temperature dropped to near freezing at night. I had nothing to wear but lightweight jungle fatigues. I did not have a jacket or long underwear because they would not be available overseas. I had to sleep on the ground in the open without a sleeping bag or tent; I had only a rain poncho and a single blanket to wrap around my shoulders.

There were no tests and no one flunked out of jungle warfare school. Even the most blundering idiot was sent to Vietnam. Cannon fodder doesn't need a passing grade, but it isn't comforting to wonder about whether the guy who is crouched in the foxhole next to you knows what to do when the shooting starts.

Eight weeks of basic training and nine weeks of jungle warfare school were considered adequate preparation to pit a normally nonviolent young adult against experienced guerilla fighters who had been born and raised in the jungle, and who had fought in the jungles for years.

A Confusing Age

In *Lonely Conflict*, a fictionalized autobiographical account of my experiences in Vietnam and in war-torn America, I had one of my adult characters say, "Eighteen is a dangerous and confusing age today. You're old enough to pay adult prices at the movies, but not old enough to see adult films. You're old enough to stand trial by jury, but not old enough to be a juror. You're old enough to drink if you're in the service, but not at home as a civilian. You're old enough to kill someone in the name of patriotism, but not old enough to carry a weapon for self-defense. And you're old enough to die for your country, but not old enough to vote for it."

The Surrogate War

The last sentence in the quote above is the most telling one of all. The draft age was 18; the voting age was 21. Draft-age males had no say in how their government was run. They could not vote against the draft. Their views were not represented in Congress.

The scene in *Lonely Conflict* was set in 1966, the year in which I was drafted. At that time the voting age was 21. The twenty-sixth Amendment to the Constitution was ratified in 1971. This Amendment lowered the voting age to 18. By that time, the number of ineligible voters who were killed in Vietnam numbered in the tens of thousands. The change in voting status came too late to save their lives.

The politicians who wanted to wage war in Vietnam were not willing to volunteer for military service or engage in actual combat. They were willing only to send someone else to fight for their (the politicians') ideals – someone who didn't want to fight or perhaps had different ideals.

It's easy to take a stand on issues when you have no personal stake in the outcome, or when someone else is taking all the risk. Although politicians have the authority to order people into slavery, and to force them to do unconscionable acts in self defense, they do not have the *right* to do so.

The draft is unconstitutional. According to the Bill of Rights, Amendment 4, individuals who have committed no crime are protected from unwarranted seizure. Any person who is seized without probable cause has had his constitutional right violated. Yet the government has committed this violation millions of times against targeted civilians.

Politicians may feel bad about losing the war in Vietnam. But they didn't lose an arm or a leg or a life. Politicians do not even suffer from accountability. I was one of the lucky ones who returned from Vietnam alive and in one piece (but barely).

My Country, 'Tis of Thee

Anyone who thinks that I am being petty about serving two years of penal servitude at the government's behest, should first stand in my shoes. My life and career were disrupted when I was dragged out of college between semesters, forced to suffer indignities and physical abuse, and sent to fight a war whose avowed purpose was to establish freedom for the people of a foreign country. I spent thirteen months in military hospitals recuperating from wounds that I received in battle. Too many soldiers suffered worse.

I submit that before the government commits itself to fighting for freedom on foreign soil, it should first ensure that its own citizens possess the very freedoms that the government wants foreigners to enjoy.

Although *America* fosters lyrics about the sweet land of liberty, the American government has committed itself to let freedom ring everywhere but at home.

I wonder how many hundreds of times I recited the Pledge of Allegiance in school, never knowing that "liberty and justice for all" was not meant for me or any other suitable males between the ages of 18 and 26.

Teenage Limbo

My character in *Lonely Conflict* hit a number of proverbial nails on the head, but he did not swing his fictional hammer at other real-life nails. He talked about giving automatic rifles, machine guns, grenade launchers, and anti-tank weapons to males who were not old enough to drink or vote, but he didn't mention that in many States those men were not allowed to marry without permission from their parents.

I wanted to marry when I was twenty years old, but according to Pennsylvania law, my parents had to sign a document in which they gave their consent to my marriage. On the other hand, my fiancé – who at eighteen years of age was two years younger – was allowed to marry without parental consent. The consensual age for men was twenty-one; for women it was eighteen. My parents objected but I eventually persuaded them to give their consent (if not their blessing).

After my return from Vietnam, my wife and I accompanied some friends to a restaurant at which liquor was served. We were "carded" because we all looked under the Pennsylvania drinking age of twenty-one. We told the waiter that we wanted only soft drinks with our meal; that no one was going to order alcohol. It didn't matter; underage people were not allowed in an establishment that served liquor.

Every one of us was over twenty-one except for my wife. The waiter informed her that she would have to leave the premises because she was under the legal drinking age. An argument ensued – primarily involving me because the waiter proclaimed that I could stay but that my wife had to leave. I was furious because, after having nearly died for my country, my country would not allow me to share a meal with my wife in a public place.

The manager intruded. He insisted that no exceptions were allowed. If my wife did not leave voluntarily, he would call the police and have her forcibly expelled. We all left and ate dinner elsewhere.

The final irony is that we could have driven three miles, crossed the bridge to New Jersey, and drunk to our hearts content – either in a bar or in a restaurant that served alcoholic beverages. We also could have gone to a liquor store and bought beer, wine, and spirits. The drinking age in New Jersey was eighteen.

I tried to get a credit card at Sears & Roebuck while I was still in the Army. I filled out the application and answered the questionnaire. They declined to issue a credit card to me because I was "not gainfully employed." Sears & Roebuck did not consider that a man who was serving his country had a worthwhile occupation.

I figured that it must be a mistake. I submitted a second application. Again it was declined, and for the same reason. My third application was also declined.

Finally, my wife applied for a Sears & Roebuck credit card. In the space that asked for her occupation, she wrote "housewife." Her application was approved at once. Within weeks she received her credit card in the mail.

I could not obtain a credit card because I was not gainfully employed, but my unemployed wife got one because she was married to someone who was not gainfully employed.

Rules of Engagement

Admiral Sir John Arbuthnot Fisher, Britain's First Sea Lord during World War One, wrote, "Violence is the essence of war, and moderation in war is imbecility."

War is not a game or a sporting event. War is a lethal activity. War is death and destruction. War consists of deadly adversaries, not tokens or contestants or players. War is not a club meeting at which *Robert's Rules of Order* determines conduct.

Having rules for war is like having rules for muggings and child abuse. Fair play is great for backgammon and canasta, but not for mortal combat.

To invert a common sports motto, "It isn't how you play the game, it's whether you win or lose." The sole object of war is to defeat the enemy. There are no fair means or foul; there is only winning.

In its purest sense, the opponents in war are the attacker and the defender: one country that wants to conquer and enslave another country, and the other country that does not want to be conquered and enslaved. To suggest that a country that is fighting for its life, its freedom, and the existence of its culture, should tie its hands behind its back and fight a humanitarian war is totally absurd.

Using humane bullets – steel-jacketed instead of soft lead, which expands upon impact for maximum damage – is like encasing the metal bar of a mousetrap in thick foam rubber, so it won't bruise the mouse's neck. Bullets are designed to kill and maim, not to count coup as a feat of bravery.

The Geneva Convention seeks to prevent atrocities. This Convention conveniently overlooks the fact that attack or invasion is the first atrocity. The Convention has no provision to prevent attack or invasion; its provisions apply only after one country attacks or invades another. Then both countries are supposed to abide by rules of humanitarian conduct.

What does the Geneva Convention mean by "humanitarian conduct"? It can mean a number of things.

It means that when you get the drop on an enemy soldier who just killed your companion or blew off his leg, you should capture him and treat him with respect.

It means that a captured enemy soldier should not be interrogated beyond establishing his name, rank, and serial number – despite the fact that he may have information that can prevent additional deaths to your side or thwart total annihilation.

A captured soldier should not be mistreated or embarrassed, despite the fact that your fellow soldiers were beaten and humiliated far worse in the process of training.

It means that you may kill a soldier in the field of battle, but not the civilian who manufactured his guns and ammunition.

It means that you are allowed to use napalm to incinerate an enemy, but you are not allowed to use mustard gas because it would damage the enemy's lungs. In Vietnam, I saw a napalmed enemy soldier whose skin was burned off 100% of his body. He screamed at the top of his lungs for twelve hours straight, without stopping except to gasp for his next scream. I was glad for his sake when he died – because I couldn't imagine the pain that he must have been enduring. Yet napalm is legal whereas mustard gas is not.

It means that you can bayonet an enemy soldier in the gut, but if he doesn't die right away, you have to do everything in your power to save his life instead of killing him as you intended to do in the first place.

It means that you may use more than a thousand bombers to drop nearly 4,000 tons of high-explosives and incendiary devices on   , but not use a single bomber to drop one atomic bomb on Hiroshima or Nagasaki, despite the fact that the amount of destruction and number of fatalities were equivalent.

Some historians are still arguing about whether Dresden was a bona fide military target; instead, they should be arguing about whether it was right for Germany to invade Poland. Other historians are still arguing about whether it was fair to destroy two Japanese cities, when they should be arguing whether it was fair for Japan to attack Pearl Harbor. You can't expect to start a war and not suffer the consequences.

I am not against humanitarian principles except when they are misapplied. If a man tries to rape a woman in a back alley, I think that she should use every means at her disposal to protect herself from violation. She shouldn't have to refer to a rule book to determine what protective measures she is allowed to take, or have to explain afterward to a male judge who had never been raped why she used what he perceived to be excessive force.

My point is that war is horrible, but that the horror of losing is worse.

A Woman's Place

In retrospect, it is obvious that the "unalienable Rights" of women were not self-evident any more than they were for slaves. Had the situation been otherwise, womankind would not have had to struggle for more than a century to obtain the right to vote and to hold public office. The very necessity for women's suffrage was insufferable.

Furthermore, if females had been granted the same "unalienable Rights" as males, they would not *still* be struggling to obtain equality in the workforce: seeking equal pay for equal work, equal consideration for promotion, and equal respect for a job well done.

Discrimination against women is an age-old pursuit that likely goes back to prehistoric times. These discriminations ran the gamut of human activities. The framers of the Constitution perpetuated those discriminations, perhaps without malice aforethought, but certainly in the backs of their minds.

Throughout the history of the suffrage movement, suffragettes were condemned, vilified, and even imprisoned. The movement wasn't as bloody as the anti-slavery campaign. No women were shot, hung, or tarred and feathered, although some female protesters were hospitalized when their parades were assaulted by violent crowds of sexists. (The phrase "male chauvinist pig" had not yet been coined.)

Battles were won incrementally as various States folded under pressure, and granted women the right to vote – at least in local elections. Not until 1920 was the nineteenth Amendment to the Constitution ratified. This Amendment granted the right to vote to every citizen over the age of 21. This included black women.

There is no need to belabor an obvious point. The continuation of slavery and the perception of women as mere chattels make it abundantly apparent that the "Rights" in the Constitution were intended to apply only to a certain class of males.

The very cornerstone of American freedom and democracy is fraught with gratuitous exclusions. Interpretations have changed to fit new and open-minded modes of thought.

I mean no disrespect by suggesting that perhaps it is time to stop amending the Constitution, and to rewrite it. As I have already written, if this sentiment sounds like heresy, so be it. The Constitution is now more than two hundred years old. The world has changed while the Constitution has remained static. It was a great document in its day, but in too many ways it has outlived its usefulness.

Amendments are like patches that serve to cover flaws and imperfections. Perhaps the best way to repair the Constitutional defects is to rewrite the Constitution in light of modern mores and ethics.

The Fallacy of Equality

All people are not created equal. If they were, everyone could become a rocket scientist, a brain surgeon, a fighter pilot, a general, or President of the United States. Instead, most people struggle to become proficient cooks, clerks, secretaries, teachers, street vendors, construction workers, authors, and employees in thousands of other occupations which boast varying difficulties and job descriptions. No amount of education can make a person something that is beyond his physical ability or intellectual capacity. Everyone has limits of strength, endurance, and brain power.

By making the broadest possible interpretation, I think it is fair to assume that the Declaration was written not just to secede from foreign rule, but to formulate a government whose Constitution could dispense human equality with respect to life, liberty, and the pursuit of happiness. Yet, as I have shown above, the framers failed miserably not only in not achieving the expressed goal, but they failed in even *attempting* to achieve that goal.

Despite their firm avowals, the framers did not create an ideal egalitarian democracy. Instead, they created a stratified society in which they and their peers occupied the upper stratum, which governed and looked down upon all the other strata.

John O'Sullivan was co-founder and editor of *The United States Magazine and Democratic Review*, a periodical that was published from 1837 to 1859. His motto was, "The best government is that which governs least."

As I will demonstrate in the following chapters, his prophetic words are even more pertinent today than they were when he printed them. The role of a truly democratic government is not to *control* the people, but to protect them from external harm. It must do this by adhering to its Constitutional precepts in a manner that is both rational and humanitarian.

Constitutional Flaws

I will not go as far as to state that twenty-first-century America is encumbered with a Constitution that is antiquated and irrelevant, although there is a bit of truth to this allegation. The underlying principles of the Constitution are laudatory and still largely applicable. As noted above, the Constitution is an awesome document in its breadth and scope with regard to freedom and human rights.

The main problem with present-day jurisprudence is the inclination to ignore the Constitution's guiding principles. All too often, Congress passes laws that contravene the Constitution, and the Supreme Court makes rulings that are based upon partiality and political expedience.

I will not state categorically that the answer to all of America's problems and ideological disputes can be found by strict adherence to the once-hallowed document. But I will assert that, while some updating is needed and necessary in order to respond to technological advances, the basic values and doctrines are as sound today as they were when the Constitution was written.

On one hand, America should not cling to the Constitution as if it represented some universal law or cosmic decree that will remain valid or binding until the end of time. On the other hand, the country should not overthrow the Constitution by refusing to abide by its inherent dogma.

I have raised the issues of slavery, suffrage, and sexual discrimination. Despite the clear language of the Constitution, these fundamental human values were not only allowed to exist after the Constitution was ratified, but they have been wrongfully perpetuated throughout America's history. Indeed, slavery and sexual discrimination still persist despite grass-roots attempts to eradicate them.

Violation of the Constitution has been all too common a practice, from the time of the Founding Fathers to the very confused present. Americans are best advised to live up to the precepts that are embodied in the Constitution, even though the authors of that document did not.

In matters both lawful and interpersonal, perhaps the question that people should be asking is not whether a particular issue is Constitutional, but whether it is morally right. Americans and their representatives must coordinate their efforts to rebel against and overthrow the reins of injustice and legalized absurdity.

That is the way to create an enlightened society.

Section Two
Dirty Politics
(Is There Any Other Kind?)

Travesty of Justice

In theory, a democracy is a form of government that is controlled by the people through elected representatives. In practice, representatives all too often ignore the people who elected them and pursue their own agendas. The following forlorn saga is a case in point about how representatives circumvented Constitutional assurances in order to attain their personal goals – unfavorable legislation that was not in the best interests of the majority of affected parties.

I was intimately involved in this particular piece of legislation, first as a protester and then as an investigative journalist. My endeavors in both realms proved to be an eye-opener for me about how those in power can so easily abuse their power and get away with it. I predict that it will be an eye-opener for most if not all of my readers.

Wrongful Passage

In the early 1980's, a minuscule minority of marine archaeologists and petty bureaucrats first attempted to force upon an unwilling public a bill that would take from American citizens every shipwreck within the territorial waters of the United States, and turn them over to the adjacent States. This was done in the wake of the fantastic trove of treasure found on the *Atocha* by Mel Fisher and his investors after sixteen years of dedicated and self-funded searching for the Spanish galleon's mother lode. Instead of locating shipwrecks on their own – and at their own expense – marine archaeologists, estimated at less than fifty in number, sought to usurp the tremendous efforts of treasure salvors by bureaucratic fiat. Their philosophy was: why earn something when we can take it by passing laws? That might make theft legal but it doesn't make it right.

The case of the *Atocha* was particularly absurd because the wreck site lay in international waters, where neither the State of Florida nor the U.S. government could exercise jurisdiction.

The story is one of epic proportions, with enough conflict and background material for a full-length book. Perhaps someday I'll write it. The most appropriate title would be *The Treasure Wars*. Here is a condensed version of the plot.

Under the guise of "historic preservation," marine archaeologists lobbied for the nationalization of American shipwrecks as a way to ensure future employment among their ranks. Quick to jump on the bandwagon were opportunistic bureaucrats who came to perceive shipwrecks as a valuable political ploy. Historic preservation was enjoying enormous popularity, and popularity equates to votes. Thus there were economic incentives to such an endorsement, not only for the politicians' continued occupation of office, but for the States they represented – in the form of tax impositions, licensing fees, tourist attractions, and so forth. The proposed legislation was unequivocally anti-democratic, at the expense of private enterprise, and against every principle on which the Constitution was founded. This didn't bother some lawmakers, however.

The bill that was framed was called the Abandoned Shipwreck Act, a semantically appropriate title. "Abandoned" was intended to refer to shipwrecks without traceable ownership and those that were derelict or had otherwise been deserted by their owners: in other words, every wreck on which there was no current claim of commercial salvage – and this included unknown and as yet undiscovered wrecks. The dictionary also defines "abandoned" as "shameful" and "immoral" and "corrupt," terms which come closer to the truth as descriptions of the Act and the purposes for which its passage was sought, especially considering the manner in which the Act was ultimately passed.

The underlying theme of the Abandoned Shipwreck Act was control and the lust for power. In their shotgun approach to shipwreck "preservation," archaeologists sought to possess totalitarian authority over all wreck sites in the country, aggregating to some tens of thousands of wrecks of which only a trivially small fraction were historically significant. The majority of wrecks had already been destroyed by time and the elements. Nearly all were the remains of commonplace vessels such as barges, ordinary sailing ships, and twentieth century steamships.

It is patently absurd to spend taxpayers' money to "preserve" a wreck when ships just like it still ply the seven seas. It's even more absurd to suffer unfounded beliefs that a wreck under water is preserved from the awful forces of nature. One might just as well "preserve" rare works of art by exposing them on windy, snow-covered mountaintops.

The archaeological community was a juggernaut gone wild on bad faith.

Founded to contest the ASA was the Atlantic Alliance for Maritime Heritage Conservation, a nonprofit organization that was headed by Charles McKinney, an archaeologist with the federal government and whose full-time job was to investigate proposals for historic landmarks and places; and Duncan Mathewson, the outspoken and volatile consulting archaeologist who worked with Mel Fisher on the *Atocha*. Seed money and primary financial support for the Atlantic Alliance was provided by Mel Fisher and other treasure salvors who sought to protect centuries-old Admiralty jurisdiction and to preserve private enterprise. Fisher had already made his millions so he had little if anything to gain by jumping into the brawl, yet not only did he travel to Washington, DC to protest the ASA, he brought with him his brilliant oratorical attorney, Dave Horan.

I began supporting the Atlantic Alliance as soon as I found out about it, in 1983. I attended meetings, and later joined some of its members in testifying before the

House of Representatives in opposition to the ASA, citing my tribulations with the National Oceanic and Atmospheric Administration (NOAA) over denial of access to the *Monitor* as an example of bad faith on the part of the government. By that time the fracas had reached a virulent level of hostility. I feared that my testimony would be purely incidental and largely ineffective, particularly in light of the opening statement made by Minnesota Representative Bruce Vento, who was the head of the subcommittee to which I presented my evidence. He announced haughtily that the hearing was a mere formality and would not affect the outcome of the bill. Bureaucratic minds were already made up.

I testified on May 3, 1985, along with other members of the Atlantic Alliance, including Mel Fisher and Dave Horan. We sat together at a long table, and took turns in presenting our views. We also submitted materials to support our convictions. I doubt that any Committee members bothered to read our supporting documentation. Listening to us – those members of the public who were the most adversely affected by the proposed legislation – was merely a formality which the Committee was forced to endure.

Here is a transcript of my testimony:

Dear Madams and Sirs:

You will find enclosed a manuscript which is the bulk of this letter. It is copyrighted, but I encourage you to photocopy it and pass it around in order that its importance be understood by members of the Committee involved with H.R. 25.

Although it is self explanatory, I will make further comment. As implied at the end of the article, divers are not merely concerned with recovering artifacts: they are proud to display them. Unfortunately, there are few opportunities presented to divers to display their finds. In the past ten years there have been only two such occasions in the Philadelphia area: 1976 at the

Philadelphia Civic Center, and 1982 at the New Jersey State Museum in Trenton. While diver attendance at these displays was good, the plain fact that there has not been more need for shipwreck artifact displays leads to an obvious conclusion: lack of interest from the nondiving public.

This lack of interest reached its epitome for me when I offered my entire collection of several thousand artifacts to the Philadelphia Maritime Museum – and they refused! Even a maritime museum was not interested enough in shipwreck history to make an effort to educate the public. So where do we go from here?

It is apparent that only a select group of people really care about recovering artifacts: wreck divers. They are the ones who hold impromptu displays at club meetings and underwater seminars. The world in general does not care. If they did, there would be no problem in starting repositories where artifacts could be kept on display. Most divers would love to give up their artifacts if they could be put somewhere and be seen and appreciated by more people.

I conclude, therefore, that instead of working against divers, the Committee should consider ways of working with them. After all, you'll never get a force as large, or as cheap, as wreck divers, to recover all those relics that the antishipwreck bill is supposed to preserve. I think that education is the way to go: by competent and interested archaeologists, and with a positive influence. People like being involved, they want to be included in projects, and will gladly volunteer their services – if only they were asked. I invite your comment.

Neither Vento nor any other Committee member deigned to comment.

Despite his stance of arrogance, Vento was mistaken. The bill did *not* pass, his presumptuous prediction to the contrary notwithstanding. Although we won the battle, we eventually lost the war. But at least we were able to stall a gross injustice for a few years.

By 1987, the Abandoned Shipwreck Act had been proposed for seven years straight, and had been defeated every time. It would seem that the people didn't want it. But what the majority wanted didn't matter to the infinitesimal minority whose personal agendas and ambitions denied accountability to the American public that they were supposed to represent.

Communism may have its politburos, but democracy has polit. burros and donkeys of a shadier kind. Chief ass in this case was Senator Bill Bradley of New Jersey. Since he couldn't get the ASA passed honestly, he resorted to chicanery and deceit in the bill's ultimate session. On the surface it appears that he presented a forceful oral argument to a full and attentive Senate, pleading that the august body should overlook seven years of undesirable legislative proposals and the strong opposition that they engendered, and should this time pass the bill. His speech was published in the Federal Register, which purportedly records all Senatorial dialogue as well as preliminary discussions on proposed bills and the votes themselves. The Federal Register duly noted that on December 18, 1987 a vote was taken and the Abandoned Shipwreck Act was passed by majority consent.

Like a merchant vessel, a proposed bill requires two passages in order to complete a voyage. The bill was required to pass in the House before it could be signed into law. Congress generally rubber-stamps bills that are already passed in the Senate, and vice versa, on the supposition that an unpopular or controversial bill wouldn't have gotten passed by the majority in the opposing house. Representatives don't like to appear antagonistic toward their counterparts in the legislative assembly unless there is a compelling reason to do so. Otherwise, one house might find itself opposed by the other when the situation was reversed and some other pet bill was proposed for vote.

Furthermore, representatives don't generally like to go against the tide. If they do, they get a reputation as obstructers, they lose the favor of their constituency, and they find themselves without backing in their own favorite causes. Since nearly half the States in the Union have no coastline, and therefore were not affected by the Act, those State representatives had no vested interest in the bill, and no self-serving reason to oppose it.

The Atlantic Alliance was quick to organize a protest before the bill came up for vote again in the House of Representatives. This afforded another opportunity for me to testify before the so-called august body.

A hearing was scheduled before the Subcommittee on National Parks and Public Lands, of the House Committee on Interior and Insular Affairs. I delivered the following testimony on February 4, 1988:

> In an already overlegislated country, where new laws continue to erode the premise of personal freedom and free enterprise on which this great nation is founded, the Abandoned Shipwreck Act serves as yet another harness strapped to the taxpayers. While the reins of injustice are boldly yanked by bureaucratic puppeteers, we cannot allow the blinders of political rhetoric to take the place of reason and foresight.
>
> In a democracy, the purpose of the state is not to own or to rule, but to protect the rights and property values of its citizens. Abandoned shipwrecks, by the very nature of abandonment, are not the possessions of the government merely by the fact of their existence. If shipwrecks belong to anyone, it is to those individuals with the will and the incentive to dive on them at their own cost and expenditure of time. The confiscation of this property under the guise of "the public good," coupled with the subsequent denial of public access, runs against all the grains of the democratic principle.

As an example of the manner in which government has already dealt with these issues, consider my confrontation with the *Monitor* National Marine Sanctuary. Despite its location in international waters, the U.S. government has laid claim to, and placed off limits to all Americans, the site of this historic Civil War ironclad. Under present law, those charged with the responsibility of preserving that wreck for the American people, have been empowered to monitor access to the site. They have instituted a permit application system which, in the words of one Sanctuary spokesperson, "was specifically designed to keep divers off the wreck."

Furthermore, meeting the requirements of the permit application is costly and time consuming to the applicant. My own permit application, including detailed descriptions of objectives, equipment, diving methods, and resumés and complete medical examinations for all participants (all of which is required by the Sanctuary before it will consider a permit application) was over one hundred (100) pages long. My purpose was not to salvage, not to damage, but merely to behold this piece of history, to photograph the remains, and to share those images with the public. Yet, despite the sincerity of my purpose, my efforts were preordained to fail by the very nature of the permit system. My permit application was arbitrarily denied on the grounds of safety. Reviewing personnel wholly ignored my extensive diving experience, despite submitted proof that I had already made *hundreds* of dives identical to that proposed for the *Monitor*.

Legally, the *Monitor* has been set aside for public benefit. But, in actuality, it has been spirited away in the name of "preservation." Since its inception as a Marine Sanctuary, no private citizen has been allowed to visit the site. Photography has been permitted only by expeditions sponsored by the Sanctuary. Clearly, the Sanctuary has failed to serve the American public; it serves only those government employees whose livings are earned by their positions on the Sanctuary payroll.

The result in this case of government aggrandizement is a complete abrogation of popular sovereignty, against which this country once waged revolutionary war. This is what can happen when government takes control. This is what *has* happened in the case of the *Monitor*. This is what will *continue* to happen should a select few paid government employees be allowed to dictate the terms of freedom to the American public. I felt strongly enough about the *Monitor* debacle to take it to Federal District Court, where a decision is now pending (*Gentile v. NOAA et al.*, C.A. #87-2192 (E.D. Pa).

In order to advance the cause of freedom in this country, and to set an example for the world of democracy, it is important that we not give in to any form of wholesale takeover. The Abandoned Shipwreck Act seeks to appropriate vested interests that have been in the public domain for the entire history of the United States. In many cases, these shipwrecks are known only because of diligent research by private individuals. To take away from them the fruits of their labors is equivalent to nationalizing a business after it has been shown profitable, with the stockholders ousted of their ownership.

While the issues in this case have been clouded by proponents of the Abandoned Shipwreck Act, who have arbitrarily assigned every shipwreck as a national resource without adequately describing what makes that shipwreck a national resource, one truth is self evident: that individual property rights in a free democratic society must be preserved in order to uphold the integrity of that society. Legislative action should not take away those rights. The brash enactment of laws that prohibit free enterprise is not within the spirit of the Constitution, nor within the bounds of freedom for all.

The sea is ever changing, ever destroying. As a shipwreck disintegrates, it passes before our eyes like a movie in extreme slow motion. Each frame is ephemeral, existing only for a brief instant in time, and must be viewed quickly before it dissolves.

Only by permitting unrestricted access to these shipwrecks can public awareness be expedited. To place off limits the tens of thousands of shipwrecks (most of which have no historic or archaeological significance) that are sunk off the American coast, and to usurp from more than four million (4,000,000) wreck divers their rights, is grossly unfair to the majority of shipwreck enthusiasts. Admiralty Law, as codified by HR-2071, has worked for over two centuries. Let it continue to work.

My plea fell largely on deaf ears – or, more properly, on ears that were closed by their own agenda. Nonetheless, I continued to write to my Congressional representative, Bob Borski, in order to voice my opposition to the bill. I also sent stern letters of protest to other representatives. Congressional advocates of the bill proceeded to bring it up for vote, but not without strong opposition from fellow members of Congress.

On March 28, 1988, the ASA was raised for discussion before the House. Concerns of opponents of the bill were typified by Texas Representative Jack Fields, who not only stated his reasons for opposing the bill, but who added historical context for its origination. I quote his speech in full:

"I rise in strong opposition to S. 858 [the Congressional version of Senate bill H.R. 74], the so-called Abandoned Shipwreck Act of 1988. "Frankly, this bill has no business being considered under suspension of the rules. It is flawed in a number of important ways and Members of this body should have an opportunity to offer amendments to improve it.

"I believe the amending process is particularly important in light of the fact that our colleague from California, Congressman Norm Shumway, has an amendment to protect the rights of sport divers, which I have yet to hear a single word of opposition. In fact, the House sponsor of this bill, Mr. [Charles] Bennett, has not only indicated that he supports the Shumway amendment, but that he would introduce legislation to eliminate this major deficiency in S. 858.

"Mr. Speaker, this is the wrong way to legislate. Let's improve S. 858 here and now and let's stop worrying about what the other body will or will not do. In their unrelentless [sic] attempt to avoid real debate, the proponents of this legislation have asked us to accept a flawed bill by denying this body its legitimate right to work its will.

"During our committee's consideration of S. 858, there were several amendments offered which address the concerns of our Nation's 4 million sport divers, the Department of State, and several other groups which are deeply troubled about certain provisions in this bill. "What is wrong, Mr. Speaker, with giving this body the chance to vote 'up or down' on each of these amendments? Isn't that how our legislative process in this, the people's body, is supposed to work?

"Mr. Speaker, in addition to the procedural problems I have in bringing up S. 858 today, I also have a number of serious reservations about this legislation which I would like to discuss.

"Before doing that, however, I would like to briefly touch upon the origins of this legislation. As many of my colleagues may know, this bill is a direct result of the failure of the State of Florida to win its battle against Mel Fisher in Federal district court.

"After more than 7 years of litigation and hundreds of court challenges, the State of Florida was unable to convince even one Federal judge that it had any legal basis or right to the *Atocha* treasure.

"While the State had no success in court, Federal District Judge James Lawrence King made admiralty law work in that case by establishing an 'East Coast Shipwreck Project.' As a result of this cooperative effort involving private salvors, archeologists, and sport divers, more archeological data was gained from the shipwrecks of the 1715 Spanish Plate Fleet in Florida waters than had been collected during the entire 20-year program controlled by the State of Florida.

"Unfortunately, the State of Florida refused to accept the mandate of the courts and instead turned its attention to the U.S. Congress. As a result, the first Abandoned Shipwreck Act was born.

"While proponents will argue that their sole interest is the protection of the abandoned shipwrecks, the real goal of this legislation is to severely restrict, if not prohibit, access to these vessels.

"S. 858 is a blatant political attempt to throw out 200 years of admiralty law, and the precedents of hundreds of court cases, by granting to the States, with little or no guidelines or restrictions, ownership to these vessels.

"And, once States have these vessels, how will they manage these resources? Well, if past history is any indication, the answer is: Not very well. We have already seen a number of States, including my own, enact regulations which outlaw all private salvage operations and restrict sport diver access.

"Mr. Speaker, there are no reported cases where a shipwreck under the jurisdiction of Federal admiralty court has been destroyed. Yet, States have a number of blights on their record. For instance, no one talks about the H.M.S. *Debraak*, an 18th-century British warship which sank off the coast of Delaware. In this case, the State of Delaware attempted to salvage this important vessel and ended up destroying it. Instead of following prescribed archeological procedures, the State yanked the ship from its watery grave, deposited it in the open air for several weeks without proper preservation, and then dumped it into a big hole at one of its State parks.

"What you ended up with was a shattered piece of junk instead of a beautiful underwater monument which could have been enjoyed by thousands of recreational divers.

"And what about the 572 artifacts found by Mel Fisher that the State of Florida confiscated and then lost during the 7 years of court litigation. If a State can't even safeguard a few valuables, can we really expect that they are going to protect hundreds of shipwrecks. Sadly, the answer is no!

"Mr. Speaker, these examples clearly indicate that State ownership is not a guarantee of historical preservation or protection. The private sector can and has provided adequate protection for the public interest. And the *Atocha* is a good example of that – more than half of the *Atocha* treasure will end up in museums and galleries for the enjoyment of all Americans.

"Mr. Speaker, sadly, I must conclude that by enacting this legislation we will end up doing far more harm than good. Without the incentive to find these vessels, they will not be found, and they will continue to deteriorate off the coast of States throughout America. And, the real losers are the American people – as they will be denied the opportunity to enjoy and appreciate this important part of our history.

"Finally, while much has been said about the protection of the rights of the 4 million sport divers in this Nation, there is nothing in S. 858 which guarantees or mandates sport diver access to any shipwrecks in State waters.

"While it is true that the author of this bill has included a 'Sense of Congress' statement about reasonable access to the general public, this provision is unenforceable and nonbinding. Once enacted, the State can and will restrict access to these vessels.

"I was hoping that at a minimum we would include language in this bill which guarantees sport divers the opportunity to continue to enjoy their hobby. As one of my constituents so articulately stated, 'There is no desire on the part of sport divers to destroy items of historical significance. In fact, more items are on public display as a result of artifacts that they have donated to museums and galleries than from any other source, including archeologists.'

"To restrict sport diving access is also counterproductive because there is no question that it is the sport diver and not the professional archeologist who finds the vast majority of shipwrecks. According to the Atlantic Alliance for Maritime Heritage Conservation, in 1 year, sport divers discovered more than 2,500 wrecks while Federal and State archeologists together found less than 200. And of all these finds, there has never been anyone who has sighted [sic] examples of looting, scavenging, or destruction of these ships or their artifacts.

"Mr. Speaker, the authors of this bill don't like to hear this but admiralty law worked well: shipwrecks and artifacts have not been destroyed. Moreover, admiralty law provides the necessary incentive for private individuals to go out and discover shipwrecks and it assures access to all interested groups.

"Mr. Speaker, we must not discriminate against these 4 million Americans and those latter-day Christopher Columbus' who are willing to find and salvage these shipwrecks in a proper, safe, and archeologically sound way.

"I urge my colleagues to vote 'no' on this bill so that it can be considered, as it should, in the normal and proper legislative manner."

Fields was not the only one to recognize that wreck-divers were being struck by shrapnel that was intended for commercial salvors. Michigan Representative Robert Davis spoke next:

"Mr. Speaker, the recent discovery of a number of historic shipwrecks, whether they be in Federal or State waters, underscores the interest the American public has in these underwater treasures. My office has been flooded with mail concerning S. 858 that we are considering today.

"Recreational divers have urged me not to support these bills because of the danger that a State could shut the door on diving access to many of these wrecks, depriving them of an enjoyable and harmless hobby and driving those who operate diving operations out of business. Salvors also protest this legislation, citing the Admiralty law provisions in our Constitution and the specter of huge penalties.

"On the other hand, historic preservationists admonish me to vote for passage of the Senate bill with no changes, fearing that if the bill should be returned to the other Chamber, it would never see the light of day again."

If Davis only knew how close to the truth he hit. But more on that later.

California Representative Norman Shumway repeated the concerns of Fields and Davis, with special emphasis on collateral damage against recreational divers:

"Mr. Speaker, this bill should be voted down today on both substantive and procedural grounds.

"First, the substantive reasons. In my mind, there is a constitutional question as to whether this bill is a good idea, even in theory. At the very least, however, if the House is to pass S. 858 and send it to the President for his signature, the bill should be amended to correct the legal and policy problems it poses in its present form.

"First, by far the most glaring problem with the bill is that it fails to protect the interests of sport divers, and the private sector generally. Proponents of the bill point to section 4's so-called rights of access provision as protection for sport divers. That is simply not true. Section 4 contains only nonbinding recommendations regarding rights of access.

"Simply stated, there is no legal, binding, or enforceable way, under this bill as it is written, to ensure that sport divers' right to dive on these wrecks, even for purely recreational purposes, will be protected by States. Moreover, there will no longer be the same private sector incentive to go out and discover wrecks as there is now under the present system. I can't stress these points enough. These two factors – the failure to protect sport divers and the elimination of private sector incentive to discover shipwrecks – more than any, are, in my mind, why this bill should be voted down under suspension.

"Because of these gaps in S. 858, the 4 million sport divers throughout the United States are virtually unanimous in their opposition to the bill. And they are by far the largest constituency group affected by the bill."

Shumway went on to cite numerous instances in which States had acted irresponsibly with regard to shipwreck salvage, as opposed to the responsible conduct of recreational divers and commercial salvors.

He also repeated Davis' sentiment, one that demonstrated prescience: "I offered amendments to correct all of these problems with the bill last Wednesday. The only argument that was made by Members, including the author of the House bill, Mr. Bennett, was that if we change the bill and improve it, *there is no guarantee that the other body will pass it again.* No one raised a substantive or policy reason as to why my amendments shouldn't be adopted." (The italics are mine, and are intended to emphasize a point that I will make later.)

California Representative Walter Herger reiterated the key objections to the bill: "We have been told by the proponents of this legislation that S. 858 would help preserve and protect shipwrecks of historical significance. As some of my colleagues have pointed out, however, this particular bill does nothing of the sort. The bill creates no systematic means for preserving shipwrecks beyond ceding control over these vessels to the States. There are no guidelines for States to follow which would enhance preservation. In fact, taking the right of exploration away from individual divers might easily prove counterproductive from a preservation standpoint.

"As I mentioned earlier, the bill grants all control over certain shipwrecks to the States, and unfortunately, few of those States have the economic resources necessary to launch publicly financed exploration and recovery efforts for the numerous wrecks which might lie in their coastal waters. Under this bill, States may restrict access to ships and prevent private divers from working to assist in their preservation. The vast majority of these divers share both an appreciation of the importance of the wrecks, and the resources and the time to search for them and ensure that adequate steps are taken to preserve their remains.

"In fact, history has shown that those States which have title to vessels in their waters, have gone so far as to completely deny sport divers the right to even search for such wrecks. Texas for example has taken this very approach, and many interested parties are worried that as a result, important archeological treasures will never be discovered.

"The bill only serves to further expand Government's control over yet another area which has previously been left to private individuals. Individuals who have contributed substantially to our understanding of our Nation's history. Sport divers have been instrumental in the discovery of a number of shipwrecks which have proven to be extremely valuable to those interested in history.

"I do believe that the Government has a positive role to play in the discovery and recovery of such vessels. I do not, however, feel that it is wise for us to establish a system that will actually discourage sport divers, who historically have been far more successful than the States at locating ships lost for centuries on the ocean floor, from helping to preserve a piece of American history. For these reasons, I oppose S. 858 and would urge my colleagues to do likewise."

Adherents were silent against these reasoned arguments against the bill's obvious and objectionable deficiencies. Other representatives also questioned the validity of the bill, as well as its constitutionality.

Only two representatives rose to speak in favor of the bill. (Neither of these was Walter Jones of North Carolina, the Chairman of the House Merchant Marine and Fisheries Committee. He was the most aggressive proponent of the bill when I testified in opposition.)

The most vocal proponent was Bruce Vento. He glibly attempted to gloss over the bill's inequities by disclaiming the objections of his fellow Members. His repudiation was weak: while pronouncing the bill's so-called intents, he admitted that those intents would not be binding upon the States.

In other words, although he stated that the bill was not intended to deny diver access, he hoped that the States would comply with the guidelines to that effect. He then admitted that those guidelines would not be written until after the bill was passed. This was equivalent to asking Congress to issue a signed blank check on which the recipient could write any amount.

Florida Representative Charles Bennett, the sponsor of the House bill, committed perjury by claiming that the Senate version of the bill had been passed "enthusiastically." Bennett was more honest when he stated, "The Senate sponsor, Bill Bradley, of New Jersey, said that probably won't happen again."

He was right about that. You will soon see why.

Despite the momentous objections, Vento moved "to suspend the rules and pass the Senate bill." Suspension means "that no amendments were allowed to be offered." In other words, Vento wanted the bill passed exactly as written, without modifications or alterations.

Shumway took exception. "Mr. Speaker, I object to the vote on the ground that a quorum is not present."

The Speaker agreed. He ordered the Sergeant at Arms to notify absent Members. A vote was taken the following day "by electronic device."

Of the 432 Members who were polled, thirty chose to abstain. After the votes were cast and counted, it was found that Congress "failed to gain the two-thirds vote required for passage in the House on March 29 [1988]."

One way to get an unfavorable bill passed is to keep reintroducing it, in the hope that the next time the defeated bill is put to a vote, a sufficient number of its opponents would not be available to vote against it, so that the proponents could succeed in having it passed.

S. 858 was reintroduced two weeks later, on April 13, 1988. This time it squeaked through, helped no doubt by Bennett's lying proclamation that the Senate had already cast its vote of confidence in favor of the bill.

President Ronald Reagan signed the bill into law on April 28, 1988.

When the Abandoned Shipwreck Act became law, it became the greatest land grab since the Louisiana Purchase. The submerged territory added untold thousands of square miles to State ownership and control.

Yet, as I discovered, the ASA was based upon a fraudulent premise and was passed by Machiavellian machinations that, although technically legal under the present system of government, are not condoned by the spirit of the law under true democratic principles.

The Atlantic Alliance has been unfairly criticized by some for failing to achieve its objective to overthrow the Abandoned Shipwreck Act, partly because of in-fighting among the competing salvage outfits that were its sponsors, and partly because it did not effectively coordinate the voices of recreational divers who were adversely affected by the pellets of archaeologists' shell fire aimed primarily at the treasure salvors. This isn't true. Salvors may have had their differences, but they offered a unified front, else the Atlantic Alliance wouldn't have existed.

Regional directors such as Joyce Hayward and Pam Warner expended considerable personal energy toward galvanizing sport divers for the cause – and were greeted largely with yawns and inertia. Recreational divers were content to let someone else fight the battle. They weren't willing to be inconvenienced. They languished with indifference and, through apathy, let their shipwrecks be legislated away from them.

The opposition camp, on the other hand, was not only strongly organized but it was infinitely well subsidized – by taxpayers' money. And whereas Atlantic Alliance members were volunteers, all the archaeologists and politicians who framed and supported the bill were paid full-time to do so. That was part of their job. De-

spite these obstacles to freedom, the Abandoned Shipwreck Act was overthrown seven times in seven consecutive years.

What ultimately enabled the bill to get passed was
trickery and conspiracy: the hoodwinking of the American people through political opportunism. McKinney
told me that, according to rumor on the Hill, only a
handful of senators were in session when the bill was
passed: perhaps as few as three. I didn't believe him –
didn't want to believe him – and spent years tracking
down the facts. When I blew the lid off the truth, it was
more sordid than I could possibly have imagined.

I became suspicious right away when Bill Bradley
refused to meet me in person, refused to talk with me
on the telephone, and refused to reply to my letters.

After more than a year of persistence, one of his un-
derlings condescended to speak with me on the telephone. All he would tell me was that the bill was not
passed with a roll call vote, and that therefore the names
of the voters were not recorded.

I immediately protested, "But Bradley was there. It
was his bill. He must remember how many senators
were in attendance."

The aide would tell me nothing. A follow-up letter
(written by a Bradley aide and stamped with Bradley's
signature) reiterated Bradley's refusal to provide information. The following letter was dated June 8, 1989:

> Dear Mr. Gentile
>
> I recently received your letter of April 14,
> 1989, asking for additional information on the
> passage of the Abandoned Shipwreck Act. I un-
> derstand that you have spoken to members of
> my staff regarding your request.
>
> I am enclosing a copy of the Congressional
> Record from December 19, 1987, showing the
> passage of the Act. In addition, I have included
> the Department of the Interior's report printed in
> the Federal Register on this subject.
>
> As you can see, the bill was passed under a

"unanimous consent agreement." Under this agreement, a bill is passed by voice vote as long as no Senators in the chamber object to the bill. All members offices are alerted that the issue is coming to the floor for vote. If no Senator formally objects the bill is then passed. Therefore it follows that if no Senator objected during this procedure than [sic] all Senators present "unanimously" agreed to the measure. Because there was no roll call vote, it is impossible to determine which Senators were present at the time of passage.

I hope that this answers your questions. Feel free to contact me on any other matters of mutual concern.

This letter certainly did *not* answer my questions. Nor was it "impossible" to determine which Senators were present at the time a bill was brought up for vote.

What Bradley meant was that instead of requesting written ballots, the chairman simply called for a show of hands and asked for "ayes" and "nays." In such a case, the Federal Register simply shows whether or not a bill was passed, not by what percentage. It was my contention that this situation was irrelevant. Since it was Bradley's prize bill and he was there to promote it, he would certainly remember the details. Undoubtedly he did, but he wouldn't talk to me because – as I finally discovered – in order to answer my questions he would have had to admit his culpability.

On June 14, 1989, I sent the following letter to Bradley:

Thank you for finally responding to my plethora of letters (fifteen at last count), the first of which was submitted to you well over a year ago. While at first glance your June 8 letter appears to contain no information, a careful reading infers that, on the contrary, it conceals a great deal. Let me explain.

When I first asked you to respond to questions pertaining to the passage of the Abandoned Shipwreck Act (see enclosures), my purpose was to quell the rumor circulating around the District that only three (3) Senators were present during the vote: you, and two others. I did not want to believe that a United States Senator would wait until late Saturday night just before Christmas, when most other Senators had already returned to their home states for the holidays, to put on the floor a bill so controversial that it had been vigorously fought down for eight consecutive years. I sought vindication of this accusation, and reaffirmation of the integrity of the senatorial office.

Now, my heart is saddened. Your continued and blatant refusal to reply to my queries, your squirming under direct questioning, and your misleading statements, seem to point to a cover up. Your statement "it is impossible to determine which Senators were present at the time of passage," is not true. Because the Congressional Record does not list the Senators present during passage does not make such a determination impossible, only more difficult. Please note that I did not ask the Congressional Record to answer my questions, I asked you. You, not the Congressional Record, have refused to answer.

I would like to see you cleared of these charges, but you will not let me. You promoted the bill, you were there during its passage, so your notes, personal memoranda, and recollections can answer my questions. Because of the importance of the bill to you personally, and because you finally saw it pass after so many years of rejection, I am sure you have indelibly imprinted memories of that moment of triumph.

At this time I form my question in such a way that your refusal to answer will be constituted as incrimination; that is, unless you refute in writing the accusation, it will go on record that you were unable to make such a refutation, and that therefore the rumors are to be believed. (Since you rely heavily on negative communication, this method precludes my having to write multiple letters.)

If more than three Senators were in attendance, were there less than ten? Less than twenty? Less than fifty? Even the admission of only a hazy recollection allows you to pick a category of approximation. If you prefer to use the convenience of "loss of memory," please state so.

I seek only the truth. Please help me find it.

That Bradley did not deign to reply speaks for itself about his guilt.

I am not one to give up easily. I took a different tack by submitting a FOIA request for all of Bradley's "documentation, personal memoranda, telephone transcriptions, and senatorial debate" relating to the ASA; before, during, and after passage of the bill. I did this concurrently with my repeated attempts to elicit an honest response from Bradley.

James M. Kovakas, Attorney in Charge of the FOI/PA Unit, Civil Division of the U.S. Department of Justice, sent me the following letter (dated June 15, 1989):

Dear Mr. Gentile

This letter is in reply to your letter dated June 1, 1989, seeking to appeal under the Freedom of Information Act, the refusal of Senator Bill Bradley to provide you with information relating to the Abandoned Shipwreck Act of 1987. As I advised you by telephone, the federal Freedom of Information Act does not apply to the Congress or the Judiciary but only to the Executive Agencies.

Since the statute does not apply to requests made to U.S. Senators, there is no appeal procedure and this office can not assist you.

I eventually uncovered the squalid and unvarnished truth after years of persistent effort and research. All Senatorial and Congressional proceedings were video-taped by C-Span. These tapes could be viewed at and purchased from the Library of Congress. Yet when I sub-mitted a request to view the tapes of the Senate hearings that were held on December 18, 1987, after an unduly long passage of time my request was denied.

No explanation was provided with the denial. Follow-up demands for an explanation went unanswered. Even-tually I submitted a Freedom of Information Act request. After another unduly long passage of time, my FOIA re-quest was denied. I appealed, and after yet another un-duly long passage of time, my appeal was denied.

Finally, I wrote a letter to my Congressional repre-sentative, Bob Borski. I had voted for Borski because he was one of those rare politicians who kept the needs and wants of his constituents constantly in mind. Unlike politicians who made empty campaign promises in order to get elected, and who then did what they wanted when they took office, Borski was a true representative of the people.

I explained my position and described the opposition that I met in accessing public information. Borski wrote a stern letter to the Library of Congress, demanding that the videotapes be released to me. Reluctantly, and after untoward delay, the Library of Congress acquiesced to his demand.

By this time, two years had passed since I had made my initial request.

The Library of Congress notified me by mail that the appropriate tapes would be retrieved from the long-term storage facility, and made available to me (for reasons that I never understood) at the National Archives in Washington, DC. This is what I saw.

December 18, 1987 was the Saturday before Christ-mas. Nearly all the senators had already gone home to spend the holidays with their families. Only a handful remained in Washington, and of those even fewer stayed in session. Those who had bills to propose or statements to make did so in the morning, then departed. By late afternoon only two senators were present in the Senate chamber: Robert Byrd and Alan Simpson. Brock Adams stood at the podium and resided as Chairperson. Bill Bradley did *not* appear.

Byrd and Simpson extended their stay in Washington for one reason only: to pass unfavorable legislation that would otherwise have been vetoed by those senators who were not in attendance. Byrd and Simpson had their own precious bills to pass, and they were in cahoots with Bradley to pass his bill. Byrd submitted a copy of Bradley's speech and asked that it be appended to the record *as if it had been read.* Thus, one perusing the Federal Register would be deceived into believing that Bradley was present that day and delivered his pleading in person. The Federal Register doesn't distinguish between written and oral statements, and surrounding dialogue is deleted so that the truth cannot be determined.

After the false submission, Byrd asked that a vote on the bill be taken. Adams waived the reading of the bill and went through the pre-voting formality as if the Senate were in full session. "All in favor?" The camera focused on Byrd and Simpson, who stood side by side. Both stated "Aye."

Adams then asked "Opposed?" He could clearly see that behind Byrd and Simpson the vast chamber was totally empty. The camera clearly showed that every seat was vacant. Byrd and Simpson stood side by side in front of the chairperson's podium. Adams knew that they had already voted in favor. Who was he trying to kid with this sham? After a moment of silence, he said, "The ayes have it."

That was how the Abandoned Shipwreck Act was passed. And it was legal. But that's not the end of the story. Byrd went on to propose another half a dozen bills, and Simpson parroted his agreement. The pre-voting litany was repeated for each bill, the chairman called for a vote each time, and these additional bills were passed into law.

Still, the worst was yet to come.

The session closed. The Senate chamber dissolved from view and was replaced by a title screen which stated simply that the Senate was not in session. I was not able to see that the chamber was empty; I was led to believe that it was. There was no reason for me to expect the session to resume, but because it is my custom to be thorough, I fast-forwarded through eight hours of blank videotape. Incredibly, just before the official midnight closing, two senators sneaked into the chamber and reopened the session.

Byrd stood alone on the floor. Assisting him in his nefarious deeds by acting as Chairperson was John Glenn, the space hero turned senator and now a conspiratorial turncoat. Like an automaton, Glenn pronounced the procedural litany as if the full assembly were gathered. Byrd proposed a bill by name and number only, Glenn accepted the proposal as if it had been read in its entirety, then called for a vote. Byrd alone voted aye, whereupon Glenn asked the empty chamber for all opposed, and, hearing no dissenting voices, said "Passed. Next bill."

In this manner Byrd forced through another half a dozen unpopular bills, all by himself and with no one there to oppose him. When Byrd passed these bills, he did not represent the majority of the nation's voters, nor did he represent the majority of their representatives. He represented no voters; he represented only himself. Yet his whim, his personal ambition, and his single vote constituted law.

Thus were passed into law that day more than a dozen bills that were binding upon some 240 million American citizens, because one or two people wanted it so. Thus were the American people raped by Senatorial fiat.

I must have been asleep in class the day my history teacher covered the legislative process and a legislator's responsibilities to the people he was supposed to represent. I don't remember being taught that such shenanigans could be conducted in the highest office of the legislative process.

Legal it may be; ethical it is not. Laws that are passed without the majority consent of the public are wrongful laws, or unlawful laws.

In this sense wrongful means "contrary to conscience or morality; unfair; unjust." Unlawful means "contrary to accepted morality or convention."

In my opinion, one is not morally obligated to obey wrongful laws. My defense of this position is that the illicit nature of the passage of such laws is questionable, and can and should be strenuously contested.

Beware the system that allows circumvention of the people's will; beware of leaders whose only interest is their own. Otherwise, liberty may be short-lived and freedom a hollow word.

The Demise of Moral Principles

I am certain that the wrongful passage of the Abandoned Shipwreck Act was in no way an isolated event. It is simply the only such occurrence I am aware of because of my personal interest and exhaustive research. The occurrence also demonstrates the depths of depravity to which representatives will stoop in order to cover up their anti-American antics and activities.

Nonetheless, no matter how a piece of legislation is sneaked onto the books past an unwary public by means of prestidigitation, the result it still the same: it becomes law.

This fact leads to an interesting philosophical speculation: what is the ethical value of a law that was passed by unethical means?

I once published an article in which the first line stipulated, "The law is a reflection of society's code of morality." I have long since regretted having made that statement. In my defense I claim that I was naïve at the time I wrote it. I have since grown wiser. Or, more correctly, I have since encountered so many corrupt laws, lawyers, and law makers that I have revised my conception of the moral value of law. I have come to learn that law differs greatly from a society's actual code of morality.

A law may have *no* ethical value, but it's still law. Law in its purest form is considered to be the backbone of government, but how strong is that backbone when it is supported by laws that were passed by unethical means; that were in fact passed *against* the will of the majority of the people?

Legislators wear big sleeves so they have someplace to hide their legerdemain.

Riders of the Purple Mage

Perhaps the most common and pervasive method of enacting controversial or unfavorable legislation is by the attachment of riders.

A rider is a clause or provision that is inserted into a legislative bill after the bill has been written and gone through the review process, but before the bill has come up for vote. Usually a rider has little or nothing to do with the subject of the bill. It's a tagalong that has no business being there – a pet piece of legislation that would have no chance of getting passed on its own. It rides piggyback on a piece of legislation that is either likely or certain to get passed.

Riders are legion. A legislative bill might have dozens or even scores of riders attached to it, clinging like so many leeches, and often sucking the blood out of the original bill; of, if you will permit me to change metaphors, like parasitic tapeworms, draining the bill of its purpose by eating it from inside.

Riders avoid the review process. Whereas an original bill must pass through extensive committee meetings and numerous public hearings, at which the bill may be modified and the language clarified, a rider is appended fully formed and unchangeable, exactly the way the sponsor wants it to read. There is no public involvement in a rider, no hearings, no debate, no examination, no scrutiny, no feedback, and no accountability. The passage of a rider is a law unto itself.

Other representatives may not object to riders, or may not care about them, as long as they are not affected by them. Indeed, other representatives may have attached riders of their own. They will then dicker with the sponsors of other riders and make a you-vote-for-mine-and-I'll-vote-for-yours kind of deal.

If a rider is appended at the very last minute before the vote, representatives might not even be aware of its existence when they cast their ballot. This is the sneakiest and most underhanded way of tricking representatives into voting a rider into law.

The legislative bills that are targeted the most for riders are appropriations bills. These bills are vital to the operation of the government. Agencies cannot operate without funding, so legislators can't afford to delay enactment. Appropriations bills are also the most difficult to negotiate. Government agencies must justify every dollar that they are asking for. The review process is exhaustive and takes a great deal of time, so legislators are not likely to vote against an appropriations bill unless one or more line-items is egregiously improper.

A rider is an insidious way of circumventing the democratic process. I remember reading a newspaper article in the 1970's about how one representative (either a Senator or a Congressman, I don't recall which; I wasn't keeping notes in those days) slipped in a rider in which an individual who was mentioned by name did not have to pay federal income tax that year. The bill passed, and that person avoided his entire tax liability.

Misrepresentation

Most riders cater to the personal agenda of the sponsor, or to special interest groups that contributed heavily to the sponsor's campaign fund. This latter scenario is equivalent to "buying" or "bribing" a representative to effect legislation that will benefit one group at the disadvantage of other groups or collective interests.

In 1998, eighteen riders were attached to the appropriations bill to fund the Department of the Interior. These riders all sought to thwart environmental laws in order to enrich certain parties at the expense of the taxpayer. One rider would permit private timber companies to log in the Tongass National Forest of Alaska. Another rider would redirect funding that was earmarked for public road repair in national forests to instead repair unauthorized logging roads. Another rider would allow oil and gas industries to avoid paying $86 million in royalties to the federal government. Yet another rider would authorize nearly $14 million for the construction of a road through a national forest to a planned and privately owned ski resort; this rider would subsidize the developer so that he could make money.

These are just a few examples of harmful riders that representatives have sponsored for personal benefit. Here is another. In 2003, Senator Christopher Bond of Missouri wrote a rider that would prevent California from requiring emissions reductions on small engines. He did this because Briggs & Stratton, one of the largest manufacturers of lawnmower engines, had two factories in Missouri. California's strict emissions controls would prevent polluting engines from being sold in that State. The reduction of sales would put thousands of Briggs & Stratton employees out of work.

That same year, Senator Ted Stevens of Alaska wrote a rider that would change the rules for crabbing in the North Pacific, so that the harvest could be increased and promised to individual fishing and processing companies.

Fowl Politics

How do these riders go unnoticed, you might ask, when they are so blatantly prejudicial and injurious to the public at large, when they contravene established law, and when they disregard the wishes of the voters?

By way of explanation, the federal spending bill for 2003 was more than 3,000 pages in length, and substantiated nearly $4 billion in appropriations. Secreted among the verbiage was one lone sentence that made a provision for the Department of Agriculture to certify meat as "organic" even if the meat producer nourished his livestock and poultry with feed that included artificial chemicals.

A solitary sentence could easily be overlooked when it was buried in a document that was larger than most encyclopedias; especially, as it turned out, when that sentence was added at the last minute in a secret session behind closed doors. One minute the rider wasn't there, and the next minute – like magic – it appeared.

The culprit in this foul deed was Congressman Nathan Deal of Georgia, who conspired with Speaker of the House Denny Hastert to slip in the rider. Investigation revealed that Fieldale Farms Corporation, a chicken farm in Baldwin, Georgia, donated money for Deal's re-election, in return for which they expected him to make it legal to raise their stock on nonorganic feed, but to advertise their product as organic, so as to enable them to compete with meat producers who paid the extra cost of using purely organic feed that had been grown without the treatment of pesticides. In other words, Fieldale Farms wanted to lie to consumers and have their lies legalized.

When this pullet provision was discovered after passage of the bill, Senators and Congressmen of both parties were incensed nearly to riot over Deal's new deal. Chief among the legislative protestors was Senator Patrick Leahy, who was primarily responsible for introducing the Organic Food Production Act of 1990. He and Senator Olympia Snowe introduced new legislation to repeal Deal's unscrupulous provision. Scores of other senators joined their ranks to present a consolidated front. Within two weeks, Deal's rider was invalidated, and additional legislation was implemented to protect the Act from future tampering.

Despite Deal's stealth plan to subvert the law, he was not even reprimanded because, although attaching such a rider was unethical, it was not illegal. Nor was Denny Hastert reprimanded. Double dealing among legislators was simply par for the course, and dishonest shenanigans were everyday events. Indeed, I would not be surprised if many of the Senators and Congresspersons who voted to annul the inorganic rider had employed the same scurrilous tactic themselves. Manipulation of the law is a common tool in the trade of a representative.

This was only one crooked rider among thousands that have violated America's democratic principles throughout the country's history.

Naval Blockade

I had a personal stake in a rider that was inserted at the last minute à la Deal into the National Defense Authorization Act of 2005. After debate was closed and just before the funding bill was scheduled for vote in both the Senate and the House, someone managed to sneak in a rider that asserted title to the Navy of all abandoned and "sunken military craft and associated contents."

Like most riders, this one had nothing to do with the bill to which it was attached. Nonetheless, when the bill was enacted, this pernicious provision was passed into law.

According to the prohibitions in the rider, "no person shall engage in or attempt to engage in any activity directed at a sunken military craft that disturbs, removes, or injures any sunken military craft" anywhere in the world, under threat of a fine of $100,000.

A grapnel or other anchoring device can be construed as a means of causing injury. Thus the rider's fine print authorizes discretionary power to ban observing and photographing submerged "craft," the definition of which includes crashed airplanes as well as scuttled warships.

Score another point for terrorism against democracy. Worse yet, this terrorist act originated in the country that was supposed to protect its citizens from terrorism. And worst of all, the act was instigated by one of the nation's departments whose sworn duty was to fight all forms of terrorism, "both foreign and domestic."

My readers must be wondering why the Navy gives a hoot about rusting hulks that it has let lay at the bottom of the ocean since World War Two or earlier, and which have no military or salvage value. The answer may surprise you: the Navy does *not* give a hoot. The Navy is preoccupied with national defense, not with overseeing wrecks that it has abandoned long ago.

But, there is a division within the Navy called the Naval Historical Center. The NHC was established to collect and preserve Naval documents, and to facilitate historical research. The NHC is operated *not* by Naval officers and enlisted personnel, but by civilians. In the mid-1990's, a handful – literally, five – of the senior civilian employees embarked on a power trip to take control of all the Navy's sunken airplanes and warships. They did this not for financial gain, but to exercise authority that they wished to possess.

After these control freaks assumed command of the NHC, they not only discriminated against private researchers by limiting access to public records, but they started an initiative to enact legislation that would grant them total and autonomous control over all submerged Naval vessels and aircraft. They used their position in the U.S. Navy to pull political puppet strings that resulted in the rider in question. They now use the Naval Criminal Investigative Service to enforce their misbegotten authority.

Under the banner of the U.S. Navy, the NHC has prosecuted legitimate salvors who have salvaged crashed airplanes, and has threatened to prosecute divers who had recovered scrap material from sunken warships unless they turned over their junk to the NHC.

Neither the nation's voters nor the four million scuba divers who were adversely affected by this stray clause in the appropriations bill had any say in the matter.

This is just one more example of how one, or two, or a handful of individuals have dictated terms that affect every citizen in the country. Democracy lies fallow when the voters are left out of the equation.

Final Irony

I cannot help but add a final bit of irony with respect

to the current plight of sunken warships. In 2007, I embarked upon a dedicated effort to locate the site of a minesweeper that was lost by collision in Boston Harbor during World War Two: the *YMS-14*. I wanted to find the wreck so I could include a description of the site in a book that I was then completing: *Shipwrecks of Massachusetts: North*.

The hulk originally lay in the shipping lane. The Navy Supervisor of Salvage "advised there was no salvage value to the wreck and requested approval to demolish it or remove it as a menace to navigation." This advice was approved, and 750 pounds of explosives were placed in and around the sunken hull to demolish it. The U.S. Army Corps of Engineers then wire-dragged the remains in order to complete the destruction. The *YMS-14* was subsequently stricken from the Navy Register on April 28, 1945.

The NHC did all they could to thwart my research efforts by withholding pertinent documents. However, with information from local historians, and from written records that I found at the National Archives, I determined the approximate location of the wreck.

Marcie Bilinski lent support by furnishing her boat and her diving expertise. After several days of searching by means of electronic detection equipment, and many hours under water scouring the seabed, we discovered the flattened and scattered remains of the *YMS-14*. The shipping lane had been moved some time in the past half century. The wreck now lay about one hundred yards south of the channel marker buoys.

I conducted a detailed survey of the site, and took photographs to illustrate my text. Of the eight depth charges with which the minesweeper was armed, five were partially exposed in the debris field. I printed a color photograph of a depth charge on the back cover of the book. I quipped about how this picture would make some heads turn.

Little did I know!

People in officialdom read my book, and must have turned their heads all the way around, like some evil demon undergoing exorcism. They must have been appalled at the idea of inert explosives lying so close to the shipping lane. They reacted in knee-jerk fashion. Operating in secret, the Navy dispatched an underwater explosives team to destroy all vestige of the half-dissolved depth charges. They destroyed what was left of the wreck in the process.

Had the witch-hunters at the NHC caught me removing a chunk of rusted iron from the wreck, they would have prosecuted me for theft of a priceless Navy relic. Yet the Navy thought nothing of utterly destroying the wreck.

I suppose this is what is meant by Naval intelligence.

All or Nothing

Drastic measures call for drastic action.

In 1995, President Bill Clinton vetoed the appropriations bill for the Department of the Interior. With no funding forthcoming from the federal government, a number of agencies were shut down for lack of money to pay salaries. Hundreds of thousands of employees were furloughed without pay, and essential services were suspended.

Clinton did not object to the bill itself. He objected to the riders.

Attached to the bill were seventeen riders that sought to circumvent long-time environmental laws by excluding special groups from compliance.

Clinton objected so strongly to these conspicuously bad riders that he did the only thing that he was empowered to do. He then suggested that if the objectionable riders were either deleted or revised, he would sign the bill. A temporary funding bill jump-started the government several days later.

The appropriations bill was edited and re-introduced, but Clinton still found certain riders objectionable. Once again he asserted his power of veto. This time the government was shut down for three weeks.

Not until the most egregious riders were knocked off their legislative saddles did Clinton append his Presidential signature.

The repercussions of the government shut-down were severe. This was exactly the message that Clinton wanted to send to Congress with respect to riders that thwarted the law and dodged the democratic process.

The Buck Stop

Forty-four of the fifty States in the Union have a provision in their constitution for line-item veto. A line-item veto permits the governor to veto specific items within a proposed bill without having to veto the entire bill. The federal Constitution has no such provision. Thus a President is often put in the unfavorable position of either vetoing an entire bill, as Clinton did, or signing a bill that is choked with riders that favor specific States or special interest groups with exemptions and privileges that contradict established law by which other States and groups must abide. There is no other recourse.

All too often during election campaigns, you will hear a nominee accuse his opponent of registering opposition to a certain critical bill by voting against it. Undoubtedly the statement is true. What you don't hear is *why* the opponent voted against the bill. Usually it is because he objected to the riders, but that fact is overlooked or never mentioned as a possibility. Keep this in mind when you hear ruthless campaign rhetoric. Partial-truth tactics are deceiving.

After the 1995 appropriations bill was finally approved, Senators Bob Dole and John McCain sponsored a bill to grant line-item veto authority to the President. The bill passed through the House and the Senate, and Clinton signed it into law on April 9, 1996. During the following twelve months, Clinton used his new power to veto eighty-two riders on eleven bills. This system enabled the government to operate continuously, while it allowed the President to cut spending on projects that favored certain States and special interest groups while disfavoring others.

Senator Robert Byrd challenged the Presidential line-item veto bill. You may recall from the beginning of this section that Byrd conspired with Simpson and Bradley to pass the Abandoned Shipwreck Act when the Senate was not in session, and that later that same Saturday night prior to Christmas he passed half a dozen other bills all by himself. Byrd was the most contemptible abuser of riders in the Senate. Squandering federal money on make-work projects in West Virginia may have gotten him re-elected, but his extravagance did not help the country as a whole. Byrd completely obviated the will of the majority.

After a year in court, the Presidential line-item veto was declared unconstitutional. The Supreme Court overruled the decision. Then the City of New York and an Idaho farmer's market challenged the line-item veto on different grounds, with Byrd supporting the case as an amicus curiae. Once again the Presidential line-item veto was found unconstitutional. This time the Supreme Court affirmed the decision.

And there it stands.

The Fractionation of E Pluribus Unum

The machinations of elected officials such as Byrd and Deal result in raw deals that give the bird to American democracy by outwitting the voting process. These officials represented themselves and their own agendas rather than the will of the people who elected them to represent *their* interests.

This kind of mischief and manipulation of the system provided no checks and balances, no committee discussions, no public debate, and no way for voters to have their views represented. Laws are being legislated without the people knowing about them; or, if they learn about them, are unable to stop them from being enacted or having them repealed.

The absurdity here is that exploitative lawmakers are allowed to enact injurious legislation that is detrimental the majority of the population, but the President is not allowed to protect the population by preventing such legislation from passing into law.

Congress may spend months or even years in framing much-needed legislation, engaging in open and honest debate, investigating the issues, negotiating with their associates and their counterparts in the Senate – only to have their efforts eviscerated by a multitude of riders that make exceptions to the rules, and that put private interests ahead of the interests of the general public.

In nearly every case, a rider proposes a piece of legislation that could not stand up to expert scrutiny, and that would be defeated if it were proposed as a separate Act. Riders undermine the law, they avoid informed consideration, and they challenge the integrity of the constitutional system of government at its most fundamental level.

Even if the President were granted the power of line-item veto, it would not suffice as a sure-fire way of enacting legislation, because many riders are so well hidden in the massive body of text that they can be easily overlooked.

Riders must be disallowed completely. Each proposed piece of legislation would then have to stand on its own, undergo review, and pass the same threshold tests that every other proposed piece of legislation must pass. Only then can the democratic principles on which the country is based be ensured.

If it takes a constitutional amendment to outlaw riders, then voters and their representatives must push to pass such an amendment.

Miscast Votes

The bedrock of the democratic system of government is the guarantee of free and open elections. When it comes to presidential elections, however, democracy in America rests upon a foundation of mud or soft sand. In the typical presidential election, nearly half the votes that are cast go to a nominee who was not the one for whom the voter cast his ballot. In other words, a voter may cast his vote for one nominee, but the voting process is rigged so that his vote is given to the nominee's opponent.

This standard practice of sham votes in America is called the Electoral College. It works like this. A voter goes to the poll and casts his vote for, say, John Doe. The vote does not go to John Doe, but into a pool for later distribution. If Jane Doe receives more votes in that State than John, Jane not only gets the votes that were cast for her, she also gets the votes that were cast for him. Thus the voting process is more of a collage than a College.

The Electoral College is undemocratic at the basest level. It unfairly redirects a voter's ballot to a nominee whom the voter opposes.

Furthermore, campaign strategies are focused on regions in which large concentrations of people reside. States with sparser population densities are relegated to backseat campaigning. Thus nominees cater more to the interests of those regions in which they hope to garner the largest number of votes.

Congress should be flunked out of the Electoral College.

The only kind of voting system that is fair to everyone is the plurality system: whoever gets the most votes wins the election. That way, every vote has equal weight in the election process.

The Law of Diminishing Returns

The more laws that government passes, the less effective law becomes, and the more time is spent in compliance with the law than is spent on life, liberty, and the pursuit of happiness.

To say that "ignorance of the law is no excuse" is totally absurd.

The number of laws, rules, regulations, statutes, codes, ordinances, and mandates number in the *millions* in the United States alone; and they differ from State to State, county to county, township to township, city to city, and borough to borough. And many of these laws contradict each other.

The legal system is now so overly complex that no one understands it in its entirety. Judges and their law clerks spend months, sometimes years, in researching law in the courthouse library, in order to render an opinion on whether a law was indeed broken; and if so, how the unsophisticated lawbreaker must be punished for breaking a law that no one was certain existed until the case was investigated ad nauseam.

I once researched a case in which a certified skipper with thirty years experience on the ocean made a split second decision to turn to starboard in the hope of avoiding a collision with an oncoming vessel. A panel of judges and a bevy of law clerks took eight *years* to decide that he should have turned to port. This isn't law; this is legalized assignment of blame.

When lawmakers spot a loophole or inconsistency in the law, they apply a patch by passing new laws that might close the loophole or explain the inconsistency. Instead, they should rewrite the original law so that neither the loophole nor the inconsistency appears ever to have existed.

While this may sound like a time-travel paradox in which a person goes back into the past and kills his mother before he is conceived, there's a difference. Time travel is a paradox in the law of physics, which is immutable. Rewriting law is a purely human endeavor, which can be changed at any time as long as the majority agrees to do so for the betterment of the community.

In Biblical times, the world of mankind was smaller and simpler than it is today, and the eighty-three words of the Ten Commandments sufficed to regulate the difference between right and wrong. In Revolutionary times, a Constitution that was one hundred times longer was needed to distinguish between right and wrong.

Today, scientific notation is needed to calculate the number of words that are used to explain the intricacies of the law, and the difference between right and wrong has little if any relevance.

Congress spends all its time in writing new laws. They should spend at least half their time in "unwriting" laws. What America needs is not more legislation, but "delegislation" and simplification. Every rider and law that was passed fraudulently must be "unpassed" (not repealed).

America needs laws that are based on righteousness. But the trend is to pass more "gotcha" laws. Which is the perfect segue to the next chapter.

Section Three
Gouging the Public
or Government Gone Astray

Wrong of Passage

The avowed purpose of government is to protect the people it governs. The Constitution of the United States promises to uphold the "common Defence and general Welfare of the United States."

Democracy is a form of government in which the people are in control, or one in which the state is subordinate to the people. President Abraham Lincoln best described the common perception of American government in his Gettysburg Address, when he expressed his hope that a "government of the people, by the people, for the people, shall not perish from the earth."

Alas, "of" still holds true but in a somewhat totalitarian sense, while "by" and "for" stand on shaky ground.

In Section One – the "of" – I illustrated the lengths to which the American government has gone to *control* the people rather than to govern them fairly and to guarantee their freedom: how slavery and discrimination run rampant throughout society under euphemistic names that serve to hide their true interpretation.

In Section Two – the "by" – I described some of the methods by which the wishes of the people have been subverted by their elected representatives, such as Senator Robert Byrd, who used chicanery to fortify his own personal regime by passing legislation all by himself, and by attaching riders that never received any form of review or consensus of opinion: a self-appointed monarch whose policy was to do good for himself instead of for the public at large.

In this chapter, I will illustrate where "for" has changed to "against," and how the people take it for granted, probably because the transformation occurred so slowly and incrementally that few of them noticed that the changes were being made.

The Waxing of Taxing with No Sign of Waning

It has often been said that those who forget history are bound to repeat it. Everyone seems to have forgotten the Boston Tea Party. Or, more correctly, they remember that colonials dumped British tea overboard, but have forgotten why they did it. The British were taxing tea that was imported into America. The colonials protested because they had no say in how the tax money was spent.

Just as a long and complicated series of mathematical operations can be expressed by the simple equation $E=mc^2$, so can the Tea Tax be articulated by a single rationale: no taxation without representation. This four-word phrase preceded the famous tea party by nearly a generation. It became a rallying cry that led to the Boston Tea Party, the American Revolution, the Declaration of Independence, and the Constitution of the United States.

Yet today there are so many insidious forms of taxation without representation that the revolutionary phrase has lost its impact. There is hardly an American in the country who does not pay some form of tax whose disposition is made without his input (by voting, either directly or through his elected representative).

By way of example of taxation *with* representation, consider State income tax. A citizen earns income on which he pays a percentage to the State in which he resides. He is represented in that State because he can nominate, vote for, and elect officials who will determine from their constituents how the tax money should be spent. Majority rules – unless the elected official ignores his constituents and spends the tax money the way he personally wants to spend it.

Now consider State sales tax. A resident purchases goods or services from his local store or shop. The State adds a percentage to the purchase price, and uses this percentage for the operation of the State government. Because the tax money is spent within the State, the buyer has some say in the way the money is spent. At local elections he can vote on questions or referendums, or he can vote for a representative whose ideas of spending parallel that of the voter.

But, suppose the citizen buys something from a neighboring State. He pays sales tax, but because he is not a resident in that State, he is not allowed to vote in that State. He has no say in the way his money is spent. In America, this form of taxation without representation is nearly universal. (A few States have no sales tax.)

Whenever a State or county or municipality needs more money, it either raises the rate of tax structures that already exist, or it creates a new kind of tax – often over the protests of the taxpayers, whose wishes are overruled by elected officials.

Ironically, inefficiency in operating a local government does not result in greater efforts to increase efficiency – it results in an increase of the tax rate, in order to pay for increasing inefficiency. This counterproductive feedback loop becomes self-sustaining until it spirals out of control, at which point someone in authority enacts measures to decelerate the process. Until the next time it is noticed.

Taxing Situations

Another form of taxation without representation might be real estate tax. When you pay real estate tax on your primary residence, you can vote in the county which collects the tax. But if you buy a rental property or a vacation home – say, at the beach or in the mountains – you pay real estate tax on those properties to a county in which you are not allowed to vote because the property is not your legal residence. Without voting privileges, you have no say in how your tax dollars are being spent.

The same holds true for school tax when that tax is embedded in your real estate tax. In that case, you may support schools in every county in which you own property – despite the fact that you may not have any children in school.

Two fuel taxes are imposed on gasoline and diesel fuel that are sold for road use: one that is levied by the federal government, and one that is levied by the State in which the product is sold. The State tax rate is higher than the federal tax rate. The road tax that the federal government collects is dedicated to the construction and repair of federal road projects, such as the Interstate Highway System. The road tax that the State collects is used only for local roads.

All is fair as long as you don't drive outside of your State. But when you purchase gasoline or diesel fuel in another State, your tax dollars are used to repair roads in that State and not in your resident State. This system seems fair because you are driving on roads in that other State. But you can't vote in that State, so you have no representation for adjusting the tax rate.

This is (Not) My Last Territorial Demand

Consider this tax scam – certainly not as bad as Hitler invading Poland, but insidious in its own way to the people who were annexed and unfairly taxed. The sleepy town of Columbia, North Carolina is the county seat for Tyrrell County. Columbia has a population of around 800 individuals. In acreage, the county is four times the size of Philadelphia. It has a population of some 4,000 people (not counting hunting dogs and white tail deer), whereas Philly has around 1.5 million people.

The town aldermen decided that the town needed more money for town projects that they had in mind. The town's primary source of income was real estate tax.

According to the first law of thermodynamics, energy can neither be created nor destroyed; it can only be changed from one form to another. The same is true of real estate except that the wording is different: there's only so much real estate because they're not making it any more.

Since the aldermen could not create real estate to

tax, they hit upon a nefarious scheme to transform un-taxed real estate to taxable real estate. They held a secret meeting during which they decided to annex a nearby housing community which lay outside town limits. By incorporating this community into the town, the town could then assess the property owners a property tax over and above the real estate tax that they paid to the county.

This sneaky maneuver would have caught the residents of that community by surprise had it not been for one honest alderman (or alderwoman, in the present case). She was Midge Ogletree (who told this story to me). She objected to the annexation but was overruled by the other aldermen. She then telephoned the affected residents and informed them of the upcoming meeting at which the aldermen intended to pass the resolution.

The residents attended the meeting en masse, but to no avail. They had no legal rights in a town to which they did not belong. Their vocal objections were ignored. Ogletree voted against annexation, but the other four aldermen outvoted her. The motion was passed. Now the members of this isolated community pay taxes for services that they do not receive: water, sewage, street lighting, and so on.

Believe it or not, the annexation was perfectly legal according to North Carolina State law. What makes the situation even stranger is that the annexed community was not contiguous with the town. A large tract of land separated the cluster of houses from the border.

The Tyrrell county commissioners also hit upon a plan to swell the anemic county coffer. A large tract of farm land had been set aside by a developer to build a housing community at some unspecified time in the future. The commissioners claimed that the anticipated population influx would strain local services such as water treatment, trash collection, police protection, and firefighting equipment (the firefighters were volunteers). So they *doubled* the real estate taxes!

The land developer put his plans on indefinite hold, yet the county is still collecting the excessive tax. If anyone knows where this money is going, or where it is hidden, they're not owning up to it.

These are only two small examples of local government gone askew over the stern objections of citizens. I wonder how many thousands of times this gambit has been played throughout the years, throughout the country.

The Customs of the Times

The following letter is self-explanatory:

> Re: Customs inspection
>
> I am an author and photographer who publishes illustrated history books for the American market. I have been engaged in this occupation full-time for the past sixteen years.
>
> Last month, in the pursuit of my usual business, I received a shipment of books from Hong Kong for distribution in the United States. Despite a long and authenticated history of book importation, U.S. Customs decided to "inspect" my shipment. For this so-called "inspection" I was charged the enormous sum of $432.
>
> The actual inspection charge was $208. The charge for transferring the shipment from the destination warehouse to the customs warehouse was $234. These charges were outrageous.
>
> Of the 84 cartons in the shipment, the Customs inspector opened only a single carton. For this solitary and momentary act of inspection, which could not have taken more than one minute to perform, I was charged $208. Extrapolated to the hour, the rate of charge was therefore $12,480 per hour – a hefty profit for one minute's work.
>
> To add injury to insult, in the process of slicing open the carton, the inspector cut through the covers of the top layer of books, thus destroying them as sale items.

To make matters worse, Customs refused to conduct the inspection at the warehouse to which the shipment was originally delivered. This necessitated the transportation of the entire shipment to the Customs warehouse – a distance of one mile – just so the inspector could open a single carton. For this lone mile of conveyance I was charged $234.

This delivery charge is absurd considering that the entire shipment was transported 10,000 miles from Hong Kong to Philadelphia for only $400. Extrapolating from the mileage charge, if I were charged at the Customs rate of transportation for the entire distance from Hong Kong to Philadelphia, I would have had to pay $234,000 in shipping charges.

The total value of the goods in this shipment was $10,000. Thus, my cost for the Customs inspection totaled nearly one-twentieth (1/20) the value of the product. This extravagant charge effectively (and greatly) reduces the amount of profit that I can hope to make on the sale of the books. As I am a sole proprietor, the money for this so-called inspection came out of my own pocket – money that was extorted from me before Customs would agree to release the freight. Nor can I complain directly to Customs, because then my name will be blacklisted, and they will designate all my future imports for "inspection," so they can make unearned income off of me.

I cannot afford to stay in business if Customs is permitted to maintain its policy of profiteering at the expense of small business operations.

I demand an investigation into this nefarious "inspection" racket that is being perpetrated by Customs. And I demand to be reimbursed for the money that I was compelled to pay, in order to have my shipment released from ransom.

It goes without saying that I was not reimbursed. I

sent this letter to all my representatives, State and federal. None of them did anything to effect a change in policy. I received only a single acknowledgement, from Congresswoman Allyson Schwartz. She simply forwarded my complaint to the Customs Bureau. My follow-up letter to her is also self-explanatory:

> You have taken the worst possible action in my behalf, one that will cause me irrevocable harm rather than any possible good. By forwarding my letter to the Customs Bureau, they will have the name and address of the complainant, and will blacklist me to ensure that all my shipments are "inspected" at great personal expense. Furthermore, they will likely delay the release of my shipments as a way of further retaliation.
>
> Is there any way that you can contain this damage?

I never received a reply to this letter. I wished that Bob Borski was still in office, because he responded to the needs of his constituents.

Sure enough, the Customs Bureau chose my next shipment for inspection. I lucked out, though. Ever since I first started my publishing business, I had employed the Carson M. Simon Company to file my customs forms. The company was owned and operated by Bill Riddle, Senior (although I usually worked with Junior). In this instance, I called Senior and complained about the situation. He had been in the customs brokerage business for most of his life, and knew the local inspectors personally. He called in a favor and asked one of them to inspect my shipment on site (at the warehouse to which the shipment had been delivered).

His contact complied. He did a more thorough inspection than the previous one. He opened nearly a dozen cartons, most from the bottom – because that was where smuggled items were usually concealed. He was careful not cut through any of my books. He resealed the boxes with green customs tape. He cleared my shipment, processed the paperwork, and did not charge a fee.

Lest the reader think that I got away with something illegal, you should know that for the fifteen years prior to the inspection for which I was excessively charged, this was the way all inspections were conducted – on site with no transportation or inspection charges. However, by 2005, the powers that be in the Customs Bureau figured that they could rip off the public by instituting the new system in which I got snared.

The Customs Bureau had importers over a barrel. If the importer did not pre-pay the newly established transportation and inspection fees within five days, he was charged a daily storage fee until the fee was paid. If the importer delayed too long in forking over the money, the shipment was destroyed.

On the other hand, once the fee was paid, the inspectors might take weeks to get around to inspecting the shipment. The importer was powerless to hasten the process – unless, perhaps, he bribed one of the local inspectors. Once the inspection was completed and the customs broker was notified to notify the importer, the importer had only three days to remove his shipment from the Customs Bureau warehouse, or else he was charged a daily storage fee.

The Customs Bureau could get you coming, going, or just hanging around.

Worse yet, the inspection was purely perfunctory and was not designed to discover smuggled goods. It was designed to earn windfall profits. When the inspector opened only one box out of 84, he was overlooking the possibility that I could have smuggled an enormous quantity of contraband in the other 83 boxes.

Scam Artists at the NPS

Most Americans perceive the National Park Service as a nice group of dedicated rangers wearing Smokey-the-Bear hats – rangers whose sole purpose in life is to enlighten the public about the great outdoors and about the beauty and wonder of nature. This is the persona that the NPS presents to the public through its advertising propaganda.

Most people who join the NPS have that same perception. They want to become part of a beneficent agency that preserves nature and serves the public with avowed lofty goals. I suspect, however, that many of these joiners soon become disillusioned when they see the dark side of the so-called Service, and realize that they have joined a police organization instead of a conservation group: Hitler's youth instead of Greenpeace.

That the majority of these ingenuous joiners make careers in the NPS demonstrates their personal dedication. Most of them strive and contrive to maintain their lofty ideals. But enough of them are converted to the dark side of the Force that permeates the system that they propagate the maleficent program that underlies the NPS.

One time a Park ranger told me that if he and the NPS had their way, they would close the gates to the public so that they had nothing to do but oversee wild plants and animals. Unfortunately for him and the agency's preference, Congress thought otherwise, and wrote legislation to protect the right of visitation. According to that ranger's attitude, the NPS doesn't enjoy visitors; it endures them. I have experienced this outlook on more than one occasion.

The greatest joy of some NPS rangers comes from issuing violations. They are constantly on the lookout for the minutest infraction of the rules, so as to have a pretext to fine someone for breaking a rule that wasn't posted or generally known. These rangers harbor no excuses and offer no leeway. Worse yet, some of them conspire to run scams on an unsuspecting public.

I once embarked on a scuba diving trip to the vicinity of the Dry Tortugas. This group of small islands lies about 70 miles west of Key West, Florida. The purpose of our trip was not dive in Tortugas National Park, but to use the Park as a safe harbor and staging area to explore several shipwrecks that lay twenty to thirty miles farther west. We foraged out every morning in the boat, then returned that evening to the protection of the islands.

One day we took some time to tour Fort Jefferson, the centerpiece of the Park. While we were tied to the dock, I noticed through the clear water that the bottom was littered with bottles and other junk. The shallow seabed was an underwater trash heap: the accumulation of years of visitors dumping their rubbish overboard. I speculated that there might be some old bottles that were worth collecting.

I asked the ranger who was standing by the dock if it was okay to collect some of the bottles. He told me to go ahead. I donned my scuba gear and jumped into the water. After an hour of scouring the bottom of the surrounding harbor, I surfaced behind the boat and prepared to climb up the ladder onto the deck. One of my buddies was standing on shore, giving me concealed hand signals. I understood from the way he was spreading his fingers that he was signaling me to drop my bottles. I didn't know what was going on, but I dropped the bottles anyway, knowing that I could easily retrieve them later.

I climbed onboard empty handed. After I doffed my scuba gear, my friend explained the situation. He was strolling back from the fort when he spotted a ranger who was hiding in the grass. My friend thought that the ranger must have spotted some rare species of plant or animal, so he veered off the path, stooped down beside him, and asked him what he was watching. There were other boats in the harbor, so the ranger did not suspect that the questioner was my friend. The ranger explained that he was waiting for a scuba diver to surface with bottles so he could cite him for disturbing the seabed and removing Park property.

There were only two rangers on the island. They worked this scam in cahoots. The one who gave me permission went and hid in the air-conditioned office, while the other went out to crouch under cover and make the pinch.

To make this situation even more absurd, remember

that I was picking up trash that other people had left behind. This means that had the trash dumpers been caught, they would have been fined for littering. Then I would have been fined for picking up their litter! That is working both ends of the scam against the middle.

These rangers must dance to the tune of the litterbug jitterbug.

More National Park Disservice

On another occasion, my girlfriend and I went on a five-day canoe trip down the Rio Grande. The so-called Grand River separates Texas from Mexico. We quickly learned how easy it was for Mexican migrants to enter the United States illegally. The water was only ankle deep and less than forty feet wide. The keel kept scraping on rocks so that we had to pole and hump the canoe through the shallows. The river was like this for the next thirty miles.

As darkness approached on day one of the trip, the left bank was a sheer cliff face that rose to a height of forty feet. The right bank was a flat beach of soft sand that extended a hundred feet to the rock wall. To the annoyance of a herd of cattle that moseyed down a narrow arroyo to drink from the river, we pitched our tent and set up camp on the beach.

Technically speaking, we broke the law when we stepped foot on Mexican soil – or perhaps when we veered south of the river's centerline – because we had not passed through customs. Nor did we have our passports. We joked about the absurdity of crossing the border without permission. We could have been arrested on technicalities by law enforcement agents of either country. The cattle mooed but otherwise ignored us.

The next day we entered Big Bend National Park. That night we camped on the left bank in the good old U. S. of A. Night three we camped again on the Mexican side of the river, and even went hiking up a slot canyon, deep into foreign territory. Night four we camped in Texas, in the middle of Santa Elena Canyon, where a breakdown created a ledge in the wall that rose 1,500 feet high. Night five we camped on an island in the middle of the river – we didn't know which country we were in, and we didn't care. We saw no one on the river the entire time: neither boaters nor law enforcement officers.

The next day we reached the dirt road where we had parked the rental car. We put the canoe on the roof, returned it to the livery, then proceeded to the Park campground. The campground was only half full. The rangers had chained off the other half so it lay fallow, and they would not let anyone camp there. There was a very good reason for doing so.

Big Bend is one of the largest and least visited Parks in the continental system. It is also one of the most isolated. The nearest private campground is more than an hour away. Visitors who arrived late in the day, and who were planning to camp but were turned away from the empty Park campground, were faced with two choices: drive an hour to town and an hour back in the morning, or camp alongside one of the Park's vacant dirt roads. Most chose not to waste the gasoline on a hundred-mile, two-hour roundtrip – and this was exactly what the rangers wanted.

Camping within Park boundaries was permitted only in the campground. There was a hefty fine for roadside camping. At dusk, I watched a fleet of Park vehicles depart for their daily rounds to catch roadside campers: a standard practice sting operation whose sole purpose was to generate money for the NPS.

My girlfriend and I parked in a remote dirt road pullout – an ideal place to camp. I observed a distant Park vehicle drive behind some bushes and hide. I realized that the pullout was a trap that the rangers had laid by intentionally clear-cutting the pullout in order to make it look appealing.

Parking was not illegal; only camping. As long as we didn't pitch a tent or lay sleeping bags on the ground, we were not breaking any Park rules. I unpacked the camp stove, prepared freeze-dried meals, and enjoyed a leisurely dinner. We slowly sipped our coffee afterward. The ranger waited – and kept waiting. By lulling him into believing that we were going to camp, we kept him watching and waiting for an hour and a half. Then we packed up and drove to town. The next day we continued on our way to Carlsbad Caverns, New Mexico.

The only one who got stung that night was the ranger – and not by bees or wasps but by his own lack of integrity.

Unhappy Trails

The NPS is a stickler for keeping people from straying off the path of the straight and narrow, and cites them for being where they don't belong. These citations are not restricted to campgrounds.

Backpacking in National Parks is a popular activity that the NPS regulates with ruthless abandon. Backpacking permits are required (but free), and specify where the backpacker may hike, may camp, and for how long. Permits can be denied to backpackers if the NPS determines that the trail he wishes to take is overused, or if the designated campsite that he hopes to reach is overcrowded. The theory that justifies these determinations is the protection of the individual's "wilderness experience." That is, to keep backpackers from meeting other backpackers.

I have met plenty of backpackers on the trail and at designated campsites. No one has ever been disgruntled by my presence, nor have I ever been displeased to chat with people whose sentiments paralleled my own. I challenge the NPS presumption that people hike in Parks for the solitude. Everyone I have met in the wilderness was there to experience nature's awesome beauty and stupendous wonders, not to avoid other people.

Nonetheless, NPS backpacking rules are so strict that they suffer no leeway. Their rigidity may not only hamper a backpacker's enjoyment of the great outdoors, but it may make the activity more dangerous. I will cite some examples.

On one of my half-dozen trips into the Grand Canyon, the desk ranger refused to issue a permit for the trail that my group wanted to take because another group had preceded us. Most of the other trails already had backpackers on them, or the arbitrary space constraints for the designated campsites had been filled. We scrambled to find a five-day loop that was in keeping with the Park's trail use and campsite limit rules.

We compromised by taking an unmaintained route called the Boucher Trail. Working out the logistics took so long that we didn't get underway until noon. The permit specified exactly where we had to camp each night. No deviation was permitted. The late start, combined with a recent landslide that obliterated part of the trail, threw our progress out of kilter. Late afternoon found us clambering over loose rock and jagged boulders on which the footing was poor, and lowering packs down steep inclines that were made more perilous by a blinding rainfall that turned the dirt into a slippery and muddy mess. By the time the sky cleared and we regained the recognizable route, we knew that we could never reach our designated campsite by sundown.

We encountered a narrow stretch of trail that had a drop-off of a couple of hundred feet on one side. Negotiating this trail by flashlight would have been dangerous. Although it was very much against the rules, we dry-camped right on the trail: the only piece of ground that was boulder free and relatively flat (although it was sloped).

The NPS employs trail runners whose primary occupation is to catch people where they are not supposed to be. Backpackers are required to display their permit on the pack frame. Trail runners stop everyone they meet, and check their permits to ascertain that they are on the trail that they were given permission to hike, and that the trail connected the previous night's campsite with the following night's campsite. Any divergence is subject to a fine, so the runner will issue a violation notice, and advise you to get back to where you belong.

We had a right to be on the Boucher Trail, but our designated campsite was several miles away. We could have been cited had we been caught camping on the trail. But trail runners are people, too, and by dark they are usually bedded down for the night. Along with the fact that we were on a seldom used route, we figured that the odds were in our favor that we would not meet a runner at such a late hour. We didn't. We broke camp early and completed our trek before breakfast. Thus we avoided the NPS collection racket.

The Ragged Edge

On another occasion, my girlfriend and I went backpacking in Glacier National Park. On the second day of one three-day loop, we left our campsite in a light drizzle that turned to snow at higher elevation. In order to reach our next campsite, we had to traverse Dawson Pass. This pass consisted of a ledge that measured from two to three feet in width, and which extended for three miles along a precipitous slope with an angled drop of nearly 1,000 feet to one side. A stumble or misstep would result in death.

Blizzard conditions made the pass treacherous. Sixty-mile-per-hour wind, with gusts into the eighties, blew the snow against the rock wall with penetrating force. My girlfriend doesn't weigh very much; twice she was knocked down by sudden blasts. The saving grace was that the wind blew against the mountain and not off of it. We made the passage safely.

Starting from the same campsite were two other pairs: two ex-army buddies who were fit and sure-footed, and a young couple who were backpacking for the very first time, with no prior experience in "roughing it." The young couple should have turned back when they saw the conditions at Dawson Pass. They could have returned to the campsite, stayed there overnight, and hiked out the way they had hiked in the previous day. But ranger scare tactics forced them onward instead of letting them contemplate retracing their way. After seeing how helpless she was, the ex-army buddies stayed with them to help.

The woman was so terrified that the only way she could take her baby steps was by having one ex-army guy holding each arm. She hardly ever lifted her feet;

she slid the soles of her new hiking boots along the smooth rock surface. Proceeding at this snaillike pace, it took the foursome five harrowing hours to reach the other end of the pass. The two novices were exhausted from physical and mental fatigue when they reached our campsite. (The two ex-army buddies were fine.)

This was a situation in which strict adherence to the rules nearly precipitated catastrophe. It could have been avoided if the Park ranger had exhibited some leniency when he issued the permit, such as by informing the couple that breaking the rules was permissible under extenuating circumstances. Nor is leniency mentioned in the permit rule sheet that is given to permittees along with the permit, in Park brochures, or in advertising literature. Instead, permittees are harshly warned to obey all rules to the letter or suffer the consequences; as long as you comply you may enjoy your stay.

For Us to Know, For You to Find Out

On one of my trips to Canyonlands National Park, I told the desk ranger that Jack Schieber, Todd Smith, and I wanted to hike to Paul Bunyan's Potty: a natural arch in Horse Canyon, in the Needles District, and so named because it resembles a giant toilet seat. The ranger nodded okay as she issued the permit and warned us not to disturb anything in the outback.

Paul Bunyan's Potty lived up to its reputation for grandeur. The opening was roughly circular and measured more than fifty feet in diameter. It was poised above a semicircular alcove that stretched more than one hundred feet across. After taking some pictures, we decided to ascend the steep slickrock slope into the alcove, in order to take pictures of the potty from directly beneath the opening. When we scrambled into the alcove, we were astonished to find a wide ledge that extended all the way around the wall; and on this ledge were a number of Anasazi ruins: small huts and corn cribs that were formed of hardened clay. Thousand-year-old corn cobs littered the ledge.

Three days later we returned to the visitor center. I

told the desk ranger what a stupendous archaeological experience we had when we discovered the ruins beneath the potty, and asked her why she hadn't told us about them when she knew that we were going there. She said that the Park didn't want people to know about the ruins. This attitude is typical of NPS rangers.

The NPS ignores the fact that the Parks were set aside for the enjoyment of the people – all the people, not just Park people. Instead of praising the virtues of a Park and encouraging visitors to see the sights, desk rangers typically discourage comers by extolling dangers that are either exaggerated or nonexistent.

"Enjoy your visit" is an empty phrase that rings hollow in the mouth of a ranger.

The Water Purity Scam

One way the NPS has been frightening people for the past couple of decades is by nurturing a national neurosis about tainted Park water. Desk rangers alarm visitors by informing them not to drink groundwater without first treating it, otherwise they might contract deadly or debilitating giardiasis.

Giardiasis is a parasitic gastrointestinal infection caused by a protozoan (a single-celled animal) whose taxonomic nomenclature is *Giardia lamblia.* Cysts of this microscopic creature may be found in water that is frequented by such mammals as beavers, muskrats, and other rodents. Once imbibed, giardia (as it is commonly called) thrives and proliferates in the intestines. In addition to inflicting its victims with bouts of nausea, vomiting, and diarrhea, giardia reproduces and sends cysts into the world embedded in fecal matter. If this fecal matter gets into the water, the life cycle begins again and the little critters spread to the next susceptible mammal that slakes its thirst. Ad infinitum, ad nauseam – especially ad nauseam.

In the 1980's, when giardia first gained notice and notoriety in outdoor circles, it was popularly known as "beaver fever." This was because the beaver was thought to be the primary carrier. Plus, the alliteration sounded rather pleasant to the ear, and it was easier to pronounce than giardiasis. The onset of the disease commences seven to ten days after the initial infection. Not everyone who drinks infected water contracts the disease, and those who do contract it may suffer varying degrees of severity.

So rarely did the disease occur that most doctors had never even heard of it, much less know how to recognize its symptoms and treat it. The symptoms were similar to those for ulcer and gall bladder conditions. Nowadays, because so much has been written about giardia, most people returning from the great outdoors would recognize the symptoms immediately, then tell the doctor what to look for and what to prescribe for it. A stool sample will confirm suspicions.

This universal awareness is both good and bad – good in that people can take precautionary measures and obtain immediate relief, but bad because, in my humble opinion, much of what has been written about giardia is grossly exaggerated. That is, the basic facts are genuine, but the prevalence has been severely distorted and overdramatized.

For years I've been conducting my own statistical analysis of giardia. So far, I have met or heard of only two people who have actually contracted the disease in the wilderness. Bob Lester and I were both infected during a three-week wilderness canoe trip down the Mistassini River in northern Ontario, in 1980

Whenever I've gone into National Parks, the desk rangers have always issued dire warnings about the widespread presence of giardia, insisting that groundwater must be either boiled, filtered, or chemically treated. So I began inquiring, "How many cases of giardia have been reported in the previous year?" In every instance the answer was the same: "None." I then followed up by asking, "How many cases have been reported altogether?" Again the answer was none. I followed up *that* question by asking, "When was the last time the water was tested for giardia?" The answer was always the same: "The water has never been tested." I was persistent: "Then how do you know that giardia even exists in the Park?" Again, the answer was always the same (although the words may have been different): "We work on that presumption," or, "We just assume it does."

In other words, the NPS is spreading rumors that are not substantiated by a single fact.

Because of the NPS wolf-crying posture and irresponsible promotion, outdoor journals and magazines publish a continual stream of articles about the bane of giardiasis, and stress the importance of treating water that is taken from rivers, streams, and creeks. Park brochures and Internet sites follow suit. What is missing from all this hype and hyperbole is hardcore evidence: known outbreaks, number of cases, locations where the water tested positive, and so on.

The result is mass hysteria about a disease that has supposedly reached pandemic proportions, but whose victims are nearly impossible to locate. Wilderness casualties and actual case studies are few and far between. I have personally spent more than a year of my life in the wilderness – both backpacking and canoeing, and with a number of companions – and have witnessed only the two cases that I noted above. I have never – I repeat, *never* – heard through all my grapevine contacts of anyone else contracting the disease.

I am sure that other isolated cases have occurred, but nowhere near the extent to which the NPS would like the gullible public to believe. The NPS was more user friendly when Smokey the Bear had a say in the matter.

BLM – the Good Guys (and Gals)

By comparison with the NPS, the Bureau of Land Management shines like a guiding light when it comes to trekking off the beaten track. I don't mean to imply that they don't have rules and don't enforce them. I simply mean that they are not paranoid about visitors encroaching on *their* domain. Land *use* is BLM's motto.

Desk rangers are affable and helpful. I have never been turned away from a trail that I wanted to take (as

I have in National Parks), although they might suggest that a different trail is more scenic or less crowded at the moment. They tell me that I can camp anywhere I want, but suggest certain locations where water is generally in good supply. They tell me to stay for as long as I would like, and estimate the roundtrip travel time for a person in average physical condition. They say that there have been no reported incidences of giardia, but suggest that boiling water is a good idea, especially if cattle commonly graze in the area.

The outback would be a more inviting place to explore if National Parks were managed by the BLM instead of the NPS. The primary difference between the two agencies is that the BLM manages land, while the NPS manages people. It's too bad that, through political intrigue, the NPS glommed up most of the most scenic and picturesque wilderness areas, leaving the less desirable or less accessible areas for the BLM.

NOAA – Annexer of the Sea

My history with NOAA is long and sordid. It all started one normal day in 1984, when I decided that I wanted to dive on one of America's iconic shipwrecks: the Civil War ironclad *Monitor*. The wreck lay at a depth of 230 feet off the Diamond Shoals of North Carolina. What happened after that day cost me hundreds of letters, tens of thousands of dollars, four federal lawsuits, and eight years of anguish.

To tell the sad saga in its entirety would require a book. In fact, it *did* require a book: *Ironclad Legacy: Battles of the USS Monitor*. In the present volume I will recapitulate only the absurdities, stupidities, and ironies of the lengthy legal battle that resulted from my naïve decision. A decision, I might add, that I have never regretted making, even though I had to make several bank loans to pay my legal fees. It took me years to get out of debt.

In 1972, Congress passed the Marine Protection, Research, and Sanctuaries Act (MPRSA), the purpose of which was to create marine sanctuaries that would serve to "preserve, restore, or enhance areas for their conservational, recreational, ecological, research or esthetic values in coastal waters." Areas that deserved such designation were those that were "necessary to protect valuable, unique, or endangered marine life, geological features, and oceanographic features."

There was no mention of shipwrecks because man-made objects did not fall into any of the categories that the MPRSA was designed to protect. Yet once the National Marine Sanctuary Program was initiated, under the aegis of the National Oceanographic and Atmospheric Administration, the first site to be designated as a Sanctuary was the *Monitor*, in 1975.

This was only the first of a long string of violations that NOAA committed against the Act, against the law, and against the American people, in its bid for totalitarian control of the underwater realm.

The MPRSA contradicted the Geneva Convention on the High Seas, to which the United States subscribed. According to international law, no nation may exercise its authority beyond its territorial borders, which is three nautical miles from land. The U.S. State Department noted its objection to the Act because the MPRSA extended NOAA's jurisdiction to the continental shelf. They characterized this as a case of "creeping jurisdiction."

Several legislators were quick to point out the illegality of the Act. Congressman John Breaux noted, "Wrecks on the continental shelf beyond the territorial sea are not owned by the United States, according to international law. The 1958 Geneva Convention on the Continental Shelf provides the applicable rule, from which the marine sanctuaries program may not deviate."

Not only did the MPRSA establish a wrongful precedent as far as national policy was concerned, but it laid the groundwork for future illegal shipwreck acquisitions under the guise of sovereign prerogative (or, might is right). In other words, NOAA nationalized the *Monitor* by means of bureaucratic fiat.

NOAA immediately made the *Monitor* off limits to the public. This was contrary to the articles of the MPRSA, which expressly guaranteed "all public and private uses of the resources of such areas."

Because the *Monitor* lay in international waters, the ban on public access applied only to American citizens: the very people to whom the *Monitor* was an icon. While American laws apply to American citizens wherever they are in the world, they do not apply to foreign nationals outside American borders. Citizens of other countries were not constrained by American law, and therefore were within their legal right to visit the site of the *Monitor*. A group of French divers did so, with NOAA's blessing.

NOAA kept the precise coordinates of the wreck a closely guarded secret. The site was not marked with a buoy that would serve to warn transient vessels of the sanctuary's location or existence.

In response to my correspondence and subsequent permit applications to visit the site, they refused to divulge the location. My request for the location pursuant to the Freedom of Information Act was denied; my appeal was also denied. NOAA told me to stay away the *Monitor*, but would not tell me where I was supposed to stay away from.

This catch-22 had a disastrous effect. Local anglers had known the location for years. They regularly fished on the site. But they did not know the identity of the wreck. To them, it was just another seabed obstruction that produced game fish. They kept dropping their anchors on the deteriorating hull. One fishing vessel snagged its anchor in the wreckage and was unable to retrieve it. They worked the boat back and forth. When they finally broke the anchor free, it severely damaged the *Monitor*'s propeller shaft and badly displaced the propeller.

To add insult to injury, "the Act authorizes the assessment of a civil penalty of not more than $50,000 for each violation of the regulation." The Coast Guard apprehended the fishing vessel during its attempts to break free of the wreckage. The owner was then fined for fishing on a site whose location and identity NOAA knowingly withheld from him.

According to the permitting process, American citizens were not allowed to look at the *Monitor* simply because they wanted to see it; they had to submit a proposal in which they promised to perform some form of useful survey work for which they would receive no compensation. In other words, they had to work for NOAA for free, and they had to pay their own costs into the bargain.

Permit applications had to be reviewed within thirty days. Yet NOAA took more than a year to review and deny my first application. My next twelve applications received shorter shrift.

NOAA kept making hoops for me to jump through. Every time I satisfied one set of requirements, they created another. They did this piecemeal in order to keep me hanging on the review of my latest application.

After all these denials, in 1987 I filed a suit against NOAA in federal court. Despite the well-known law of full disclosure, NOAA objected to furnishing internal documents that showed its duplicity in handling my permit applications. Judge Louis Bechtle sustained their objection, and ultimately ruled against me because I could not furnish the supplementary evidence that I needed to prove my case against NOAA's capricious and arbitrary handling of my permit applications.

(Ironically, ten years later, Bechtle hired me as an expert witness and Special Master to the Court in the *Brother Jonathan* case. I testified in court on the judge's behalf. He dispatched me to oversee salvage operations on the shipwreck, which lay off Crescent City, California. He was truly a judge without a grudge.)

One summer, while I was doing survey work for my book on shipwrecks off North Carolina, NOAA had government agents spying on my activities, in case I should decide to make a sneak dive on the *Monitor*.

I then filed suit number two in Administrative Court. Before the hearing, NOAA's attorney unwittingly disclosed documents that had previously been withheld from me. This documentation firmly established NOAA's culpability and unfair handling of my applications.

During the trial, NOAA's lead witness, Edward Miller, testified that in addition to safety concerns, NOAA denied me permission to dive on the wreck because I stated that my prime purpose was photographic in nature. He claimed that visibility on the wreck was zero. I countered that by showing a NOAA videotape of the site in which the visibility exceeded one hundred feet.

Judge Hugh Dolan then interrogated Miller about some fine points that were unclear in the judge's mind. Miller didn't know that I now had the information that he had kept secret from me. When the judge asked Miller a direct question in this regard, Miller lied right to his face. As soon as the judge finished his questioning, my attorney presented the judge with the document that proved that Miller had just committed perjury.

Armed with this incontrovertible evidence, the judge ruled in my favor. Yet he did not prosecute Miller for perjury. In his written opinion, he stated that Miller had testified "with more than a lack candor." NOAA subsequently fired Miller.

The permit was duly issued. I first dived on the *Monitor* in 1990. NOAA placed an observer on board my charter boat to monitor diving activities. She inspected our wetsuits after every dive, to ensure that no one had accidentally brushed against the coral that encrusted the wreck – because touching the wreck was prohibited and subject to fine and cancellation of the permit. Yet on a NOAA expedition, their divers crawled all over the wreck, dragged umbilical hoses across the fragile hull, and were stupid enough to film it. They also placed heavy excavation equipment on the wreck, then dug into the hull in their search for relics.

My expedition was a grand success. We took hundreds of photographs and many hours of videotape. All the dives were conducted safely and without incident. The only near catastrophe occurred when NOAA got one of its divisions – the National Marine Fisheries Service – to harass us: this despite the fact that a NOAA observer was on board our boat at all times.

Our boat was flying both an alpha flag and a dive flag. These flags indicated restricted maneuverability and divers in the water. According to Coast Guard regulations, no vessel was permitted to approach a vessel that flew such flags any closer than one hundred feet. After radio contact, the skipper of our boat explained that divers were in the water, denied permission for the Marine Fisheries boat to approach, and suggested that they wait until the divers were out of the water. The Marine Fisheries boat ignored the skipper and standard safety protocol, and ran over top of four divers who were decompressing in the water. I was one of the divers in the water. I saw the propellers pass right over my head.

After the expedition, I filed a grievance against the Marine Fisheries Service for contributing to an unsafe condition. NOAA handled the grievance and whitewashed the case. The Coast Guard stated that they were unable to prosecute a fellow government agency.

Afterward, I submitted the same permit application for the following year. NOAA denied it! I went straight back to court. This time the same judge ruled against me! Apparently, the political climate had changed.

I persevered by submitting yet another permit application. NOAA duly denied it. I filed another lawsuit against NOAA; my fourth. Once again the same judge ruled against me. Yet, several weeks later, I received permission from NOAA to dive on the wreck in 1992. What had transpired in the meantime was that Congressmen Norman Lent and Tom Carper, who sat on the Merchant Marine and Fisheries Committee, and who were keeping tabs on the *Monitor* situation, held a meeting with NOAA's top administrators behind closed doors. They ordered NOAA to issue a permit to me, and to lay off the contrived excuses on future permit applications.

I never learned the names of the administrators, or what Lent and Carper said to them in private to persuade them to toe the legal line, but I do know that Lent loudly criticized NOAA's mishandling of the *Monitor* at NOAA's next budget hearing. I suspect, therefore, that as Congress holds NOAA's purse strings, they threatened to withhold funding for the Program.

NOAA's Ark

The *Monitor* was not the only scam that NOAA was running. There are now twelve Sanctuaries in the Program. Every one was created against the wishes of local residents.

NOAA is required by Congress to hold public hearings, so that affected citizens can air their concerns about the establishment of a Sanctuary, and about the rules that will govern it. NOAA pays lip service to Congress by holding such meetings. Then it routinely round-files the feedback and proceeds to do whatever the hell it wants to do. I have attended such meetings and have observed their proceedings firsthand.

NOAA has continued its policy of withholding information about shipwrecks that happen to lie within Sanctuary boundaries. For example, in the Stellwagen Bank National Marine Sanctuary lies the *Portland*, a passenger vessel that sank off the coast of Massachusetts in 1898. It lies at a depth of 430 feet. In response to a Freedom of Information Act request, NOAA declined to provide the location for several reasons, among them the allegation that knowledge of the site's location might "impede the use of a traditional religious site by practitioners." NOAA was trying to claim that the wreck lay in hallowed Amerindian grounds – 30 miles from the mainland, and 430 feet beneath the surface of the sea!

Local divers located the wreck and shared the information with me. I published the coordinates in my book on Massachusetts shipwrecks, in a special chapter that I titled "The Stellwagen Bank Robbery."

NOAA established the Thunder Bay National Marine Sanctuary in Lake Huron, where there are no fish or geological structures that need protection, and which is not even a marine environment. "Marine" refers to the ocean, not to freshwater lakes. The sole purpose of the

Sanctuary was to control the shipwrecks – manmade objects that are not within the purview of the MPRSA.

When Congress placed a moratorium on the establishment of new Sanctuaries, the only way that NOAA could continue its cancerous growth was to increase the size of existing Sanctuaries. It arbitrarily increased the size of the Thunder Bay National Marine Sanctuary by *eightfold*. This gave them control over a lot more shipwrecks.

NOAA representatives knowingly lied to the people who attended public meetings in North Carolina. When fishing boat skippers and dive shop operators questioned a spokesperson about a proposed program to expand the Monitor National Marine Sanctuary to include every shipwreck off the coast, the rep denied that such an expansion plan existed. Yet I unearthed a secret, five-year-old interoffice document which outlined in detail how NOAA planned to expand the Sanctuary more than a *thousandfold*, in order to control every shipwreck off the North Carolina coast. To NOAA's chagrin, I published the information in my free online newsletter.

The National Cash Register of Historic Places

In an attempt to make the *Portland* seem more important than it is, NOAA nominated the shipwreck for inclusion on the National Register of Historic Places. Such a pretentious designation offers a modicum of protection to buildings and other properties because they may not be torn down or allowed to fall into disrepair. Nor are they allowed to be modernized or modified in any way that would alter the characteristics of their originality.

In other words, they must be preserved exactly as they are, under threat of civil suit for failure to comply with the regulations of historic preservation. No one seems to have realized that these antique buildings do not meet modern building standards or fire codes, and certainly could not pass inspection or receive an occupancy permit without extensive repairs or restoration. Despite these hazards to human life, safety code violations are overlooked so that the owner can keep the structure "as is."

Inclusion on the NRHP is a promotional scheme that owners can use to increase tourism. It also serves as an inducement to preservation societies and government agencies to donate grant money and allocate funding for the benefit of the owner.

There can also be a downside to inclusion on the Register. For example, the City of Philadelphia decided to create an historic district in order to cater to the tourist trade. Philly commissioners selected a block to be restored to the way it appeared during the time of the city's founder, William Penn. The City did not own the buildings on the block; it owned only the street.

The street was paved with the original red bricks which were in a sad state of disrepair. At one time the buildings presented a matching red brick façade, but after two hundred years of renovations they no longer appeared as they did in Revolutionary times. The City refurbished the bricks in the street, but forced private owners to pay for the restoration of their property. Each owner was forced to shell tens of thousands of dollars out of his own pocket.

When I investigated the construct of the NRHP, I found that they conducted no investigations to determine the historic quality of a site. They merely processed applications. There are no standards or guidelines for eligibility. The merits are left entirely to the nominators to research and document. Once the NRHP determines that an application conforms to its guidelines for applicability – that is, all the blanks in the nomination form are filled in correctly, the t's are crossed, the i's are dotted, and the paperwork is complete – it rubberstamps the nomination, and the rest is history (or historic preservation).

You could nominate your neighbor's eyesore garage as an historic building and the NRHP would grant it protective status as long as you described the structure with sufficient academic pomposity and infused the text with a number of bombastic phrases and buzz words –

and they would never know the truth.

What is the value of acceptance as an historic site if no qualifications are required for granting such a status other than a nominator's knack for composing highfalutin language?

If the nomination is such a giveaway, then it follows that a site that is listed on the Register is no more significant than that of a person whose name is published in the telephone directory, because no one ever gets turned down.

One do-gooder conservation group nominated some World War Two army barracks for inclusion on the Register. The NRHP duly accepted the application and approved the designation. The U.S. Army was later sued because it failed to maintain the structures when they were in dire need of repair.

When the case came to trial, the base commander testified that he had been allocated $80,000 for upkeep of the base. He decided to use the money to renovate the base's hospital facilities so that patients could receive better care, rather than squander the money on a group of unoccupied buildings that had no useful function or military application.

Perhaps just as bad is the case of the *Portland* and other shipwrecks on the Register. By law the owners must keep the structures in good repair. Yet there is no way to maintain the condition of a shipwreck in 430 feet of water. NOAA has been able to do nothing more than occasionally deploy a waterproof video camera to observe the rate of deterioration. Thus NOAA is violating the law by not shoring up collapsing decks and bulkheads, and by letting the hull rot away.

A visit to the NRHP office in Washington, DC revealed more shenanigans. In going through some accepted nomination forms, I found a number of so-called historic sites that were "address restricted." This means that they would not reveal the location of the site. In other words, the Register contains historic properties whose locations are concealed from the public. When I filed a request for the locations pursuant to the Freedom of Information Act, my request was denied; my appeal was also denied.

At the DC office I asked for photocopies of nine nomination forms. The staff was able to find only one. They had no idea where the other eight forms were filed. They still haven't found them.

The Seal of Fate

Congress passed the Marine Mammal Protection Act in order to "save the whales" from being hunted to eventual extinction. The Act protects all species of marine mammals from human interference: whales, porpoises, seals, sea lions, otters, manatees, and so on.

It must have sounded like a good idea at the time, but the adverse repercussions were unanticipated and, once observed and acknowledged, were ignored. No one has seen fit to amend the Act in light of the absurd situations that have resulted from strict adherence to thoughtless legislation.

My good friend and oceanographer Whit Anderson created a poster that demonstrated one of the problems of meddling with nature even if there was no malice aforethought. A picture of a baby fur seal bore the caption: "Save the whales? They eat us like popcorn."

While animal rights activists were trying to save killer whales known as orcas, they were contributing to the demise of a number of species of seal, because orcas eat seals as their primary diet. Saving one species of marine mammal inadvertently put another species of marine mammal at risk. A lofty goal has therefore degenerated to sacrificing one or more species for the savior of another.

Consider the plight of West Coast boat owners. Sea lions proliferate along the entire Pacific seaboard. Their natural habitat is not in the water, where they go to feed on fish, but on boulders and rocky outcrops, where they sleep and breed. Sea lions are not picky about where they rest. A dock or finger pier will suffice for their purpose if no geological features are available. The population of sea lions that live in marinas is huge.

Under normal circumstances, boat owners could live equitably with sea lions because the marine mammals will readily move out of the way whenever a land mammal walks along a dock to reach his boat. But there's the rub. According to the Act, the most intelligent species on the planet is now prohibited from interfering with mammals that live in the sea but roost on land or manmade structures.

"Interfering" has been interpreted to mean "disturbing in any way" so as to make a sea lion jump off the dock, twitch its flippers, or bark in displeasure. This means that if a sea lion is squatting on a finger pier between you and your boat, he has squatter's rights and you have none. You have to wait for the sea lion to leave voluntarily before you may proceed to your destination. I have seen as many as half a dozen sea lions lounging on finger piers in defiance of boaters who would like to pass, but are not allowed to do so.

This problem has long since reached epic proportions. Yet no one has taken the bull by the horns (or the sea lion by the whiskers), and done something constructively to alleviate an unjust, unreasonable, and, need I say it, absurd situation.

Instead, Marine Fisheries officers lurk around marinas like so many scavengers looking for road kill. They are waiting to pounce on violators so they can stick them with hefty fines. Arguing is futile because there is no money to be made by yielding to reason.

The East Coast has similar problems. In Newport, Rhode Island, sea lions have taken to basking not only on docks but on boats. The noise they make by barking all day and night is annoying to nearby residents. Worse than that, by sheer weight of numbers they managed to sink a 50-foot boat that was moored in the harbor. Sea lions wreak havoc like a pack of feral dogs – which, except for flippers instead of paws, they very much resemble.

People are suffering more harassment from stupid laws than marine mammals ever suffered from marauding humans.

A Whale of a Tale

In May of 1992, Lee Tepley and Lisa Costello were boating off the coast of Hawaii when they spotted a pod of pilot whales in the distance. Lee maneuvered the boat so that it lay in the path of the swimming whales. He and Lisa jumped into the water wearing snorkeling gear. Lee had a camera inside a waterproof housing.

He switched on the camera as the pod of whales approached; he started filming. The whales swam past them, then stopped to play. It was an exhilarating experience – until one of the whales bit Lisa on the leg and dragged her down to 25 feet beneath the surface. The whale could hold its breath for an hour, but the woman could not. Lee was powerless to do anything to help her. He kept the camera aimed on the tragedy in progress. Lisa was slowly drowning.

As her life was in the final stages of ebbing away, the whale took her to the surface and let her go. Lisa gasped for air. Lee helped her onto the boat. They were both relieved after a close call with death.

This was real life, not a television melodrama. The couple later appeared on television, where Lee's footage was shown to an enthralled nationwide audience.

After the broadcast, both Lee and Lisa were cited for violating the Marine Mammal Protection Act. NOAA's Administrative Law Judge Hugh Dolan – the same one who presided over three of my *Monitor* cases – found the defendants guilty of interfering with the whales by placing themselves in their path. They were fined $10,000.

The whales got away scot free.

Note, too, that the pair were tried by a NOAA judge without the benefit of a jury. This kind of trial is unconstitutional. Article III, Section 2 of the Constitution of the United States clearly asserts, "The Trial of all Crimes, except in Cases of Impeachment, shall be by Jury."

This assertion is repeated in Amendment 6: "In all criminal prosecutions, the accused shall enjoy the right to a speedy and public trial, by an impartial jury."

Nowhere does the Constitution equivocate about a trial by jury.

Blue Spring Blues

Federal agencies are not the only ones susceptible to stupid regulations that work against the public they are supposed to serve.

I went on a diving trip to Florida with Bill Nagle and Jon Hulburt. On our return from exploring shipwrecks off Key West, we stopped in the northern part of the State to do some cave diving. When we pulled into Blue Spring State Park, the ranger at the gate demanded that we pressure-gauge our scuba cylinders in his presence. They had a rule that diving wasn't permitted with tanks that were filled to less than three-quarters of their rated capacity. The purpose was to ensure that divers didn't run out of air in the underground shaft.

The tanks that we loaded last in Nagle's pickup truck were only half full, but, I was quick to point out, they weren't single tanks with a capacity of 72 cubic feet of air (the standard of the day and with which it was permissible to dive) but *twin* 80-cubic-foot tanks with a total capacity of 160 cubic feet. Simple mathematics proved that half of 160 was greater than three-quarters of 72. Furthermore, our double-tank setups were equipped with an alternate air supply: a full 40-cubic-foot pony bottle with its own regulator.

Logic wasn't the rule's strong point or in any way relevant. The ranger would let someone dive with 54 cubic feet of air (three quarters of 72), but would not let us dive with 120 cubic feet of air (half of 160 equals 80, plus 40). Even without the pony bottle we had more air than a full 72-cubic-foot tank; with the pony bottle we had more than double.

The ranger was adamant. Before he would issue a permit to dive, we had to unload the truck completely and drag out tanks that were full (although we didn't have to use them once we were out of the ranger's sight). After the dive, we packed our gear and prepared to depart.

I insisted that we stop at the entrance gate so I could argue with the ranger. "Can't you see the stupidity of basing permission on tank pressure instead of the amount or air?"

He said, "I know, but that's the rule."

"But it's stupid not to let someone dive when he's carrying more than twice as much air as someone else who *is* allowed. That doesn't make any sense."

He shrugged. "I don't make the rules. I just carry them out."

"Then if you uphold a stupid rule, that makes you stupid."

He didn't like what I had to say. But I felt better for saying it.

The Corruption of America

The primary focus of a government agency is the justification of its existence. All other considerations are secondary, including the performance of its mandates.

All too often, the primary focus of a government agent is abusive exercise of his authority. All other considerations are secondary, including the performance of his duties.

Bad agents subvert a system which itself subverts the wants and needs of the public.

The public is not served by stupid or incompetent power mongers. Instead, public servants serve themselves at the expense of the taxpayers who pay for service and get servitude instead.

Government has lost sight of accountability. The democratic principle of checks and balances has gone by the wayside. Ineptitude has become a self-fulfilling function. Agents are ignored when they write bad checks. Agencies are disregarded when they fall out of balance.

Corruption can be halted, but only if government takes affirmative action to halt it.

Section Four
The Income Tax Gestapo
or The Lurking Evil and the Insidious Invasion of Privacy

The Din of Inequity

No one likes to pay taxes. Yet most people accept the need to fund the government that supposedly works for their benefit. These opposing sentiments result in a state of "discontented consent," a condition which is unbalanced toward the side of dislike by the suspicion that too much money is spent to provide too few services; or worse, that money is spent on services that are either unnecessary, unwanted, undesirable, or all of the above. The results of this suspicion – or direct observation – are feelings of confusion, frustration, resentment, and rancor, but manifested largely by dull resignation.

Legislators deliver loquacious speeches about revamping obviously unfair tax laws, but do little more than prattle. They fear to buck a system that is so entrenched in the American economy that it transcends divine essence – much like the golem in Jewish folklore, which was endowed with life by supernatural means, and thereby acquired immortality. Taxation has become a godlike entity to which Americans are now subservient.

Citizens generally feel powerless against the onslaught of escalating taxes. Confrontations with tax law rarely occur, and the few confrontations that transpire are rarely won. The reason for this is simple: it costs more money to oppose unjust tax laws than it costs to pay undeserved taxes. And the reason for *that* is that taxation bureaus enjoy the benefits of autonomous control: they are not beholden to any individual or governmental agency, and they possess unlimited resources with which to defend their position. Absurdly, the cost of defense is borne in full by the taxpayer. As a result, people grumble and complain, but accept a status quo that appears to be as inevitable as death.

Let me commence this chapter with some personal experiences.

Internal Revenue (Dis)Service

Most Americans believe that Big Brother is only a fiction that was created by George Orwell (in his landmark novel *1984*), that their privacy is guaranteed by the Constitution and its Amendments, and that law enforcement minions cannot invade their premises or confiscate their property without due process – such as an official court order which is issued by an unbiased judge and which is based upon substantial evidence of so-called "probable cause." Most Americans are wrong.

The IRS operates completely beyond the pale of Constitutional rights: without just constraints, without impartial peer review, and without an honest system of checks and balances. The IRS is practically a law until itself: one that supersedes all other laws of the land, and one which functions without adequate appeal.

The IRS is judge, jury, and executioner, all rolled into one convenient package.

This federal revenue bureau is absurdly called a "service."

Mimsy Were the Borogroves

I left the construction industry to embark upon a new career as an author and photographer. Since I had always filed my own federal income tax forms, I saw no reason to change my routine. But as an author/photographer I did not receive a salary from which estimated taxes were withheld. I earned money only when I sold a photograph or a piece of writing; and the publishers did not withhold taxes. Furthermore, my new occupation entailed investments and expenses that were legally deductible from my gross taxable income.

I needed advice about tax laws that related to my

forthcoming occupation: which expenditures constituted allowable deductions, and what record-keeping method I should employ. I decided to go to the self-proclaimed expert for this advice: the IRS. I scheduled an appointment at the local branch.

I explained the situation to my assigned tax adviser. She listened attentively, asked a few questions, then offered me some handouts. When I asked specific questions she was less than helpful and, as it developed, decidedly unknowledgeable. For example, in answer to my questions she made statements such as, "That might be deductible;" or, "It could be;" or, "I don't know, but it might be."

If the IRS didn't understand the tax laws, who did?

She made it seem as if the laws relating to tax deductions were arcane secrets, or theoretical constructs, or a guessing game. I pressed the point not only because I wanted to conform to the law, but because I wanted to be prepared in the event that my tax return was ever audited. She was unable to give me any straightforward information. She terminated the session by saying, "I don't know what kind of information an auditor will want."

The only sound advice she gave me I already knew: keep records. Idly, I wondered if she meant 45's or LP's.

First Blood

After a rewarding decade as a freelance author, photographer, and photojournalist, I expanded my business to include the publication of books that I wrote and which I illustrated with my photographs. The paperwork that was involved in categorizing business expenses, listing capital investments, calculating depreciation, maintaining inventory numbers, and generating sales receipts, was complicated. Since my closest friend was a full-time accountant for a national insurance company (and later for a large hospital conglomerate), and was therefore conversant with accounting procedures and federal tax guidelines, I found it expedient to pay Drew Maser to "keep my books." This enabled me to spend more time on the creative production of my craft.

Several years later, the IRS sent me a reminder which stated that my tax return for 1992 had been randomly selected, and was scheduled for audit two weeks hence. The letter claimed to be the second such notice, and claimed that I had ignored the first one. In fact, I had never received any first notice. Worse, I was about to depart on a long-planned photo trip, and expected to be gone for several weeks. According to the notice, a person who failed to appear for an audit was subject to severe penalties. I called Drew at once.

He scoffed it off and told me not to worry. I faxed the notice to his office. He called the auditor who was assigned to my case, explained my situation – that I was unavailable for the date of the appointment – and rescheduled the audit for two months later when I would be in town between trips. He received no argument about rescheduling the audit.

If you believe that the IRS sends an auditor to your house or place of business, where you could easily access your files and produce documents on demand, you are misinformed. I was ordered to appear at the IRS office in center city. The audit form demanded that I bring documented proof to substantiate every single deduction that I claimed on my tax return. ("Tax return" is an obvious oxymoron, as tax is never returned; only overpayments are returned). These deductions included travel expenses, shipping expenses, telephone bills, purchase receipts, depreciation justifications, and so on – quite literally, everything relating to my business.

I was also ordered to produce *all* personal (non-business) paperwork: checkbooks, bank statements, credit card statements, brokerage accounts, lists of equity holdings (real estate, stocks, bonds, and mutual funds), rent or mortgage payments, and documentation for *all* forms of income: wages, salaries, royalties, rental properties, sales, pensions, and so on. In other words, in addition to my business dealings, I had to account for every dollar of personal income as well as every dollar of outgo.

In short, I had to establish proof of every financial

transaction I made during the tax year that was under-going audit: personal as well as business. My entire life was open to IRS scrutiny. Whatever I didn't bring, the IRS could come and take by force. The IRS was Big Brother in disguise: hiding behind the mirrors in my rooms, watching everything I did.

During the breathing space that was now available, Drew did an exhaustive job of preparing my records for the audit. He photocopied all pertinent receipts, records, and documents. When I arrived at his house for a pre-audit briefing, I found that original documents and pho-tocopies completely covered both floors and all tables and chairs in his living room and dining room. He was collating the documents into folders for rapid access. Not only did he organize the files in categories the way the audit form demanded, but he arranged them in the order in which those demands were listed on the de-mand form.

His quiet advice was like the Boy Scout motto: "Be prepared." All too often, he told me, people appeared for an audit with a shopping bag full of receipts, either be-cause they were too lazy to organize them, or because they believed that they could overload the auditor with paper: a gambit that never worked and which only an-gered the auditor. Angering an auditor is worse than an-gering a lion in the jungle or a highway patrol officer. Whereas the latter can write a citation in revenge for lack of condescension, an auditor can arbitrarily dis-patch the sheriff to confiscate the entirety of your records, and can also levy heavy fines for noncompli-ance.

Drew did not want to have to fumble through a stack of disordered papers in order to satisfy the auditor's de-mand for a specific document. He wanted to be able to produce the document instantly, in order to demon-strate that I had nothing to hide and that my records were in perfect order. The saving grace was that I had saved every receipt and document that I had ever re-ceived or generated, including those for nondeductible items; and on the few occasions when I had not received a receipt, I had noted that fact in a ledger. Of the hundreds of individual expenses that I had claimed, there were less than half a dozen for which we could not find a receipt. This high percentage of producible documentation lent credibility to the claims for which the receipts were missing, and which in any case amounted to only a small fraction of my claimed deductions.

We had to take originals or copies of every requested document to the downtown office. Because my business was small, and only three years old, we needed only two briefcases and a milk crate in which to carry all the records. We arrived before the appointed hour with our paperwork in hand. The auditor had nothing more than a single slender file folder.

Grand Theft Audit

The auditor was businesslike. She introduced herself and shook hands with both of us. She indicated seats in front of her desk. She read the rules of engagement from the notice, then proceeded immediately to the audit by asking me to produce the first item on the list. Drew complied without hesitation by handing her a copy of the requested document, and informing her that it was a photocopy that she could keep for her own records. She raised her eyebrows at his state of preparedness. He explained the origination of the item, then showed her how the item tied in to the general ledger, where it appeared in the tax return, and why. She nodded silently and moved on to the next item.

For the next hour she repeated the litany, "You were asked to produce . . . Did you bring that with you?" In every instance the answer was "Yes."

I said hardly a word. Drew pulled documents and offered explanations. He was so thoroughly prepared that he even had photocopies of individual toll receipts on separate sheets of paper. She went through my deductions category-by-category and item-by-item. In most cases I had two means of substantiating an expense: the sales receipt and the payment method (credit card statement or cancelled check). Once she asked me to substantiate an expense for which I had paid cash and for which I had not received a receipt. The expense was less than ten dollars. I explained the situation. Drew showed her where the item was entered on the ledger, and how it correlated to similar items for which I *did* possess receipts. She merely nodded.

In this manner she examined every aspect of my business deductions: film purchases, photo duplication services, camera repairs, printing costs, travel expenses, equipment expenditures, postage and shipping costs, accounting and legal fees, and so on; plus the various forms of income from the sale of articles to magazines and newspapers, from lectures and presentations, from photo sales to a variety of media, from book sales, and so on.

She wanted to know exactly how I earned my income, so she asked me how I conducted my business on a day-to-day basis. When she asked if I worked out of a studio, I replied succinctly, "No." She asked me if I worked out of my house. I replied, "Yes." She asked me if I claimed part of my house and my household expenses (such as utilities) as a deduction. I replied, "No." Drew had warned me long ago not to claim a room in my house, because the IRS invariably denied such a deduction, and used the claim as an excuse to ascribe fraudulent filings for which excessive fines could be levied.

Because I specialized in underwater and outdoor photography – types of photography that could not be conducted in a studio – I traveled extensively: by vehicle, by boat, and by plane. She brought this aspect of my business under close scrutiny. I used the standard IRS mileage method to claim vehicle expenses, and maintained a vehicle log that showed destinations and mileage. I substantiated boat charter fees by means of cancelled checks. Airfares were duly noted on my credit card statements, but I saved the used ticket stubs as well. She could find no fault in my record keeping system . . .

But, she wanted to know how I could prove that all my travel was related to business, and was not vacation.

This one stumped me. It had never occurred to me that I needed any such proof. I went to work as a photographer the same as I went to work as a commercial electrician: by some means of transportation. The only difference was that I traveled farther (except for the time when I traveled from Philadelphia to Denver at a time when construction was slow in Philly).

Drew came to my defense. In addition to a vehicle log I also maintained a dive log (a copy of which we submitted to the auditor, to her surprise). The dive log showed every dive I made, where I made it, and the name of the boat that transported me to the dive site (in addition to bottom times, decompression times, and other statistics that were irrelevant with respect to my tax return, but which helped immensely in reconstructing the history and chronology of my dives for book publications and magazine articles). My checks were made payable to either the name or the owner of the boat, whose location could be verified should the auditor choose to do so. She did not.

But she *did* want to know how I could prove that a certain trip to Florida was a business venture. I thought about it for a moment, then said, "The processing date is stamped on every slide mount. I could bring in the slides that I took during the trip, and show you that the pictures were taken during that time period, and were taken on the shipwrecks that are given in my dive log." She scowled. She was not convinced, but she did not pursue that avenue any farther. She did not bother to ask about similar excursions to western wilderness areas, where I did the bulk of my nature photography.

Guilty Until Proven Innocent

Instead, she changed gears completely and harped on one of the two cruxes on which she was attempting to disavow my tax return. *She did not believe that I was an author and photographer.* I had expended so much energy in perfecting my craft that it came as a shock to suddenly realize that the occupation that I had pursued for the past fifteen years should come into doubt. My vocation was such a fulltime job – and so fulfilling an occupation – that I never took vacations: I had neither the time nor the money. Any excess profits I plowed back into my business.

At first, neither Drew nor I knew how to address this issue. How could I prove that I did what I did? I was self-employed, so I had no boss or company to vouch for me. I could prove where I was when I said I was there, but I could not prove that what I did when I was there was related to work. By the very nature of my chosen occupation, the majority of my work did not earn any profit until months or years after its consummation. I might spend a week doing research at the archival facilities in Washington, DC, but not write a derivable article or chapter in a book until many years later; and then additional years might pass before my words appeared in print. Similarly, I sometimes sold photographs that I had taken ten to fifteen years earlier. A picture that I shot today was an investment in the future. Furthermore, like all photographers, I had tens of thousands of photographs that would *never* see publication. And my books did not earn out for two to three years.

Nonetheless, I had published a respectable quantity of material throughout the years. Some of my authorship I established through royalty statements, but I had no other proof on the spot. After much discussion, it occurred to me that she might be persuaded about the validity of my employment if she saw some of the results. I suggested bringing in some of my published material. She shrugged, but thought that it might be a good idea. To jump ahead of the story, Drew returned the following week with a milk crate full of magazines in which I had published articles or photographs or both, as well as five novels and seven nonfiction titles that I had published to that time. Scores of magazines and a dozen books converted her disbelief about my occupation.

Profit or Perish

There was a second issue with which the auditor took exception. I had claimed a loss in the year being audited. After analyzing my business income and comparing it to my expenditures, she did not understand how I could afford to live if my business did not show a taxable profit. She challenged me to prove the fallacy of her conjecture.

As any accountant or businessperson knows – and the IRS should be so informed – actual profit and loss have limited bearing on taxable income. A thriving business may earn a respectable profit, yet show a loss on its federal income tax return. This paradox is explained in a number of ways.

The tax structure is an artificial construct that spans a twelve-month fiscal period from January 1 to December 31. Profits earned in the previous December or in the succeeding January appear in different years, while expenses incurred within the confines of the tax year are deductible only for the year in question, even if they were incurred on December 31 of the previous year. In addition, earnings and expenses may occur in large lump sums, and may not be spread evenly throughout the year. The owner or stockholders of a business view its profitability over a long-term period that spans several years, while the IRS sees the company in discrete, single-year segments. The performance of a company in any one particular year may not reflect its overall viability.

Extraordinary expenses that were incurred late in the filing period may represent a periodic capital investment (in my case, printing costs), but may not necessarily represent the business's liquidity or future earning capacity. However, such an expense may adversely affect the business's tax liability for that specific year. The IRS had only its own rules to blame for this inconsistency, by not recognizing the amortization of assets. This was the basis for my claiming a loss.

Furthermore, many businesses prosper despite outstanding debt. In reading my bankbook entry by entry, the auditor made this discovery in an interesting fashion. She suddenly let out a gasp of protest: "You *added* your payments!"

I asked to see the bankbook. I glanced at the page she was examining. "Yes."

Drew held the bankbook in front of her, and explained, "The way Mr. Gentile borrows money is through overdraft."

I made a large payment to my printer in December prior to the year that was being audited. Since I did not have enough cash at the time to make the entire payment, I borrowed the amount that I was short after reducing my available cash to zero. I did my banking through a brokerage firm. The brokerage firm held my stocks and bonds in an asset account. With these equities acting as collateral, I could borrow up to half the value of my investments (a percentage that was established by the Securities and Exchange Commission). This method obviated the need to make a bank loan (and going through the costly and time-consuming process of filling out an application and paying for the privilege).

When my printer was paid (by electronic wire transfer), my checking account status went from positive cash flow to negative cash flow. This meant that the numbers entered in my bankbook were *negative* numbers. Therefore, whenever I made a payment (say, to a utility company), I *added* the amount to my debt. In essence, I borrowed money to pay my electric bill. On the other hand, whenever I deposited earnings, I *subtracted* the amount from my debt, thereby reducing the amount of my outstanding loan.

The auditor was astonished by such a system of revolving credit. Now she knew how I could afford to live when my business showed a loss: I subsisted on borrowed money until I recouped my investments. This was no glib explanation or unusual concept; businesses did it all the time on a relatively short-term basis. It was no different from obtaining a mortgage on a house or a loan on a car, paying regular interest, and paying off the debt at a later date.

Beyond Unreasonable Doubt

The auditor was miffed at having her great discovery

accounted for in so exemplary a fashion. She searched harder for evidence of misconduct and for creative accounting procedures. She added all my bank deposits, and found that the total was higher than the amount that I claimed as earnings. She assumed that the difference was due to undisclosed income. Armed with this apparent discrepancy, she again scrutinized my bankbook to look for inequities. She fairly gleamed when she found a $4,000 deposit that I had not claimed as income on my tax return. Again I asked to see the bankbook.

I remembered the occasion. I flipped back a couple of pages, and showed her where I had written a check to my son in the identical amount. He wanted to take advantage of a stock option that was about to expire: a perquisite that his company offered to management personnel. He could purchase the stock at a price that was far below the market value, then sell it a couple of months later on the open market at a much higher price. I lent him the money. He consummated the deal and paid me back.

She grudgingly admitted that the transaction was legitimate, but my deposits *still* exceeded my claimed earnings. So I had to prove to her satisfaction that some of my income was nontaxable by law, and that other revenue did not represent income. My disability pension from the Veterans Administration was deposited monthly into my account by electronic wire transfer; this money was not taxable. My mother gave me cash for Christmas and for my birthday, instead of buying presents; gifts were not taxable unless the amount exceeded $10,000 per donor. The County of Philadelphia issued a refund on property taxes that had been unlawfully assessed. The State of Pennsylvania restituted a settlement claim in a State-sponsored class action suit against a roofing company's owners who had fraudulently exaggerated the necessity for repairs, and overcharged accordingly. (In addition to having all their assets confiscated in order to repay the people they had defrauded, both owners were sentenced to long jail terms.) I paid for an item that I later returned; I was reimbursed by check. My automobile insurance company returned a payment that I had mistakenly made twice. A catalogue company issued a rebate on purchases that were not business related and which I had not claimed as expenses. A vendor accidentally keyed a credit card payment with an extra zero; when he discovered his mistake, he issued a refund. And so on, and so on . . .

Eventually we achieved a balance in which every dollar of income matched every dollar of disbursement, with no taxable income outstanding.

However, in every instance it was *my* responsibility to provide proof to contradict her every allegation. Without such proof, the auditor automatically assumed that I was guilty of intentional tax evasion. This presumption of guilt contravenes the most basic tenet of America's judicial system. But there it is – guilt by imagination until proven innocent beyond all unreasonable doubt.

My hard-earned vindication earned no plaudits from the stone-faced auditor. By lack of punitive action, she conceded that I was an author and photographer whose tax return was filed in accordance with the law.

The Evil that Lurks

Several years later, another tax return was supposedly selected at random for audit. As before, my first awareness of the pending audit was the so-called second notice: delivered by ordinary mail, one fortnight prior to my scheduled appointment. I called Drew, and he called the newly assigned auditor to request a postponement to a time that was more propitious (for us). This was duly granted.

Once again, Drew went through the laborious procedure of organizing and photocopying all relevant documents and receipts – basically, every scrap of paper that had been generated or collected during the year being audited (1997). This was a massive undertaking. But when I suggested some shortcuts based upon the conduct of the previous audit, Drew disapproved and repeated quietly, "Be prepared."

I was already more prepared because of what I

learned from the first experience. I had opened a second bank account from which to transact personal affairs. I created a journal in which to chronicle sequentially my various activities: dive and nature trips, speaking engagements, research trips, and so forth. I saved nondeductible receipts that served to substantiate my travel history. Instead of a single folder for all business-related receipts, I maintained several folders which separated receipts into categories; this made Drew's work easier.

Auditor #2 was as businesslike as the first one. She explained the manner in which the audit would be conducted, then asked some questions to establish background information: What did I do for a living? How long had I worked in that occupation? Had I ever been audited before?

I thought these questions were stupid and unnecessary. The IRS had access to all my records: tax records as well as personal records. Therefore she had to know about the previous audit. Was she baiting me?

To the latter question, I replied calmly, "Yes."

"And what was the result of the audit?" she wanted to know.

I said, "My records were found to be in order."

She nodded, made a notation on her notepad, but made no comment. After several more questions and introductory remarks, she commenced the audit by asking me to produce the first set of documents that were noted on the list. Drew pulled both the originals and photocopies out of his folder. He handed her both stacks, and informed her that after comparing them, she could keep the copies. She glanced over the papers, returned the originals, and retained the copies with a "Thank you."

Drew was strictly professional. He explained how the dollar amounts tallied with the tax return, and showed her precisely where the figures appeared on the tax forms. She asked questions, and he answered. I stayed out of these conversations because they related to accounting procedures about which I was ignorant. These dialogues were for accountants only. Occasionally, when she wanted to know the generation of an item, I was called upon to elucidate.

The auditor was not overly friendly, but neither was she disagreeable. She accepted documents and explanations without skepticism. This routine continued for an hour. When she asked for documentation of my travel expenses, I was ready to pull an ace out of my sleeve that would leave no doubt as to the completion of my itinerary.

As she scanned my vehicle log, Drew showed her how the dates and destinations correlated with the activities that were entered in my dive log and my journal, and where on the tax form those activities were corroborated by expenses or income. She bobbed her head like a swimming coot.

Drew asked politely, "What would you like to see next?"

I got ready for my slam-dunk.

She scooped up all the papers on her desk, tapped them on the pressboard surface to align the bottom and sides, shoved them into her folder, and, without looking up, said, "What's the point? Whatever I ask for you're gonna provide."

My records were so complete and so organized that she realized that she was wasting her time, and terminated the audit in less than a quarter of the duration of the previous audit. She did not even question the validity of my occupation.

Still Lurking

The very next year I received *another* notice from the IRS. This time they wanted to audit my tax return for 1998: the year following the one whose audit I had passed so successfully that the auditor dismissed me before completing the audit.

I couldn't believe it. Twice so far, auditors had found my tax returns in perfect order, with supporting documentation to substantiate every single expense that I claimed for deduction, and with no claims for deductions that were not allowable. My entire financial portfolio balanced precisely to the dollar. (Drew rounded up or down from pennies.) One would think that, given my impeccable history, the IRS had other taxpayers to fry.

Furthermore, against all odds, for the third time in a row I received only the *second* notice and not any first, leaving only two weeks to prepare for the audit. I felt that the chances of the Postal Service losing three first notices was slim to none – and Slim left town. The probability factor was one in a quadrillion. I told Drew that this scheme had to be intentional. He in turn communicated my sentiments to the newly assigned auditor when he called to demand a postponement. She was totally silent on the matter, breathing not a word of denial. She ignored the issue altogether by agreeing to reschedule my appointment. Guilt by silence or by refusal to deny may not constitute admissible evidence in a court of law, but the inference in terms of logic was incontrovertible.

We arrived on the appointed day with all my records in hand: photocopies in addition to originals. The auditor started by reciting her combat orders in a manner that was, if not hostile, at the very least aggressive and accusatory: a tone that grew more antagonistic as the audit progressed. She made it clear in no uncertain terms that, despite the previous year's unblemished audit (of which she was aware), she was going to conduct a full investigation of my business activities, expenses, and deductions.

She asked me to explain the nature of my business. By this time in my career, my business had grown to include consulting work, historical research, appraisals, and expert witness jobs. But she was not interested in my various forms of revenue. She wanted to know instead how I reconciled expenses with income; or, how I recognized income as opposed to reimbursement. My system was one of utter simplicity: I counted as income any money that I received, and deducted expenses as they were incurred. Income minus expenses equaled profit.

For example, let us say that I agreed to lecture at a conference in California. When the organizer sent a check as payment in advance, I counted the full amount as income – even though part of the money was reimbursement for plane fare. Then, when I purchased the plane ticket, I deducted the cost of the ticket as an expense. I entered every transaction individually on a worksheet, which I gave to Drew at the end of every month; he subsequently entered the information in an accounting program. If the organizer sent me a plane ticket instead of the money with which to buy one, I entered neither income nor expense, because I neither received any cash nor laid any out; no transaction appeared. The same was true if the organizer paid for my meals and lodging. However, if I paid for my own meals and lodging, then submitted an invoice for reimbursement, I counted the meals and lodging as expenses at the time they were incurred, then counted the reimbursement as income when it was received. In the latter scenario, expenses and reimbursement canceled each other out, with no profit showing on the year-end balance sheet. (If this accounting method sounds too straightforward to require explanation, the reader is reminded that I was merely answering the auditor's question.) Thus, a large portion of my gross income was not taxable because it was offset by expenses that were directly related.

Likewise, book sales were offset by printing costs, magazine article payments were offset by research expenses (such as photocopy charges for historical documents), photo sales were offset by film purchases and processing fees and equipment repairs and purchases, and so on. In order to justify my deductions, the auditor examined each and every receipt, and asked me what expense the receipt represented. Most receipts were company receipts (printing company, camera repair shop, museum, and so forth), on which the company name and the service performed were provided. Fortunately, I had annotated cash register receipts which provided only dates and amounts; Drew showed her where these expenses appeared on the accounting program printout and on the tax return.

Answer the Question, Not the Implication

As the audit progressed, the auditor's face grew longer with every item of supporting documentation that I presented. I produced everything she asked for.

She took exception to my vehicle log. "This is nothing but a piece of paper. It doesn't prove anything." This comment was gratuitous and ridiculous: a daily vehicle log was precisely what the IRS required from truckers and from anyone who relied upon the mileage method for computing vehicle expenses (instead of actual travel costs such as vehicle repairs, gasoline purchases, insurance costs, and so on). This was not *my* method of accounting; it was the IRS method.

"How do I know that you actually traveled that many miles?" Drew was waiting for just such an argument. He handed her my vehicle repair receipts. She said angrily, "You can't claim repairs when you use the mileage method."

Drew calmly explained, "No, and we didn't. But if you will look at the dates on the receipts, you will see that he had repairs done in January, a State inspection in April, tires purchased in September, and an oil change in December. All those receipts have the mileage entered on them by the dealer. The number of miles that are authenticated by the receipts almost equal the number of miles that are claimed as business travel."

She scowled. "If you're gonna have an attitude about it." Her comment was misplaced. I suspected that she had a litany of negative comments that she used to back taxpayers into a defensive position. She took a moment to absorb Drew's information, then admitted grudgingly, "You *have* done your homework."

She re-inspected my vehicle log with biased vigor. "Thirty miles to UPS?"

There was no inflection in my voice when I asked, "May I see that?" She handed me the log and pointed to the entry. "Yes, thirty miles is correct."

"*Thirty miles?*" she said incredulously.

I knew that she was baiting me. "That's roundtrip."

"*But thirty miles?*"

Her repetitious accusation was designed to make a submissive taxpayer lose control of his temper – to display an "attitude" that she could utilize against him. I was not falling for her gambit. I knew that the distance from my house to the drop-off station was fifteen miles; I drove it often enough, and the odometer recorded the identical distance on every trip (unless I took a roundabout detour in order to avoid traffic jams). I felt like saying, "*You stupid jerk. If you don't believe it's thirty miles, drive it yourself and see.*" But of course, that was precisely the kind of comment that she was trying to evoke, so she could claim that my antagonism implied (to her way of thinking) that I was evading tax liabilities.

From where we sat, the distance to UPS was about five miles.

I said calmly, "I live in the Northeast," and let her make the inference.

"But why so many shipping charges? What are you shipping?"

The answer was obvious, as we had already discussed the publishing aspect of my business. Her question was another attempt to inspire anger.

I said, "Books," and let it go at that.

In reality, I did not *have* to drive to UPS. I could have delivered book orders personally. Had I chosen to do so, I could have taken a leisurely Sunday drive to Virginia Beach – a roundtrip distance of 550 miles – to deliver an order to one of my dive shop customers, and the mileage would have been tax deductible. That I had chosen a less expensive and more time-effective means of delivery was *my* business, not hers. Neither she nor the IRS had the right to tell me how to run my business in order to make it more profitable. The IRS was empowered to tax my profits, not to penalize me for inefficiency in earning.

She took a deep and expectant breath, but I did not offer elucidation unless she asked for it.

She returned to my vehicle log. "What are all these other destinations?"

Drew repeated his explanation from the previous

audit, and showed her how the dates and destinations tallied with those that were given in my dive log and my journal (which also listed speaking engagements), or how they coincided with photocopy receipts from museums and archives that I had visited. My heart began to race, because I was close to making the slam-dunk that I had been prevented from making the year before.

Her evident dissatisfaction played right into my hands. "But how do I know that you really went to these places?"

I handed her a stack of receipts that were stapled in chronological order. The toll receipts were deductible and were tabulated on my tax return. I also kept all my meal and gasoline receipts. I could not deduct my gasoline receipts because I used the mileage method of deduction. Meals were not deductible unless I was wining and dining customers. But all these receipts were useful as supporting documentation.

"Every receipt is place, date, and time stamped. Together they draw a track of my travels, like a child's connect-the-dots drawing, that will corroborate the entries in my dive log and journal."

She looked as if she had been pole-axed. Her jaw dropped so hard that it nearly bounced off her chest. Anger flushed her face as she came to realize that she had been outwitted and outmaneuvered.

Down and Dirty

The auditor had no more to say on that subject. But her bag of tricks was far from empty. She was out to get me at the commencement of the audit; now she was even more determined to find some flaw in my tax return. She kept us there for hours while she questioned every aspect of my record-keeping methods and Drew's accounting procedures. Whereas before her questions had been suffused with innuendo, now they were openly denunciatory.

My biggest investment during the tax year under audit was the construction of a rental property. I had purchased a building lot the year before. Construction commenced in the spring, and the house was completed by autumn. A tenant occupied the premises in October. Construction costs came out of my savings until I ran out of money; then I borrowed. I provided the auditor with copies of the deed, the builder's invoices and proof of payment in full, incidental completion costs for materials for which I paid out of pocket, the bill for the homeowner's insurance policy, the real estate tax assessment, rental income, and so forth. She examined these papers item-by-item and line-by-line.

Suddenly she squawked, "*Six dollars for a switch plate?*"

I had compiled a list of incidental purchases. I asked her to let me see the item in question. "That's correct."

"But *six dollars* for a switch plate?"

She made it sound as if she had some particular expertise in the cost of switch plates. Before I became a photojournalist I was an electrician. I had done all kinds of electrical work: residential, commercial, industrial, and maintenance. I had worked in new construction and in renovation. During my electrical career I installed literally thousands – perhaps tens of thousands – of switch and receptacle plates. Thus I felt confident that my knowledge of switch plates was greater than hers. Instead of repeating my answer, I showed her the receipt.

The cost of the switch plate was irrelevant with respect to the IRS. If I had paid six *hundred* dollars for the switch plate, the cost would still have been deductible. The auditor had no business in telling me that, in her opinion, I had overpaid for construction materials. But I didn't say that.

"Only fifteen hundred dollars for rent?" she protested.

I asked to see the entry. "That's correct."

"But only fifteen hundred dollars?"

Now she was presenting herself as an expert in the real estate field. I could charge as much or as little as I wanted, but I could expect to obtain only what the market in the area would bear. She knew nothing about the locale – didn't even know where the house was located when I told her – so her opinion about rental fees was worthless. There were properties in the poorer sections of Philly which would have had difficulty in bringing in fifteen hundred dollars per *year*. But construction of my rental property had not been completed until October: a fact that the auditor already knew but apparently overlooked.

"That's for three months rent."

She nitpicked at every entry. Her blatant attempts at intimidation continued in this vein for hours. I responded to her accusations in soft, smooth tones. I never raised my voice. I had a great deal of trial experience on the witness stand as an expert. I had been cross-examined by hostile lawyers who were experts in the art of intimidation, who connived vigorously to distort the simplest answer into a statement that misrepresented the truth, who browbeat me unmercifully in futile attempts to discount my expertise. This auditor was a milquetoast by comparison. Not only that, but she refused to accept the fact that I had nothing to hide; it was impossible for her to trip me or to get me confused.

As Mark Twain said, "If you tell the truth, you don't have to remember anything."

Neither did her condemnatory tactics work on Drew. He could not be rattled. He dealt with the IRS on a daily basis. He had defended company audits whose complexities made mine seem like a first grade reader, and for amounts in millions of dollars. To him, this audit was nothing more than another day at the office. Furthermore, he knew that I had nothing to hide, so neither did he.

Fault by Default

Ultimately, the auditor found only two items that were in any way questionable (in her mind). Drew had placed one deduction in a Schedule which she thought was inappropriate; she believed that the deduction belonged in a different Schedule. In either Schedule, the deduction was still deductible.

Secondly, she objected to his switch to an alternative

accounting method because it resulted in a reduction of my tax liability for the year that was being audited. According to federal tax laws, one may use the accrual method for claiming deductions. In the accrual method, one may deduct not only an expense that was incurred during the fiscal year, but may also deduct related expenses that accumulated, or accrued, in the subsequent year. In my case, I paid printing costs for one book in two adjacent years: a down payment in the year being audited, and the remainder after the end of the year when the books were delivered. When Drew completed a trial tax return for the year that was being audited, he switched to the accrual method in order to reduce my tax liability for that particular year.

An accountant's job is to file a tax return that abides by the law yet is advantageous to his client. My tax return did not violate any law or IRS ruling.

Nonetheless, the auditor proclaimed, "You can't do that without permission."

Drew disagreed. Due to the complexities of federal tax law, such disagreements occur commonly between tax accountants and the IRS. Even if Drew were found in error, the disallowance would not constitute a violation for which the IRS could impose a penalty.

The auditor could find no clear-cut faults in my tax return. She maintained her two objections like a cliffhanger clinging to a ledge. She terminated the audit by proclaiming, "You'll hear from me in three weeks."

Filling the Quota

I did not hear from the auditor for more than eight *months.*

I have no way of knowing how much time and effort she wasted on investigating my tax return. I saw only the final, meager result of her work. She did not disallow a single deduction (not even the six dollar switch plate to which she objected so strongly). She moved the deduction that she claimed was misplaced from one Schedule to another, but it made no difference in my tax liability. The only thing she could "get" me on was

Drew's switch in accounting methods. She refused to grant permission for the switch.

She did not – *could* not – disallow the deduction, because it was a bona fide expense. The only thing she could do was to disallow the expense for the year that was being audited. This left me with a greater tax liability for that year.

Drew laughed off the absurdity of her ruling. He told me that I had three ways of handling the situation. One: I could file an appeal to a higher authority that *would* grant permission for the switch. Two: I could pay the tax that she had calculated was now due, then submit an amended return for the subsequent year. If the deduction was not taken in the year being audited, then by the regular accounting method it could be taken in the subsequent year (in which the expense was actually incurred). This amendment would reduce the subsequent year's tax liability by the identical amount that the auditor wanted me to pay for the year that was being audited. However, he opined that in retaliation for this action, the auditor would likely demand an audit of the amended return. This would cause more work for us in preparing for the audit – although ultimately it would make no difference to my overall tax liability. The payment and the rebate would zero out.

Three: I could pay the tax, then claim the deduction in the present year as an unclaimed expense, or a "loss carry forward." The payment would therefore be canceled out by the reduction in my present tax liability. In effect, I would pay the IRS with one hand, and take back the money with the other. The net result was still zero: the IRS would be no richer and I would be no poorer. Drew thought that this way of "getting even" would not result in a recommendation for audit, since the IRS would have no way of knowing about the loss carry forward unless and until an audit was conducted for the present year. He was right, because that is what I did, and there the matter rested.

The auditor was smug when Drew handed her my check. Was she stupid, or didn't she know that she had fooled no one but herself? I simply paid my current year's taxes in the form of two checks instead of one; the total amount was the same because the money that I paid to the auditor reduced my current year's taxes by the identical amount.

This begs the question: Why did the auditor go to such extreme measures to disallow a deduction that she must have known I could deduct in the subsequent year? Did she believe that I would let the matter go? Wouldn't it have been simpler to authorize the switch in accounting methods?

I later met an ex-auditor who provided the explanation: the quota system. In order to justify her continued employment, an auditor had to "earn" at least half a million dollars per year. That is, she had to disallow enough deductions in the conduct of her audits to generate five hundred thousand dollars of revenue for the IRS. Otherwise, she would be replaced.

The IRS Inquisition

All three of my auditors possessed abrasive personalities. They were hard-core, roughshod, down-and-dirty browbeaters, eager to pounce upon me for the slightest perceived infraction. Not one of them ever cracked a smile. Each comported herself in an aggressive, condemnatory manner.

Auditor #1 did not want to believe that I was who I said I was, but she was forced to accept the truth when it was flung at her face. Auditor #2 was firm, but knew when she was beaten. Auditor #3 was openly belligerent, intent on "getting" her taxpayer no matter how much dirty-dealing was required. (She once put Drew and me "on hold" while she called her daughter on the telephone, and chatted about her school work. She should have done this on her own time, not on my time and while she was being paid by the taxpayers, including the taxpayer who sat patiently in front of her.)

Each auditor worked on the presumption that I had cheated on my taxes, that I had something horrible to hide, and that I was lying. The tenor of all three audits was one of interrogation, as if I were a mass serial killer or a dread prisoner of war instead of a patriotic citizen. This attitude went a long way toward alienating me against auditors and the auditing process.

Worse than their attitude, however, was their conduct. The lengths to which Auditors #1 and #3 went to intimidate me were uncalled for. While they had the right to demand proof and supporting documentation, they could have done so in a friendly and non-threatening manner. Not until after the third audit did I learn that each auditor was concerned more with achieving personal financial gain than with conducting a fair and objective audit of my tax return.

The Auditing Prejudice

All three of these audits were grossly biased, without so much as a pretense of impartiality. All three auditors had only one goal in mind: to obtain money by hook or by crook, by fair means or foul. Auditor #2 bailed out of the audit when she realized that her investment in time was unlikely to produce any worthwhile return. The other two auditors overzealously carried the audits to the extremes of absurdity in their vain attempts to discover illicit activity where none existed. In each of these audits, the one-sidedness of the auditing system was overtly evident – not only by the documentation for which the auditors asked, but by the documentation for which they did *not* ask; and which, when the issue was approached, Auditor #3 intentionally avoided.

For example, in discussing my travel expenses, Auditors #1 and #3 saw every receipt for expenses that I had claimed. Both could see that my business kept me on the road for up to six months of the year. Both had documentation of the places I visited: libraries, museums, and archives that were located primarily in Washington, DC, in addition to other research facilities that were located in a number of other States; dive sites all along the eastern seaboard, from Canada to Key West, and in the Great Lakes; wilderness areas that were located largely west of the Rockies; and so forth.

Yet neither one asked me why my expenses for lodging were so low. Neither one volunteered to inform me that I was permitted to deduct motel fees as a business expense. On the contrary, while I was establishing proof of my whereabouts during a discussion of my travel itinerary, Auditor #3 abruptly changed the subject when I showed her my credit card statement on which a motel location was given.

My lodging expenses were low because I could not afford to stay in motels during my travels. I camped in a tent for weeks at a time. I slept on dive boats whenever it was possible to do so. I bivouacked in my van at Interstate Highway rest stops, or along the side of secondary roads, or in marinas. I stayed with friends and often slept on the floor. But none of the auditors asked for these explanations, or offered so much as a speck of advice on expenses that I *could* have deducted, but didn't.

In short, the auditors intentionally withheld information that might have reduced my tax liability by increasing my allowable deductions.

They offered absolutely no advice on any other expenses that I could have deducted.

All three audits were discriminatory in that they did not seek to achieve a fair and balanced tax return, but sought only to disallow expenses for which I might not possess receipts. Nor did I get any pats on the back because my records were so well organized. Instead, I got annoyance and open hostility.

The taxpayer deserves better treatment.

For What It's Worth

Two things I learned from all these audits were that a purchase receipt was almightily meaningful to the IRS but the purchased item was totally irrelevant.

By this statement I mean that if I showed up for an audit and tried to prove an expense by, for example, showing the auditor the actual camera whose purchase I claimed on my tax return, she would disallow the deduction. On the other hand, if I brought in a *receipt* for a camera – even if I hadn't bought the camera but ob-

tained a receipt elsewhere – she would have accepted it
readily as proof of purchase.

Most receipts do not have the purchaser's name
written on them: toll receipts, post office receipts, cash
register receipts, and so on. This means that a taxpayer
can easily get away with claiming deductions for purchases that he did not make, simply by collecting receipts from friends, relatives, and trash cans. It is this
kind of blind stupidity that makes the auditing process
so absurd.

If the IRS were to do a thorough job of investigation
into a person's deductions, they would insist on seeing
the purchased item, and on tracing every receipt to the
issuer. This is the only kind of investigation that would
constitute proof in a court of law – but then the IRS is a
law unto itself.

It Ain't Over Till the Fat Lady Sings

The IRS was not done with me. Having found nothing wrong with three of my tax returns, they hit on me
again in 2001 for the 1999 tax year: another so-called
"random" audit. For reasons that Drew and I never ascertained, the audit was cancelled before a date was set
for my appointment. I suspect that the terrorist attacks
of September 11, 2001 caused a reorganization of IRS
priorities, and focused attention on nonrandom selec-
tions.

This saved us a lot of work, and it saved the taxpayers a lot of misspent tax dollars. But the IRS left the
back door open. In a letter that was dated November 26,
2001, the IRS sent me a cancellation letter that stated,
"We examined your tax return for the above period and
made no changes to the tax you reported. However, we
could change your tax later."

But that wasn't the end of the matter.

The IRS decided to audit my 2005 tax return. This
time, the audit was "to verify the correctness of income,
deductions, exemptions, and credits," and was to focus
on gross receipts, and publishing and printing costs.
They did not use the "second notice" tactic for this audit.

They set a date which, as usual, was inconvenient for me, as it fell in the middle of my summer travel plans. The auditor, who signed herself as an "Examining Officer," appended, "If you do not respond to this letter, we will issue an examination report showing additional tax due."

This was preposterous. In essence, the IRS was threatening to tax my nonappearance. Taxes are based upon income minus deductions; nothing else. According to the law, they were not allowed to affix a tax liability arbitrarily. They were supposed to have some kind of evidence that I had underpaid my taxes. The IRS was not empowered to create a tax liability out of whole cloth or wild imagination. There had to be some justification for doing so. In my mind, a so-called "random" selection for examination was not sufficient cause.

Leave it to the IRS not to be concerned with legalities or with an individual's right of due process. The veiled threat here was that if I didn't defend my tax return, they would assume that I had no defense. They would then disclaim *all* my deductions on the assumption that I earned my income without incurring any expenses. This presumption of guilt flew in the face of three successful defenses of my operating expenses in past audits.

Drew and I went through my schedule, then he informed the auditor when I would be available. Nonetheless, I still had to drive home from Boston for the unhappy occasion. Drew tried to circumvent the appointment by photocopying all the pertinent materials pursuant to the auditor's request, and sending them to her in advance. He reasoned that if she had in hand all the documents that she had requested, there was no need for us to appear in order to present them to her in person. She demurred. She wanted me to appear.

Furthermore, she refused to let Drew appear with me. As you can see from my previous audits, having expert advice and a competent defender placed the IRS at a disadvantage. Auditors would rather deal only with bewildered taxpayers. They don't know the law and were in a poor position to defend themselves from the on-slaught of ruthless examiners. The auditor claimed that Drew's capacity as my accountant did not qualify him to act as my representative at the audit – this despite the fact that he was the one who had prepared my tax return, and therefore was the person who best under-stood why my return was filed the way it had been filed.

Drew, of course, knew that this was poppycock. He drew up a power-of-attorney form and had me sign it. Once he submitted this to the auditor in my behalf, she reluctantly acknowledged that he had the right to ap-pear and represent me.

Repetition Ad Nauseam

The audit was held in the top floor of a bank build-ing. The IRS occupied the entire floor. Drew and I arrived on time, but the auditor was nowhere to be found. She did not answer calls from the receptionist. We were kept waiting in a reception room. I needed to get rid of some of my morning coffee, so I went to use the rest room. The rest room door was locked. This seemed odd – were they afraid that a disgruntled taxpayer would steal the toilet paper or vandalize the facilities?

Back in the reception room, I asked for the key code to the lock. The receptionist told me that the rest room was reserved for employees, and that visitors were not allowed to use it. He suggested that I leave the building and go elsewhere to find a rest room – perhaps to a diner that was half a mile down the road.

I could understand the rationale: keep the taxpayer on edge by making him hold in his urine during the audit. I didn't argue. Instead, I moseyed along the hall-way until an employee from a different workstation ex-ited the rest room, then I let myself in before the door slammed shut.

The auditor called us into her office twenty minutes after the scheduled time of my appointment. There was only one corridor between the elevator and the reception room. The offices lay beyond the reception room. As the auditor had not passed us by walking through the reception room, I quickly inferred that she had been in her office all the time that we were cooling our heels.

To give her credit, this auditor was not abrasive. She explained the procedures that we would follow during the course of the examination, and managed to do so in a kindly and non-accusatory manner. Throughout the entire morning she was never aggressive or hostile. She grinned on occasion. She treated Drew with professional courtesy, often leaving me out of the conversation so they could discuss the fine points of tax law as it related to my return.

Nonetheless, Drew and I were suspicious, and were not fooled by her show of cordiality: it could have been an act. Perhaps she was trying to seduce us into her clutches like a Venus flytrap using sweet-scented sap to lure an unsuspecting insect into its maw, to be dissolved and ultimately consumed. Or, to change metaphors, perhaps she thought that she could kill more bees with honey.

Be that as it may, Drew went to bat first by informing her that, while organizing my paperwork for the audit, he found a $530 deduction that he had overlooked when he had prepared my tax return. He handed her the substantiating documentation. She accepted it with equanimity.

She wanted to know all about my business: what I did, how I did it, how I showed my income, where I posted expenses, and so on. This took more than an hour because my vocation had become so complex. In addition to writing books and magazine articles, and shooting and selling photographs to book and magazine publishers, I now did consulting work in a wide range of disciplines that were largely related to my expertise in the underwater world. I did historical research for treasure salvors, I appraised artifacts that had been recovered from the sea, I testified in court as an expert witness, and so on. Some of this work I could do from my home; sometimes I had to travel to distant job sites.

After she had a handle on everything that I did to earn a living, she began to ask for documentation that supported my expenses. As before, Drew was ever ready to produce everything that she asked for in duplicate. First he showed her the original paperwork, then he handed her photocopies to keep. As he did in the previous audits, he explained how the money – either income or expense – tied in to the tax return, and how all the numbers tallied. There was nothing subversive about my tax return or the substantiating documentation: it was done purely by the numbers.

After an hour of this, she said, "You did all my work for me."

Drew merely smiled.

We wound up the audit by lunchtime. Still amicable, the auditor said that she would get in touch if she found that she needed additional paperwork. We didn't hear from her until six months later. She returned the two-inch-thick packet of photocopies that Drew had furnished, along with this annotation: "We've completed the examination of your tax return for the year(s) shown above. We made no changes to your reported tax." She now signed herself as a Tax Compliance Officer.

By Foul Means Only

Note that the auditor's wording was noncommittal. She did not write that she found no discrepancies; instead, she wrote, "We made no changes." There certainly *was* a discrepancy. Drew indicated a discrepancy at the beginning of the examination. The auditor agreed that all my deductions were legitimate business expenses, but she neglected to mention the deduction that was mistakenly omitted. She should have given me credit for that $530 expense, but she didn't. Her smiles were merely facetious.

The IRS has never been accused of fair play.

It is ironic that no auditor ever demanded supporting documentation for my income. I wonder what would have happened if I had informed an auditor, who was questioning the validity of my expenses, that I was unable to validate all of my income; if I said, for example, that I could not substantiate several thousand dollars of my reported income because I was paid in cash, and that in retrospect I would have to amend by tax return by reducing my reported income.

I wonder.

Statistical Improbability

By way of example, 132,275,830 individual tax returns were filed in 2005. The IRS audited 302,785 (full field examinations). By simple mathematics, this means that 2.289% of individual tax returns received full field examinations.

The IRS recouped an average of $17,944 additional tax dollars per full field examination. (None from me.)

Furthermore, a number of additional audits were conducted via correspondence. That is, the IRS sent letters to people informing them that, according to an examination of their tax return, they owed more tax than they had paid because one or more of their deductions had been disallowed. The IRS recouped an average of $7,758 per tax return examination by means of correspondence.

Most people paid the putative delinquent amounts without question: in the case of full field examinations, in order to avoid penalties and the cost of defense; in the case of correspondence tax return examinations, in order to avoid a full field examination.

If the auditing process were truly random, an individual taxpayer would have one chance in 43.69 of being called in for a full field examination. For ease in calculation, let's round 2.289% up to 2.3%, and round 43.69 up to 44. If a person starts to file tax returns at the age of 20, and continues to the age of 65, then he will have filed 46 tax returns. According to probability theory, he can expect to be audited at least once during his lifetime. Some can expect to be audited twice, some may never be audited. All in all, not bad odds for a lottery.

But the IRS targets certain individuals to be penalized with audits. Wage earners with straightforward salaries and few or no deductions are generally left alone. Those who receive the brunt of the audits are self-employed taxpayers who have to spend money in order to earn it. But even discounting the fact that one class of taxpayer is more likely to be audited than another, what are the chances of being randomly selected twice?

Again by means of simple mathematics, the answer is calculated by multiplying 2.3% by 2.3%, or 0.023 times 0.023, which equals 0.000529, or 0.0529 %, or slightly more than one-half of one percent, or about one in 200.

For three audits, multiply the previous product by 2.3% again; this equals .0000121.

For four audits, multiply the previous product by 2.3% again; this equals 0.0000002.

For five audits, multiply the previous product by 2.3% again. According to my calculator, the new product is 0. In reality, there is not a zero percent chance of being audited five times; my calculator simply cannot display enough digits to calculate the percentage, and the closest approximation is zero.

According to probability theory, I had a better chance of being struck by lightning in clear weather at the exact same moment that a baseball-size meteorite pierced my heart while I was exploring an underwater cave, than I had of being selected to have five full field examinations purely by random.

But the IRS wasn't done with me yet.

Lurking Six: the Inevitable Sequel

One would think that the IRS wouldn't bother to harass a senior citizen who had a perfect tax payment record for his entire life, and was now collecting retirement benefits from the Social Security Administration. One would be wrong.

One evening I ran down to the mailbox unit that was located a mile and a half from my new house. I retrieved my mail, stuffed it in my fanny pack, and jogged back home. I tossed the pack on my desk without paying attention to its contents, then showered and sat down to dinner. I returned to my desk around 8:30 that night. In my mail was a letter from the IRS.

They didn't try to pull the "second notice" gambit. Instead they got right to the point: "We have selected your federal income tax return for the year shown above for examination." The year chosen was 2007.

Note that the letter did *not* state that the audit was the result of a random selection. They didn't try to pull that gambit either.

The IRS wanted to examine every expense that I claimed for supplies, to whit: "Copies of cancelled checks, receipts, and statements to show who was paid and the amount paid for supplies. If the payment was made to a company that sells a variety of items, then a receipt will be needed to show exactly what was purchased and the cost of the item(s). If various items and/or supplies were purchased together, please provide an itemized list and be prepared to verify each item on the list with back-up documentation. For example, a detailed receipt, invoice, statement, etc. If the expense includes payments made on a regular basis for services or products, then provide a copy of the contract or agreement detailing the services performed or products used."

As everyone knows, in modern day banking protocol, canceled checks are no longer returned to the account holder. That practice ended a couple of decades ago. To obtain copies of canceled checks, I would have to first identify which canceled checks related to my business, then visit my bank and have them make copies for me. This process could take weeks, or months. My bank charges a hefty fee for every canceled check request. Furthermore, the IRS had timed delivery of the audit letter so it was impossible for me to obtain copies of my canceled checks in time for the audit; my bank did not open until an hour and a half after the scheduled appointment.

As I noted above, it is perhaps a revelation to taxpayers who have never been audited that a receipt for a purchased item carries validity whereas the actual item does not. In other words, if I brought a newly bought camera to the examination room as proof of purchase and possession, its expense would be disallowed unless I had a receipt to establish its purchase. By extrapolation, you don't need to buy the cereal as long as you have the box tops.

They also wanted to examine my vehicle expenses: "Repair receipts, inspection slips, or any other records to show total mileage driven for the year. Log books and other records verifying the business mileage claimed. If you did not keep a log or other formal records of your business mileage, reconstruct the business use of the vehicle. This information should include current mileage reading on the vehicle used for business purposes, mileage reading on the vehicle when you acquired it, mileage reading for January 1 and December 31 of the year being audited, and mileage distance between your residence and your business location. Also bring an appointment book or calendar of your business activities during the year. If you claimed actual expenses, invoices and cancelled checks for automobile expenses you incurred during the year. These include gas, oil, tires, repairs, insurance, interest, tags and taxes. For depreciation of actual expenses provide a bill of sale or other verification to establish the cost or other basis of the vehicle, including the trade-in of another vehicle."

How many individuals had that kind of information at their fingertips? This brings to mind the age-old legal strategy: if you can't win a lawsuit on its merits, paper your opponent to death by demanding irrelevant disclosures. Furthermore, what possible relevance could the current mileage reading have when it was two years after the year being audited?

The IRS had already scheduled an appointment for me – *for the next morning at 8:30, at a location that was a two-hour drive from my house.* They gave me twelve hours notice to appear with all my expense receipts properly organized, as well as copies of my 2006 and 2008 tax returns. Under the heading "What will happen if you do not respond" was written, "If you do not respond to this letter, we will issue an examination report showing additional tax due." Once again, they intended to disallow all my expenses unless I appeared and defended them.

This offensive strategy would have sent the ordinary taxpayer into a panic. I merely ignored the idle threat, and scoffed at the absurdity of the situation. Nor was I worried about a greater tax liability. As always, I had filed my taxes by the book – the IRS book of rules and regulations – so I had nothing to worry about.

Because it was way past office hours, I was unable to call either the auditor or my accountant. I rested easily that night, knowing that in the morning I had no intention of showing up for the audit, and that auditor could effect no reprisals as a result of my nonappearance. The law specified that any examination had to be conducted at my convenience.

I opined that, depending on how long the auditor had been at her job, I may have had more experience in conducting tax examinations than she had.

The request for copies of my tax returns for 2006 and 2008 was superfluous. The IRS already had those tax returns in their computer database. The auditor had access to them at the touch of a few keys on her keyboard. Asking me to provide them was just another way to burden me with work, and to intimate that they might also examine those tax returns if I didn't comply immediately with their audit demand.

The next morning at 8:10, I called Drew at his office and told him that yesterday I had received yet another audit notice and that the date for a full field examination had already been scheduled. He calmly asked when they wanted me to appear. I told him 8:30. He asked what day. I said, "Today." He was appropriately aghast.

We discussed the situation for several minutes. At 8:20 I called the auditor, told her who I was, and informed her that I was not going to appear in front of her ten minutes hence, for the reason that I had received the notice only the previous evening. She did not strike an adversarial pose, but immediately took a defensive posture by claiming that the IRS computer system had been slow in sending audit notices to taxpayers.

"Even so," I challenged, without missing a beat, "the letter is dated only last week. Even if the computer had sent the notice right away, one week is not enough time to prepare for a full-scale audit."

She apologized and admitted that I was right. "When the computer selected your tax return for examination, it should have given you more time."

She had just admitted a mouthful without knowing that she had done so. She had tacitly confirmed what I had suspected all along: *my name had not been selected at random, but had been programmed into the IRS computer for periodic audits.* More on that later.

Without giving her credit for commiseration, I charged straight ahead but in an even tone that was not accusatory. "But the audit location is a hundred miles from my house. Why wasn't it scheduled for someplace close to where I live?"

This loaded question put her even more on the defensive. She claimed that the IRS didn't know that I had moved the year before. (The audit notice had been sent to my old address, and forwarded by the Postal Service.) I found this statement impossible to accept, but didn't mention it to her. The IRS knew everything about me. All they had to do was type my Social Security number into their database, and my entire life history would unfold in front of them. They were pleading ignorance so they could systematically disrupt my life in the most inconvenient manner possible.

Without pause I asked, "Are you aware that the IRS audited my tax return a couple of years ago for the very same reason?"

She said "No," but followed her negation immediately with "What was the outcome of the 2005 audit?" If she didn't know about the audit, how did she know the specific year that had been audited? I was certain that she had the information in front of her, yet she had pleaded ignorance.

"No change," I said. "My tax return was accepted as submitted. Don't your records show that?"

"I don't have that information. I can get it, but it will

take several weeks to go through the system."

Again I didn't believe her, but I played dumb. "How about if I send you a copy of the confirmation letter?"

She allowed that if she showed her supervisor a no-change letter from the previous examination, he might suggest that my case be handled differently. I hoped this meant that she and her supervisor were going to be smart about this latest contrived audit, and realize that they weren't going to find any tax liabilities in my return – much the way that Auditor #2 closed my examination prematurely when she realized that she wasn't going to get any money out of me because my records were in such good order and in full compliance with federal tax laws. I entertained the hope that I could circumvent the audit altogether.

I declined to mention that this was the sixth time in fifteen years that my tax return had been selected for examination, and that all previous audits had been resolved in my favor. In the unlikely event that she didn't already know this, I figured that such an admission might force her to infer that the IRS kept calling me back because of chronic tax evasion practices.

She gave me her e-mail address. I promised to scan the confirmation letter and send it to her as an attachment as soon as we disconnected, which I did.

The last item that we discussed was representation. She refused to allow Drew to represent me because he did not have power of attorney. I corrected her, and told her that Drew's power of attorney was already on file with the IRS from the previous audit, that I had a copy of it in my tax records, and that I could send it to her if (as she claimed) she had no record of it. She refused to accept the previous power of attorney, and said that I would have to obtain a new power of attorney.

I ended the phone call on the note that after she received the new power of attorney, she should communicate directly with Drew about rescheduling the audit and a change of venue. I called Drew and recapitulated the conversation. He drew up a new power of attorney (Form 2848).

That same day (February 3), the auditor sent a follow-up letter to my legal residence. It stated, "The request for transfer of an examination will be considered only after the taxpayer or representative submits the written statement including the following: A. The reason for the transfer; B. The taxpayer's current address and current phone number; C. The address/location of the taxpayer's current principal place of business; D. The address/location at which the taxpayer's books, records, and source documents are maintained; E. Sufficient information to establish that the transfer will result in an examination where the books, records, and source documents are maintained; F. Why the requested location is more efficient for the examination of the taxpayer; G. Other factors which indicate that conducting the examination at a particular location could pose undue inconvenience to the taxpayer."

If this sounds overly burdensome, I am certain that it was intentional. By the time the letter was delivered, I had departed for a trip of several weeks duration. Upon my return I found in my mailbox a letter from the IRS which stated that power of attorney had been denied.

I shot an e-mail to the auditor: "I am confused. My accountant has received no communication from you during my absence. I returned from a trip of several weeks to find a letter from the IRS (dated February 18, 2010) in which the IRS denied my right to give Power of Attorney to my accountant (Drew Maser) so that he can represent me, the reason given being 'we could not verify that the return is under Examination at the IRS.' "

She replied, "Your case was closed out of our office on 02/03/2010 and you should of or will be receiving a letter stating that your return was accepted as filed. A letter with a number of 1024 in the bottom right hand corner should of explained this. This is why they could not locate your case in examination. The case must get approval before it is released from our offices but once the approval is given it could take up to 45 days for the letter 1024 to be mailed out. I apologize for any inconvenience this may have caused you."

The Government Gets Revenge

All these tax examinations beg the obvious question: Why did the IRS keep picking on me when they had firmly established that I kept excellent records of my business operations, and never once cheated on my tax returns?

The chances are literally astronomical that my name was selected six times in fifteen years purely by random. If my calculator couldn't figure the odds on being selected five times, the sixth selection defied the bounds of reason and probability theory. The number of zeroes that must precede the percentage integer is calculable only by a sophisticated mainframe computer that contained a floating-point processor which supported scientific notation. I won't go as far as to state that the number of zeroes exceeds the number of elementary particles in the known universe, but the figure must be pretty close.

As I noted above, the sixth auditor just as much as admitted that my name was programmed into the IRS computer for periodic selection. I can think of a good reason for being included on the hit list.

As noted elsewhere in this volume, in the late 1980's I initiated a suit against the United States government for the right to dive on the Civil War ironclad *Monitor*, which was sunk off the Diamond Shoals of North Carolina. The wreck site was controlled by the National Oceanic and Atmospheric Administration (NOAA). During eight years of correspondence and litigation, the case was heard once in federal court, three times in administrative law court, and ultimately ended with congressional intervention in 1992. I succeeded in winning the right of access for all American citizens to see for themselves this icon of U.S. naval history. This protracted legal action cost me tens of thousands of dollars and hundreds if not thousands of hours of my time.

The astute reader will remember from the beginning of this chapter that my first full field examination was for my 1992 tax return: coincident with end of the final case in which two Congressional representatives overruled NOAA's position of denial and decided in my favor. This ultimate action put paid to NOAA's totalitarian control of the *Monitor*, and established a precedent for succeeding generations. NOAA's administrators were sorely stung by the diminution of their control, and the administration continues to hold a grudge against me for usurping some of their authority.

It is widely known that the government uses the IRS as a cat's paw to harass citizens who are suspected of criminal behavior or subversive activities, and to get even with constituents who have caused political grief. I fall into the latter category. There may be no way to prove it, but I see no reason to doubt that NOAA instigated a lifelong tactic of revenge against me by using extreme political influence to have my name programmed into the IRS computer for periodic examination.

I could be wrong. Perhaps there *are* enough zeroes in the known universe to account for my selection by purely random means.

The IRS Flimflam

I believe that most taxpayers are inherently honest. They pay their taxes on time and in full.

I also believe that the average taxpayer is not well organized. Add to this the fact that many people have trouble in simply balancing their checkbook, and we have a recipe for error that has nothing to do with deception or tax evasion.

I am compulsive about saving receipts. (I even save my grocery receipts.) I am also a meticulous organizer. If I were not perfectly organized, I could not locate a specific photograph among the tens of thousands that I have in stock, when a publisher submitted a request. Organization is the nature of my business as well as part of my personality. But I am an aberration.

The IRS "banks" on the fact that people are poor record keepers, not that they are dishonest. In the usual bustle of modern day life, people are generally overwhelmed by affairs that require immediate attention: earning a living, paying bills, raising children, maintaining homes, staying healthy, and so forth. Saving receipts and organizing files are not their primary goals. Such activities appear unimportant, and are likely to be a waste of time.

The same is true if not worse for self-employed taxpayers. They spend so much time and energy on running their business, that keeping records for tax purposes is often put by the wayside. A sole proprietor seldom thinks that, when he enters an expense on a worksheet, he may some day be called upon to *prove* that expense beyond a shadow of doubt. When the day does arrive, incomplete records that are haphazardly arranged will prove his undoing.

The IRS not only banks on a taxpayer's disorganization, it helps to accentuate it. The last thing the IRS wants is a taxpayer who is prepared for an audit. In order to achieve its nefarious goal, the IRS often sends a fake "second notice" which threatens the taxpayer with penalties if he fails to present his records for audit within an impossibly short time period, perhaps within the next few days, or possibly overnight. No one can afford to stop his life in midstream so he can work full time to organize files. The taxpayer then arrives with his records in disarray, and the auditor chews him up and spits him out for failing to *immediately* provide requested documents to support his deductions. Any expense that the taxpayer cannot verify instantly is automatically discounted.

The auditor puts the taxpayer on the defensive, first by intimidation and then by outright threats. She paws through every private part of the taxpayer's financial life, exposing his most intimate transactions. She questions his activities. She makes unsupported accusations. She informs him that she can sanction severe penalties against him for less than full disclosure, for failing to report income, and for claiming deductions that he cannot support. She blackmails him with threats of reprisals such as fines and incarceration (although I suspect that few people have actually been jailed for income tax evasion since Al Capone was imprisoned in the 1930's).

The taxpayer is so badly shaken by the auditor's threats and almighty authority that he is willing to pay any amount that she devises rather than to suffer more humiliation and anxiety. Because he never wants to go through the sordid experience again, he pays the exaggerated amount as soon as he receives his adjusted "liability." He hopes that he will be forgotten, and that the IRS will pick on someone else the next time.

Since the typical taxpayer is disorganized by nature, he is no more prepared for a subsequent audit than he was for the first one. So the IRS stings him again by preying upon normal human weaknesses and character flaws.

Infernal Revenue Service

Aside from my name being posted on the IRS hit list, why pick on me? And why six times? Why not audit a large corporation instead?

The individual taxpayer is often unprepared, disorganized, intimidated, and alone in his defense. An auditor can easily bully him into submission. Persecution is the auditor's primary stock in trade.

A corporation cannot be debased or terrorized. A corporation consists of a large number of individuals, none of whom can be held personally accountable for tax disparities. A corporation employs certified public accountants to defend its tax returns, and employs attorneys to file appeals and to argue in court. These highly paid professionals are educated, well trained, and experienced.

IRS tax advisors are not as conversant with federal tax law as one would expect. IRS auditors rely on human nature and terror tactics to cheat an individual out of his hard-earned income. An auditor does not need to know much about tax law – she needs to know only a little more than the taxpayer knows. A taxpayer who is not accompanied by his accountant or tax consultant is at a distinct disadvantage, because he is at the mercy of the auditor for interpretations of the law.

A corporation will fight the IRS because it has nothing to lose by fighting, and everything to gain by prolonging the fight and by postponing the payment of taxes. When millions of dollars are at stake, a CPA or a company executive can more than earn his salary by finding loopholes and by negotiating settlements.

Furthermore, a corporation's hired hands know federal tax law better than IRS auditors know it.

The individual taxpayer is at the mercy of an unscrupulous auditor, whereas an IRS auditor is little more than a mouse in the claws of a corporate legal team.

Screw the IRS

There are ways to prevent yourself from being screwed by the IRS. First and foremost: save your receipts. Even if all you do is stuff them into a manila envelope or toss them into a file folder, at least your expenses can be reconstructed should the need ever arise.

Second: take your tax consultant with you to the audit. His presence alone sends a message to the auditor that she cannot take liberties with the law. His knowledge and experience pitted against hers can save you a great deal of anxiety as well as costly misinterpretations of federal tax law.

Third: do not be afraid to argue. Your attitude has nothing to do with your rights as a taxpayer. Be cool, be firm, but do not ape the auditor in being hostile or aggressive. And remember: answer the question, not the implication.

Fourth: do not volunteer information, because you may inadvertently open other lines of questioning to your disadvantage. You have nothing to gain by being unnecessarily straightforward with an auditor who is not being honest with you and who has your worst interests at heart.

Fifth: keep in mind that the auditor's goal is not to help you to file a more accurate tax return or to advise you on deductions that you could have taken but did not, but to cheat you out of money by dint of intimidation or by your ignorance of federal tax law. Do not expect to be treated fairly, or even decently.

Sixth: in filing your tax return, err on the side of pre-sumption. If you have any doubt about whether an item constitutes an allowable expense, deduct it. Let the au-ditor disallow it (if you are audited). It is not a criminal offense to make a mistake.

Seventh: instead of selling household items that you no longer need or want, consider donating them to char-ity and obtaining a receipt to be used as proof of a char-itable contribution. Do the math to see which way works best for your tax bracket. For example, say you pur-chased a paperback book whose retail price was $10. If you sell it to a used book store, you'll be lucky to get a dollar for it; maybe less. But if you *give* it to a church for its annual bazaar, you can deduct the full cover price from your taxable income. If you're in the 25% tax bracket, that means that you will realize $2.50 when you file your tax return. And you'll be doing the church a favor into the bargain.

The Flatworm Stimulus

The federal government uses income tax laws to nudge taxpayers the way a rancher uses a prod to herd cattle, or the way a scientist uses a stimulus to evoke responsive movement from a flatworm. For example, when the government wanted to save energy, it offered tax incentives for the installation of storm doors and windows. Multiply this one example by tens of thou-sands, and you can understand why federal tax laws are so complicated.

Tax incentives are like friction: the rougher the sur-face, the more energy is lost in motion. Add enough com-plexity and the tax system takes on the consistency of Swiss cheese: riddled with loopholes that corporate tax-payers worm through, and which ignorant auditors try vainly to plug.

The system would operate more smoothly if it were simplified, and it would save money for the country in the long run.

For example, Pennsylvania's State income tax is a

straight 3% of the taxpayer's adjusted income, whereas brackets for federal income tax range from 10% to 35% (a spread that is based upon the greater number of loopholes that are available to high-income taxpayers). The reason for the great difference between State and federal taxes is that the State income tax has neither incentives nor loopholes. Everyone pays the same percentage. The savings in administration of the system are enormous when compared to that which is spent on administering the federal income tax system. And the savings overall – for the State and for the taxpayer – are even more enormous.

The expense of administration and the price of defense from the federal income tax system is outrageously high because of the necessity to employ large numbers of administrators and auditors to implement the system, versus accountants, tax consultants, and lawyers who are hired by taxpayers to defend them against the system. The cost of tax compliance is colossal.

Tax Fraud . . .
. . . is alive, well, and shows no signs of dissipating. The biggest perpetrator of tax fraud in the United States is the Internal Revenue Service. It replaces codified laws with arrogant bullying techniques as a way to extort money illegally from an ignorant or naïve public. It employs an arsenal of threats, intimidation, and blackmail to divest honest earnings from people who are unfamiliar with the rules of engagement. It lies to its taxpayers. It cheats when fair means fail. Yet it expects nothing less than total honesty and full disclosure from the people it is supposed to serve.

Federal tax laws are so complicated, ambiguous, contradictory, or all of the above, that it is easy for the IRS to take advantage of an individual's ignorance and to frighten him into paying taxes that he doesn't owe.

It has often been quoted, "Nothing is certain but death and taxes." In reality the situation is worse, for even dead people pay taxes. Death is taxed under the euphemism "inheritance tax." This is the government's way of extorting a person's heirs after he has left this mortal coil.

Tax reform is an issue of constant debate. Yet tax reform is treated like the weather: people complain, but no one does anything about it.

I take that back. Congress has done something about taxes – they keep adding them. As recently as July 1, 2010, Congress created a new tax on, if you can believe it, indoor tanning services. That's right; from now on, there will be a 10% tax for people who don't get enough natural sunlight and opt to bask under a commercial sunlamp. What absurd tax is next?

Before you know it, Congress will emplace a tax on air and sunlight.

In my opinion, the federal income tax system is far too perverted to be overhauled into an equitable means of collecting taxes. The IRS operates a system of abuse that is far beyond the pale of democratic acceptance.

The IRS can no longer be tolerated. It needs to be abolished completely. A federal tax collection system could then be reincarnated equitably like the State tax system; or, even better, federal taxes could be collected in a different manner entirely.

Taxes are a necessity, and are not necessarily or inherently evil. The government needs to be supported financially so that it can perform its function to protect its citizens. Only hardcore radicals believe in anarchy.

But there are better ways to collect taxes. Fair ways.

Consumption Tax

A consumption tax known as FairTax is a revolutionary plan to collect federal tax money in a way that is fair to most taxpayers. In one fell swoop, the adoption of the FairTax would abolish all other forms of federal taxation in a simplified manner that is nearly identical to the collection of sales tax. Instead of collecting tax on income, the FairTax would collect tax on spending, incrementally throughout the year at the nation's cash registers.

FairTax can best be described as a personal consumption tax.

The leading proponents of the FairTax system are Neal Boortz and John Linder. Boortz is a syndicated talk show host. Linder is a Congressional representative from the State of Georgia. Together they authored a book that is entitled, appropriately, *The FairTax Book*. Let me distill the salient features of the theory behind this innovative taxation system.

One beauty of the FairTax is that it cannot easily be evaded. Tax is imposed on new goods and services, and is paid the same way in which sales tax is paid. The tax is calculated as a percentage of the purchase price, and is shown on the sales receipt at the time of purchase. The more purchases you make, the more tax you pay. In this manner, although the tax rate is the same for every individual, people with higher incomes will theoretically pay more tax because they spend more money.

Another beauty of the FairTax is that it cannot be manipulated. Like sales tax, it incorporates no convoluted system of deductions or exemptions, and therefore contains no loopholes.

Multiple taxation is avoided because the only ones to pay FairTax are individuals: not companies, corporations, partnerships, foundations, organizations, or any special interest groups.

No penalties can or need to be applied through the FairTax system.

An individual does not need to maintain records or keep receipts of any kind for FairTax purposes.

No complicated year-end tax forms have to be completed and submitted.

Unfair tax practices are avoided.

No accounting services are required.

No tax return audits need to be conducted.

The threat of invasion of privacy is eliminated.

The fear of political reprisals is eradicated.

Tax life is uncomplicated.

FairTax Losers

Not everyone will benefit from the FairTax. The hardest hit group will be tax evaders: those people who either do not file tax returns, who deal in cash, or who cheat on their federal income tax returns.

As Boortz and Linder are quick to point out, drug lords and illegal aliens are the biggest tax evaders. Their unlawful income goes untaxed under the present system which taxes *reported* income. Under the FairTax system, they would contribute to the support of the government and its public services every time they made a purchase or paid for a service.

The next largest collective group that would be disadvantaged by the FairTax system are people who do not report all their income: those who collect money under the table, who make barter arrangements in lieu of payment, who operate cash businesses, and so on. All these revenues are lost in the current tax system. The FairTax means no more freeloading off honest citizens.

Foreign tourists would help to pay for government services – such as police protection, fire departments, and emergency medical services – when they visit the United States and spend money for food, lodging, transportation, and souvenirs. Under the present system of federal income tax, they receive the benefits of these services without putting money into the pot that pays for them.

In short, every individual who spends money in the United States would pay consumption tax in proportion to the amount of money spent, regardless of where or how that money was earned (or stolen).

Even thieves, robbers, swindlers, embezzlers, smugglers, scam artists, bookmakers, gamblers, loan sharks, and confidence people would support the country by paying their share of tax when they spent their ill-gotten gains. It could no longer be said that crime doesn't pay. Criminals would most certainly pay – taxes.

FairTax Naysayers

It should come as no surprise that the most invective lobbyists against the FairTax are those who use the present system of federal tax collection to their personal advantage – politicians. They have everything to lose and nothing to gain by a tax collection system that strips them of authority and bargaining power.

Politicians use and abuse the current tax system as a matter of course in their everyday (mis)conduct. I could cite thousands – perhaps tens of thousands – of ways in which elected officials bend tax rules in order to curry favors, pay personal debts, even get elected. A list of misuses would fill not just a book but a multi-volume series.

The most recent gross example has been completely overlooked by a befuddled public and star-struck media. In the old days, it was common practice for candidates and their henchmen to stand by poll booths and bribe arriving voters to cast their ballots for them or their favorites. This practice has long since been outlawed, yet it was used to great advantage in the 2008 Presidential campaign. When Barak Obama promised to give every American taxpayer a $600 rebate on his federal income tax if he was elected, he was in essence bribing the taxpayers to vote for him. And it worked!

Tax Extravaganza

The abolishment of the IRS would serve several great causes. It would force some 160,000 federal employees to seek useful employment. It would obviate the need for individuals and corporations to hire tax consultants. It would enable people and companies to concentrate their efforts on doing productive work. It would allow American citizens to earn a living without fear of being audited. It would let life in America proceed without government intervention or Big Brother invasions of privacy.

Large corporations have entire departments whose staff members sometimes occupy one or more floors of an office building, and whose sole purpose is to handle tax related issues. A so-called "tax compliance" department is a euphemism for a group of accountants whose primary job is to find loopholes in tax laws so that they can save money for the corporation.

The cumbersome laws that govern the collection of

federal income tax are printed in a series of large tomes that exceed 67,000 pages in length. By way of comparison, this is more than twice the length of the full-sized comprehensive library edition of the *Encyclopedia Britannica*, which details the whole history of the world as well as the sciences, arts, religions, and philosophies of mankind.

The Tax Ax

The IRS has constructed tax brackets with artificial demarcations. Most Americans are middle-class wage earners who fall in the 25% tax bracket. This means that they pay two and a half tithes, or one quarter, of their hard-earned income in federal tax. By way of example, an individual who grosses $60,000 per year only nets, or takes home, $45,000 (minus other taxes such as Social Security tax, Medicare tax, State income tax, school tax, gift tax, personal property tax, capital gains tax, and so on).

(In aside, Social Security tax is called a "contribution." This is absurd: with regard to money, a contribution is a voluntary donation, not a forced payment.)

In the FairTax system, that same individual would take home every penny of his $60,000. Thus he would start the year richer by $15,000 that he would not have to pay on April 15. But it gets better.

The FairTax system would do away with multiple taxation. Under the present system, companies and corporations pay corporate tax. Actual profits of these legal entities are thereby reduced by the amount of their tax liability. When dividends are paid to stockholders, the stockholders are then taxed when they file their individual tax returns. Thus the stockholders pay double tax: first they pay corporate tax on company earnings, then they pay individual tax on the portion of those earnings that they receive as dividends. The IRS gets you coming and going. And it gets worse.

The IRS taxes every stage of production within a company. Let's take a company that builds clocks as an example. Clocks are built from various parts and subassemblies: springs, faces, hands, cases, movements, and so on. Movements consist of a variety of components such as gears, pins, cams, and so on. Every individual who is involved in the manufacture of every part pays personal income tax: the miners who dig the ore, the smelters who convert raw ore to metals, the chemists who create steel and brass alloys, the machinists who mold raw metals into bar stock and sheet metal, the fabricators who make metal fittings, the lumberjacks who chop down trees, the lumberyard workers who make lumber from timber, the woodworkers who fashion slats from blocks of wood, the people in the assembly plant, the teamsters who transport the raw materials, the parts, the components, the subassemblies, and the finished product. And this is to say nothing of the designers, engineers, marketers, advertisers, wholesalers, and retailers who are involved in the overall process of making a clock available to the consumer.

The income taxes that all these companies and individuals pay are embedded in the production cost of the clock, which drives up the retail price by approximately 22% (according to Boortz and Linder).

The FairTax would eliminate this embedded tax.

Boortz and Linder estimate that an individual consumption tax of 23% is required to finance the government at its existing state of operation. Additionally, this tax rate would compensate for the elimination of all other federal taxes: Social Security tax, Medicare tax, corporate tax, capital gains tax, import duties, and so on.

Thus when a consumer paid for a clock, he would pay about the same price that he would have to pay now. The difference is that he would not pay tax until he actually purchased the clock, and then he would pay the same amount of tax that everyone else would pay, no more and no less – unless, that is, he decided not to buy the clock, in which case he would pay no tax. And the amount of tax paid would be shown on the cash register receipt the same as State sales tax.

None of this takes into account the vast savings that

would result from not having to support a top-heavy Internal Revenue Service, and the immense cost of collection and tax return examination. Or the cost of hiring tax consultants. Or the time wasted on preparing income tax returns and follow-up audits.

Understand that the FairTax would not do away with federal taxation; instead it would make taxation easy and equitable.

Abolition of the IRS has my vote – if only my representatives would offer it as a referendum.

A New State of Affairs

Most States impose sales tax, income tax, excise tax, luxury tax, inheritance tax (a euphemism for death tax), and numerous other niggling taxes. Most counties impose personal property tax, real estate tax, and school tax. It would be a simple matter to abolish all these targeted taxes and replace them with a Statewide consumption tax as a means of compensation. This would enable local governments to collect their operating expenses by way of a single utilitarian and universal system. It would also reduce the costly overhead of the multitudinous collection processes that nibble away at the taxpayers.

If the federal government established the local rates, the system would not violate the principle of "no taxation without representation" that I discussed in Section Three, because voters would be represented by their federal Congressional and Senatorial electees.

The Competitive Tax Plan

While I adore the simplicity of the FairTax system, I cannot ignore the inequity that Michael J. Graetz pointed out in his book *100 Million Unnecessary Returns*. Graetz is Professor of Law at Yale University. His major bone of contention against the FairTax is that it favors high-income earners and disfavors low-income earners.

Low-income earners must spend all or most of their income on survival needs, whereas high-income earners have some of their earnings leftover either for savings or for investments (such as real estate, stocks, bonds, and mutual funds). Money that is spent on investments would not be taxed under the FairTax system because it would not constitute the purchase of a product or service. Thus the purchase of new products and services would be disproportionate among the masses.

Graetz proposes to reform the current tax system with what he calls the Competitive Tax Plan. The major component of his system for raising money to support the government is a Value Added Tax. According to him, "The VAT would work like a national sales tax, but instead of depending only on retailers to collect the tax, a VAT is collected piecemeal at all stages of production."

Let's say that it costs $5 for a company to manufacture an item. When the item is sold to a wholesaler for $10, tax is imposed on the increase in value. When the wholesaler sells the item to a retailer for $20, tax is imposed again on the new increase in value. When the retailer sells the item to a customer or end-user for $30, tax is imposed once again on the final increase in value.

Graetz concludes that this graduated system of tax collection is more difficult to evade than a tax that is imposed only on the ultimate sale price when the item is paid for at the cash register. He bases this conclusion on the premise that an unscrupulous retailer might collect the tax but not turn it in to the government.

Graetz also finds fault with FairTax mathematics. He thinks that a national sales tax rate of 23% is not enough to equal the present amount of revenue that is generated by the federal income tax and all the other taxes that supplement it (excise tax, luxury tax, inheritance tax, and so on). He thinks the rate might have to be as high as 35%.

To keep the VAT rate low, he proposes to keep many of the other taxes: corporate tax, estate tax, gift tax, and so on.

Furthermore, he wants to keep the IRS as the country's tax collector. And he wants to impose a federal income tax on individuals who earn more than $50,000 per year; or, in other words, he wants to exclude individuals who earn less than $50,000 per year from having to pay federal income tax. This taxation and exclusion are intended to overcome the inequity between low-income earners and high-income earners by making the wealthy pay more because they can afford to do so.

Counterpoints

Although the Competitive Tax Plan appears to be more equitable in the distribution of tax impositions among individuals with different earning levels, I have a number of objections to the plan. I will list these in order from the least objectionable to the most.

The artificial line of demarcation at the earning level of $50,000 creates a disparity. An individual who earns $49,000 is not taxed. An individual who earns $51,000 is taxed at the rate of 15% (according to Graetz's plan). This means that the $49,000 earner keeps all $49,000 of his earnings, whereas the $51,000 earner pays $7,650 in federal income tax and keeps only $43,350 of his earnings. Ironically, it pays more to earn less.

Furthermore, who will arbitrate the filing status of individuals and small businesses when they do not file returns because of their belief that their earnings were not large enough to necessitate their filing? If people don't file tax returns, who is to say that perhaps they *should* have filed? And who tracks individuals or small businesses that did not file returns because, although their gross income exceeded $50,000, their net income after allowable deductions was less than $50,000? Who determines the allowability of deductions?

The plan calls for keeping such unfair taxes as corporate tax, wage tax, gift tax, and estate tax (alias inheritance tax, alias death tax). The problem with the death tax is that all too often it totally disrupts the ability of the heirs to keep their inheritance and to maintain a living. Estate tax is currently in a state of flux: it is coming and going, and the rates are changing annually. As of this writing, the rate can be as high as 55%.

As a simplistic example, take a large farm or ranch

that has been in the family for several generations. This farm has never been sold, yet it is arbitrarily valued at $12 million. The farmer dies and leaves the farm to his four sons and daughters. Each sibling receives one quarter of the farm that is worth $3 million. Each sibling must then pay estate tax of 55%, or $1,650,000. The farm is the only family asset; it is land, not cash. The only way the siblings can obtain cash to pay the tax is to sell the farm. The farm is then broken apart and the siblings have no land to farm. The heirs are essentially disinherited of their birthright. The government gets richer while the people get poorer, or go broke in the process of excessive taxation.

While the majority of Americans are relieved from the onus of filing a tax return under Graetz's plan, a sizeable portion of the population – including businesses whose gross income exceeds $100,000 – is still bound by the insufferable rules of the federal tax system: all 67,000 pages of it, including exceptions, exemptions, and numerous addenda. Americans currently squander more than 150 *billion* dollars a year on federal tax compliance and collection. Graetz's plan would not reduce this wastage by any significant amount.

The complexity of federal tax collection would remain essentially the same.

And worst of all . . .

Eliminate the IRS

Imposing a limit on the number of people the IRS is permitted to harass and investigate is like stopping the Allied armies at Germany's borders as long as Hitler promised to reduce the number of non-Aryan executions to a level that was considered acceptable to all.

As I noted above, the only solution to IRS excesses is abolition.

A government agency develops an identity that is equivalent to a child developing a personality. Many factors are involved in this developmental process: Congressional mandates, managerial emphasis, individual conduct, and so on. Once an agency is imprinted and its identity is solidified, it is almost impossible to alter its base characteristics. Rehabilitation eventually yields to recidivism.

By way of example, when I proved victorious against the National Marine Sanctuary Program (a division of the National Oceanic and Atmospheric Administration), the enmity that was created between me and Sanctuary personnel spread rapidly throughout the agency, then crept to other NOAA agencies. I was a pariah; my name was anathema.

Agency animosity did not diminish with the passage of time. As low-grade employees rose through the ranks, they were inculcated by their superiors about the way my court case had reduced Sanctuary authority. Newly hired personnel were similarly indoctrinated. This pathology continues even today, so that a whole new workforce – people who didn't work for NOAA at the time of my litigation, and who were not affected by the outcome – has been taught to hate me. Most of them probably don't even know why. They just accept it because that's the way it is.

The same is true of the IRS. The people who work there are an unalterable part of the mindset. They can no more divorce themselves from the Service's mean attitude than a junkyard dog can learn to be nice.

Not only must the IRS be abolished, but no one who ever worked there should be hired by the replacement federal tax collection agency, lest they bring their malicious attitude with them and infect innocent employees with a malignancy that would spread uncontrollably until the replacement agency became as corrupt as the Internal Revenue Service.

Down with the IRS!

Section Five
Mass Media Deception
or Misdirection, Miscommuni-
cation, and Misanthropy

Product Disability

In a capitalistic society, the primary goal of private enterprise is to earn a profit. How that profit is achieved is of little concern to the shareholders. The communications industry is no different.

The problem with this economic system with respect to mass media is that it harbors no product liability. The government does not force the media to issue warning statements to the effect that the information that they are about to impart may not be true, factual, or accurate. Indeed, truth, factuality, and accuracy are too often in abeyance in the portrayal of information that is published, broadcast, or televised.

Published nonfiction may be poorly researched or exaggerated. Radio broadcasts may be slanted to make a point that is not predicated on the facts. Televised news shows are sometimes just that – a pretense or ostentatious display of knowledge that seeks to entertain rather than to educate. Society's mental health is put at risk by such a lackadaisical attitude or intentional dishonesty.

The media prey on sentiment and natural gullibility to entice readers, listeners, and viewers to pay attention to their gaff, in order to sell their product and to make money on the sale. But by subverting honest endeavor in the name of profit margins, they drastically alter the way the world is perceived, either by knowingly distorting the facts or by committing sins of omission.

The result is the creation of urban legend – a fairytale or piece of fiction that people *want* to believe despite its obvious implausibility, because the romantic elements trigger an emotional response that is as strong if not stronger than long-term drug addiction.

The fallacy of fictitious news is that many people accept as gospel whatever they see or hear *first*. No amount of subsequent evidence to the contrary can sway them from their newly conceived notions. People actually come to believe information that is unsupported by evidence because the belief is more comforting than the contradictory truth. Some people ascribe to the theory that a lie that is believed by enough people then becomes fact.

An industry with no sense of accountability can be worse than the Ministry of Truth that was depicted in George Orwell's *1984*. Spoon-fed delusions can be far more palatable than harsh and uncomfortable reality. The media industry thrives by telling undiscerning individuals what they want to hear.

Publish or Perish

It has often been said in academia that a scientist must publish papers in journals or perish through anonymity. A scientist must establish the priority of his ideas and scientific findings by making public announcements to the scientific community.

The fallacy of the system is that submitted manuscripts must undergo peer review prior to acceptance for publication. Some science articles are rejected because a reviewer has a personal dislike of the submitter, or because the submitter's facts or the results of his experiments disagree with those of the reviewer, whose prejudice and desire for fame is greater than his quest for the advancement of science.

As a result, papers that contain new and radical ideas or experimental data that challenge traditional thought or established notions, or that conflict with the pet theories of the reviewer, are rejected as a way of suppressing same. Unorthodox viewpoints have little or no opportunity to obtain recognition.

Some scientists have resolved the rejection issue by publishing on the Internet. Their detractors cried "Foul!"

and claimed that the tactic was unfair because of the lack of peer review. Nonetheless, publication established the priority of ideas, even if the presentation wasn't made in an established scientific journal. It seems fair to me.

Publish More or Perish

The "publish or perish" sentiment is even truer in the publishing industry.

Publishing houses make money not by publishing books, but by selling them. If they don't sell enough books, they go out of business. Therefore they resort to a number of schemes to promote and advertise their wares – schemes to trick the reader into making purchases based on misleading or patently false information.

There are laws against false advertising but they do not apply to the publishing industry.

The book business is one in which I have been involved for practically my entire life: first as a reader, then as a buyer, as a writer of short stories and articles, as a photographer, as a novelist and nonfiction author, and as a publisher. I have encountered every kind of scam in the business – at least, I hope I have.

The most common method of swaying potential buyers to purchase a book is to misrepresent the author. For example, a publisher will use a famous individual or media personality as a byline, then hire a real author to do the actual writing. There are variations of this common scam. A look at the history of this unethical practice will prove edifying.

Bait and Switch

In the 1930's and 1940's, Helen Traubel was a celebrated singer in nightclubs, cabarets, and opera. By 1950 she was at the height of her career. In 1951, Simon & Schuster published a mystery novel that was entitled *The Metropolitan Opera Murders*, as by Helen Traubel. The title was appropriate and associational because she had sung at the Metropolitan Opera House. But Traubel had nothing to do with the book other than lending her name to the title.

The actual author was Harold Q. Masur, a hard-boiled mystery writer who was famous in his own right. His first book, *Bury Me Deep* (1948) was an instant best-seller. Nonetheless, Traubel's byline graced the cover and title page, and ghostwriter Masur was banished to anonymity.

Readers who thought that they were buying a book that was written by the famous opera star in actuality bought a book that was written by an up and coming mystery writer. The publisher obviously thought that they could sell more copies by advertising Traubel as the author of a novel that took place in an opera house.

In more recent times, the Putnam Publishing Group published a series of nine books that started with *Tek-War* (1989), as by William Shatner. Shatner was a well-known television star, most fondly remembered for his role as Captain James T. Kirk in the 1960's *Star Trek*. His byline enticed *Star Trek* fans (known as trekkies) and science fiction readers alike. The publisher printed the actor's name on the cover in large bold letters, and advertised him as the author in the company's promotional literature.

It was later divulged that the actual author was long-time mystery and science fiction writer Ron Goulart. Readers who praised Shatner's gift for writing words, as well as for voicing words on the boob tube, were hood-winked by a clever marketing campaign.

Perhaps the best known case of byline deception involves Virginia Cleo Andrews, who wrote gothic horror novels under the name V.C. Andrews. She had published eight books by the time of her demise, in 1986. Yet over the next quarter century, an additional *sixty-seven* books have appeared under her byline, and they still continue to appear. With seventy-five books now published under the name of V.C. Andrews, it seems as if she became more prolific after her death than she ever was during her lifetime.

It is not unusual for authors to leave behind unpublished manuscripts when they die. In this case, however, the situation was different. Simon & Schuster conspired with the heirs of Andrews' estate to hire a ghostwriter to complete two unfinished manuscripts . . . and then to produce multiple new series of books under the V.C. Andrews byline. The true and truly prolific author was Andrew Neiderman.

Neiderman has published books under his own name as well. In 1990, Berkley Books published his *Bloodchild*. The front cover bore this curious blurb: "A Master of Psychological Thrillers." The blurb was attributed to V.C. Andrews, who by that time had been dead for four years. She must have been speaking (or writing blurbs) from beyond the grave, perhaps by means of a ouija board.

Today, a new generation of young readers is probably unaware that the person whose byline is printed in huge bold letters on the cover of a newly published V.C. Andrews novel, expired before they were born. American readers, that is . . .

England didn't stand for this publication swindle. A suit was brought in British court to put a stop to this nefarious practice of lying to the public about the Andrews authorship. In England, the truth will out.

What's in a Name, or the Meaning of "With"

When Madison Books decided to assemble a coffee-table volume called *Lost Liners*, they called me for underwater photographs to illustrate the text. The premise of the book was "ocean liners I have visited," as by Robert Ballard. The list of ironies and hanky-pankies that led to the production of this book is monumental. It is worthwhile to provide some background in order to achieve an understanding.

Ballard was an oceanographer who worked for Woods Hole Oceanographic Institute. His specialty was deep-sea submersibles and remotely operated vehicles. He became an American icon after the discovery of the *Titanic*. The hypocrisy of his sudden launch to fame was that it was a media creation. The American media either downplayed or neglected to mention the fact that the discovery expedition was jointly sponsored by WHOI and IFREMER (Institut Francais De Recherche Pour L'Exploitation de la Mer).

Three-quarters of the work that it took to locate the wreck of the *Titanic* was led by French scientist Jean-Louis Michel, aboard the research vessel *Le Suroit*. Ballard made no attempt to correct the media misconception, but instead took full and solo credit for the 1985 discovery. Only in France did Michel emerge from the shadows to have his valuable contribution acknowledged.

The discovery of the *Titanic* led to national recognition for Ballard and the shipwreck. Stirred to fever pitch by media hype, the country went *Titanic* crazy practically overnight. Savvy hucksters polluted the marketplace with such ridiculous novelties as *Titanic* T-shirts, postcards, mugs, snow globes, wall plates, photographs, cigarette cases, models, medallions, commemorative coins, lapel pins, calendars, pennants, hat bands, napkin rings, refrigerator magnets, stuffed toys, posters, ball caps, poker chips, blankets, music boxes, ashtrays, plus replicas and reproductions of everything you can imagine and some that you can't.

Not to be left out of these money-making schemes, the publishing industry waded into the collectible feeding frenzy with both feet shod in seven league boots. I walked into a bookstore whose central display offered 27 newly published books about the sinking of the *Titanic*. Not one of them presented any new information that had not been published three-quarters of a century earlier. Only the formats and layouts were different. Each was a clone of the other; each regurgitated previously known facts and figures with the panache of Archimedes stepping into his bath and crying "Eureka!"

You would have thought that the *Titanic* was the only shipwreck in history. Although there have been tens of thousands of shipwrecks, and although thousands of books have been written about them, they all took a back seat to the promotional extravaganza of the

Titanic. The bookstore in question carried no other shipwreck titles.

The folks at Madison Press assembled *Titanic*-era photographs and research materials, and hired Rick Archbold to write the text of a book that was published under Ballard's byline. For his efforts, Archbold got a "with" on the cover and title page. The book was ostensibly written by Robert Ballard "with" (assistance from) Rick Archbold. Ballard may have written the introduction - or maybe not.

Chances are that whenever you see a celebrity's name in giant capitals on a book cover, and a subordinate name appended after "with" in small case letters, the "with" did the actual writing. I learned this for certain when I spoke with the people at Madison Press. To continue . . .

The National Geographic Society, which years ago shifted its emphasis from scientific studies to vapid entertainment, was quick to jump on the *Titanic* bandwagon with a series of television shows, with Ballard as the showman. They funded expeditions whose sole purpose was to obtain enough footage to produce a one-hour special. These so-called expeditions were relatively short – usually on the order of a week or two.

I first met Ballard in 1992. The Boston Sea Rovers hired me to give a presentation about my successful lawsuit against NOAA and my subsequent dives on the *Monitor*. Ballard was a long-time member of the club and was asked to introduce me at the annual film festival.

National Geo funded a film shoot on the *Lusitania* in 1993, with Ballard as titular leader. I dived on the wreck in 1994. When Madison Press got around to doing the photo layout for the predictable book, they found a paucity of close-up photos from the National Geo shoot, because the robotic camera was unable to get near the wreck. This triggered the call to me from the art department, where I learned who actually wrote their *Titanic* book. They contracted with Spencer Dunmore to write the text for the *Lusitania* book, and used some of my underwater photos to illustrate it.

Not only did the *Lusitania* book byline Ballard as the author (Dunmore got a "with"), but my name did not appear in the captions for my photographs. Instead, a credit sheet in the back of the book printed my name in fine print, along with the page numbers where my photographs appeared. Thus the casual reader was led to believe that Ballard himself had taken all the photographs. Even the film crew and still photographers who accompanied the shoot received no acknowledgement for their work.

And so we come to *Lost Liners*. Madison Press wanted to do another Ballard book. The format called for name-dropping the most famous sunken ocean liners – names that the buying public could associate with. Ballard was sent to the *Andrea Doria* for a two-day photo shoot. He obtained pictures of nothing but utter blackness.

A quick trip to the *Empress of Ireland* fared only slightly better, with very few images that were of publishable quality. This left Madison Press without sufficient illustrative material for the project. Not only did I have photographs of the *Lusitania*, but I had interior shots of the *Andrea Doria* and *Empress of Ireland*. Once again my credits were relegated to small print in the back of the book.

Ballard even admitted that until the project was brought to his attention, he had never even heard of the *Empress of Ireland*. Yet he was being touted as a world-class authority on shipwrecks.

What did Ballard contribute to *Lost Liners* other than his name? I don't know.

Disillusionment

I grew up reading about the adventures of Tom Swift Jr. The author was given as Victor Appleton II – supposedly the son of the Victor Appleton who wrote the original Tom Swift series in the early 1900's. Imagine the letdown I felt when I learned that there was no such person as Victor Appleton, or the son who continued in his father's tradition. Both Appletons were house names.

A house name is a made-up byline that is used when a number of different authors are contracted to write a series of books. The reader is led to believe that the byline is the name of the author, when in fact there is no such person, and the books could be written by any number of authors.

Grosset & Dunlap went so far as to state on the flyleaf of the Tom Swift Jr. books, "The author of these exciting stories about the son of the original Tom Swift has inherited the wonderful storytelling ability of the first Victor Appleton." Howard Garis wrote the original series. Elizabeth Stratemeyer wrote the early titles in the second series; she wrote outlines for the later titles and farmed out the writing to a stable of authors who worked for hire for the publishing house.

Other house names have received complete biographies – sometimes *auto*biographies – that were obviously fictitious.

At least a dozen authors wrote Nancy Drew books under the house name Carolyn Keene. Franklin W. Dixon was the house name that was used for the Hardy Boys books. The Bobbsey Twins books were bylined with the house name Laura Lee Hope.

The Doc Savage pulps were bylined Kenneth Robeson. Lester Dent wrote the early novels, until he ran out of steam and other writers were hired to take his place. Walter Gibson rather than Maxwell Grant knew "what evil lurks in the hearts of men," the line that introduced the Shadow to pulp fiction readers. There never was a Brett Halliday; the Michael Shayne mysteries were written by other hands.

House names are legion: there are hundreds, thousands of them, lurking unknown in the vaults of publishing houses. Usually they are created as a way of associating a byline with a specific character, series, or formula.

My point is that the public has the right to know the true author of a book, just as they have the right to know the amount of fat and cholesterol in a can of soup. Honesty should take precedence over marketing cons.

What's in Another Name

Some actors have stage names, but if they do, they have only one. Writers, on the other hand, may have dozens or scores of bylines. The purpose of a pen name is to hide the writer's name from the public: sleight of pen hand, so to speak, so that readers won't know who was responsible for producing a particular piece of writing. Blindsiding readers effectively prevents them from declining to buy works by writers whose work they would rather not read.

In the days of pulp fiction, some wordsmiths were so prolific that the over-appearance of their names gave readers the impression that they focused on quantity rather than quality, and that therefore they were not worth reading because of their lackluster and machine-like prose.

Some entire magazines were written by a single person – under a host of noms de plume.

Occasionally, a writer's alter ego became more popular than his real name. The works of Don A. Stuart were more respected than the works of John W. Campbell, Jr., although Campbell wrote science fiction under both names. Henry Kuttner was less popular than his alias Lewis Padgett. In both cases, the pen name was employed for a specific style of writing that differed from the style that was commonly associated with the real name.

Hardly anyone has heard of Salvatore Lombino. He wrote science fiction under the bylines Richard Marsten, Hunter Collins, and Evan Hunter (which he adopted as his legal name, and under which he published *The Blackboard Jungle*). He wrote under a host of other names, the most famous of which was Ed McBain.

One of the most prolific authors of all time was John Creasy. He cranked out more than 600 books under several dozen assumed names. The use of his own name on all these titles would have diluted his reputation to commonplace writing. Vying for the same reputation was Frederick Faust, who wrote millions of words under various pen names in the pulps; his most well-known pseudonym was Max Brand.

Some authors have used pen names that designate the opposite sex. When prolific author Harry Whittington wrote a series of stories about a female nurse, he used the byline Harriet Kathryn Myers. This was probably done for marketing purposes, in the belief that women would be more prone to buy a nurse book if it was written by a woman. Whittington also wrote under a slew of other names.

When Alice Sheldon entered the field of science fiction – which was read more by boys and men than by girls and women, and in which male authors predominated – she created the byline James Tiptree, Jr.

Sometimes a writer chose a fictitious byline because he didn't want to be associated with his work – for example, if he was writing pornography.

While the use of pen names might sound innocuous, writers and publishers sometimes evoke them as marketing ploys. When a byline goes out of vogue or is no longer acceptable to the reading public, the byline can be abandoned and another one created. This means that readers who determined that they didn't like reading works that carried a particular byline, could be tricked into buying the same writer's works under a different byline.

To unravel this mess of phony names, I use a hefty tome whose 1,100 pages of fine print provide tens of thousands of pseudonyms that were used by nearly as many authors. This gives you an idea of how prolific is the use of bogus bylines that are used to dupe readers into buying a book that they might not have bought had they known the truth of its authorship.

Titles in Disguise

The use of false names is not the only deplorable practice that publishers employ to sell their product. Perhaps the most common method of fooling readers is to re-issue a book by an author whose work a lot of readers liked, but to change the title so it seems as if the author had written a new book that the reader hasn't read. Not until the reader consummates the purchase, and takes the book home to read – perhaps weeks or months later – is the flimflam recognized for what it is.

The books in Isaac Asimov's Foundation trilogy were all retitled by Ace Books: *Foundation* became *The 1,000 Year Plan*, *Foundation and Empire* became *The Man Who Upset the Universe*, and *Second Foundation* became *Galactic Empire*. His *The Stars, Like Dust* was retitled *The Rebellious Stars*.

Arthur C. Clarke's *Prelude to Space* was retitled twice: first as *Master of Space*, then as *The Space Dreamers*. Likewise with Frank Herbert's *The Dragon in the Sea*: first as *21st Century Sub*, then as *Under Pressure*. I could list scores, perhaps hundreds of such shenanigans, but you get the point.

Many books are retitled after an author has died, quit writing, or become famous. A change in cover art helps to conceal the book's true nature. Eager fans will then purchase the new edition in the belief that it is a newly written book by one of their favorite authors – a book that they haven't read. This lends truth to the saying that "you can't tell a book by its cover."

The most egregious retitling deception that I have encountered was perpetrated by the publishing house of Robert Hale. In the 1950's, E.C. Tubb wrote nine Westerns under various pseudonyms. In 2000, Robert Hale reprinted these books not only under different titles, but under different bylines!

Men of the West as by Chet Lawson became *Hills of Blood* as by Frank Weight. *Drums of the Prairie* as by P. Lawrence became *The Dying Tree* as by Edward Thompson. *Wagon Trail* as by Charles S. Graham became *Cauldron of Violence* as by Gordon Kent. And so on for six more of Tubb's Western titles.

This kind of trickery leads modern readers to believe that these books were newly written, and were not nearly half a century old. Where is consumer protection when you need it?

The Booby Prize

Fourteen years after the discovery of the *Titanic*, and after hundreds of undistinguished but lengthy and well-illustrated volumes had been written about the sinking, I saw yet another new title that purported to be *The Last True Story of Titanic*. The author was James G. Clary. I wondered what new information this latest addition to the titanic mythos could possibly impart.

What drew my attention to the book was neither the overstated title nor the name of the shipwreck, but the front cover blurb: "Nominated For a Pulitzer Prize."

The slender volume was only 152 pages in length. The all-too-few black and white pictures were poorly reproduced. I thumbed through the pages and read a few passages. I expected that a Pulitzer Prize nominee would be written with the verve and outstanding style of John Krakauer's book about the 1986 Mount Everest catastrophe, *Into Thin Air*. I was greatly disappointed.

The writing standard was so juvenile that it defied description. The text was replete with run-on sentences and grammatical inconsistencies. The treatment of the subject matter was superficial at best. It was worse than a simple regurgitation of what had already been expounded by better-skilled authors too many times in recent years. How could such unoriginal tripe have been nominated for a Pulitzer Prize?

It couldn't. It wasn't. The author published the book himself. The fake announcement was a shifty marketing ruse by an unscrupulous author who was more deserving of a Putz Prize.

As I have already noted, there are laws against false advertising, but those laws are ignored in the publishing industry. On the contrary, false advertising is the meat and potatoes that drive an industry that operates above the law and without any sense of decency or ethics.

The Prevarication Gambit

When the truth doesn't sell, write lies. If fibs don't work, embellish and exaggerate the falsehoods beyond believability. The prevarication gambit is based on the premise that the public is stupid and gullible, and will believe anything they are told, no matter how impossible and ridiculous the story. This ploy is the trend that is overtaking the publishing industry. I know from direct knowledge.

Let me preface my pair of firsthand accounts with a publishing hoax that perhaps is still the best known. In 2003, Random House published a book under its Doubleday imprint: *A Million Little Pieces*, by James Frey. The book purported to be the true personal memoir of a drug addict, written by the addict. There does not appear to be any doubt that Frey wrote the book. The doubt lies in the "true" nature of the content.

In 2006, investigative reporters William Bastone and Daniel Green blew the whistle on Frey's so-called true memoir. Their website – thesmokinggun.com. – habitually published accounts of bizarre but little-known criminal activities that were overlooked by the press and by broadcast media. They discovered that much of Frey's book was fabricated.

This created a national furor because the book had been a bestseller – and was made more so when Oprah Winfrey promoted it on her talk show. Faced with irrefutable evidence, Frey confessed and made a public apology. Nonetheless, because the book was such a commercial success, Random House continued to publish and promote it, albeit "with notes from the author and from the publisher" about its lack of authenticity. These notes were not likely to be read until a buyer bought the book and took it home to read.

Stranger Than Fiction

Only parts of *A Million Little Pieces* were invented. *Shadow Divers*, while less well known, was almost entirely a work of imagination and fictitious creation. I know this for a fact because I was intimately involved with the subject matter of the book while the events were unfolding. Not only that, but some of my own personal achievements in the world of wreck-diving were attributed to the book's two central characters.

Shadow Divers was subtitled, "The True Adventure of Two Americans Who Risked Everything to Solve One of the Last Mysteries of World War II." The essence of the story was that John Chatterton and Richie Kohler discovered a German U-boat, then took seven years to identify it. Instead of writing the book themselves, they hired Robert Kurson to write it for them; all three shared the royalties. Kurson's only previous book was a biography of the Three Stooges, which perhaps set the stage for what was to come.

In going through *Shadow Divers* scene by scene, I highlighted hundreds of instances of gross exaggeration and outright falsehood. In my exposé– *Shadow Divers Exposed* – I wrote 380 pages of refutation against events that I could prove were untrue in *Shadow Divers*. I interviewed a score of witnesses who either did the things that Chatterton and Kohler claimed to have done, or who were present during depicted events and who witnessed those events the way they actually occurred, in contradiction to the way those events were portrayed in the book. In some cases I relied upon published or archival documentation. I cited my sources so that follow-up journalists and fact-checkers could corroborate what I had written.

In the final analysis, Chuck Wine discovered the wreck, Mark McKellar identified it, and Chatterton and Kohler took the credit.

I submitted the manuscript to Random House – the publisher of *Shadow Divers* – in order to give them the opportunity to disavow their book, issue a retraction, acknowledge *Shadow Divers* as a work of fiction, and publish a factual account. They did not have the courtesy to respond. They had invested millions of dollars in publishing and promoting *Shadow Divers*. They continued in the same vein as if the truth about the book were unknown.

Publication of *Shadow Divers Exposed* did not hinder Random House from continuing to claim that *Shadow Divers* was a "true adventure," when in actuality it was almost a complete fabrication, or, as I blatantly called it, "the greatest literary hoax since the invention of moveable type."

The Federal Trade Commission has laws against false advertising. Random House broke the law egregiously when it promoted *Shadow Divers* as a "true adventure," when in reality it was far more fictitious than *A Million Little Pieces*. It continues to break the law by continuing to advertise the book as a "true adventure" now that the truth is out.

Although the evidence that I presented was overwhelming and verifiable (because I cited my sources), I received a couple of dozen "nastigrams" from readers who did not want to be disabused of the fictional notions that *Shadow Divers* had implanted in their minds. They castigated me for dispelling a myth that they were comfortable in believing. Such is human nature

This brings to mind two relevant quotes. Napoleon said, "History is a myth that men agree to believe." In *1984*, George Orwell wrote, "Who controls the past controls the future; who controls the present controls the past." These people were prescient. If the Random House novel had gone uncontested, the fictional events in *Shadow Divers* might have become urban legend.

Out of Ammo, or the Empty-Headed Magazine

I once read an article in *Reader's Digest* about the wreck of the *San Diego*, an armored cruiser on which I had made more than 150 dives, and about which I had written the book. The premise of the article was so absurd that only a non-diver could possibly fall for it. But then, most of the magazine's readers knew nothing about wreck-diving.

According to Richard Miranda, author of "Trapped in a Sunken Ship," he was exploring inside the wreck when a bulkhead collapsed behind him. He was alone in the dark with only a flashlight to help him find his way out. He worked his way "through a maze of narrow corridors" in fading light as the flashlight's battery slowly failed. When he found a crack in the hull, he put one of his neoprene gloves on the end of a length of copper pipe, poked the pipe through the opening, and waved it to attract attention.

When a diver appeared, Miranda stretched his arm through the crack, and with his knife scratched on the side of the hull: "Trapped . . .Air . . . Rope."

The diver went for help. Miranda was nearly out of air when a diver shoved a spare tank through the crack. Miranda donned the tank, then worked his way through collapsed wreckage until he found an opening to a gun turret. He squeezed through by doffing his tank, but dropped the tank in the process. He was about to expire when the diver reappeared and shoved his regulator into Miranda's mouth. The diver then led Miranda out of the wreck and to the surface.

An accompanying sketch depicted a trapped diver scratching his message in what to him was in reverse: he was inside and had to write intelligibly on the outside. Try sticking your hand out a window and writing words on a tablet that you can't see, and writing those words from right to left. The sketch showed bare metal, whereas in reality the hull was thickly encrusted with barnacles, algae, sea anemones, hydroids, and other marine fouling organisms.

Miranda was an acquaintance of mine. The next time I saw him, I chastised him severely for writing such obvious rubbish. He did not take offense. He explained how he came to write the article in the preposterous form in which it was published.

He had always wanted to write a real-life article about the history the *San Diego*, and what it was like to dive on the wreck. When he finally did, he submitted the article to *Reader's Digest*. The editor liked the concept but thought that the piece didn't contain enough action. He suggested that Miranda spice it up a bit. He wrote a second draft with some exciting action sequences. The editor still thought that it wasn't sensational enough. Miranda then rewrote the article in accordance with the editor's suggestions for increasing its dramatic appeal. Still the editor wasn't satisfied.

So Miranda made up a completely outrageous story

and sent it in. The editor loved it! And that was the version that was published. The magazine's naive and unsuspecting readers were led to believe that every word of the article was true.

I know I've written it before but I reiterate: if ever there was a need and a place for consumer protection, it is in the publishing industry, which unfortunately shapes the human perception of reality – or more correctly, which distorts the perception of reality worse than a funhouse mirror distorts a person's physical characteristics.

The Making of a Bestseller

I cannot remember the name of the author or the title of his book, but in the 1980's I read an article about a prospective author who wanted to prove that he could make the bestseller list. He had never written a book before, and he had no aspirations of achieving literary fame. He simply wanted the recognition that was associated with bestseller status.

After writing and publishing his novel, he spent approximately $50,000 of his own money to promote it. As near as I can recall, he placed large eye-catching advertisements in the *New York Times*, *Publishers Weekly*, and other newspapers and magazines that had book review columns. The continued onslaught of visibility convinced enough readers to buy the book that he accomplished his loftless goal. He demonstrated the true value of a bestseller: if you put enough money into a book's promotion, and if you tell people hard enough and often enough that a book is worth reading, you can turn any mediocre book into a bestseller.

The moral of this story is that bestsellers are not written; they are promoted. This is not to say that all bestsellers are mediocre. Many of them deserve the recognition they receive; many do not. A bestseller is determined by the number of copies that are either sold in bookstores or ordered from the publisher within a certain time frame, not by the book's inherent quality or literary merit.

Bestsellers can be made in other ways, too. In 1956, radio personality Jean Shepherd objected to the manner in which bestsellers were selected: not by total volume of sales but by customer requests. As a practical joke, he decided to test this arrangement by promoting a book on his radio show. He raved about Frederick R. Ewing's latest raucous title, *I, Libertine*, and encouraged his listeners to purchase the book forthwith; or, if their local store was out of stock, to request that they order it. Shepherd confided to his flock that the book was so overtly salacious that it had been banned in Boston

So many listeners followed his advice that in due course, *I, Libertine* was placed on the bestseller list. The only problem with this bestseller was that it didn't exist. Shepherd had fashioned both the author and the title out of whole cloth. He even created a fake biography of Ewing: he was a retired British officer, a radio announcer, and an expert on eighteenth-century erotica.

The nonexistent bestseller then became a white elephant around Shepherd's neck. People everywhere were asking for the book. Shepherd rather sheepishly admitted to a newspaper reporter that he had perpetrated a hoax. Next he discussed the situation with science fiction writer Theodore Sturgeon. Sturgeon put Shepherd in touch with Ian Ballantine (the owner of the publishing house Ballantine Books). The three of them made a deal. Sturgeon ghostwrote the book based upon Shepherd's radio outline; Ballantine published the book under the Frederick R. Ewing byline (adding another pen name to Sturgeon's repertoire); a picture of Shepherd was reproduced on the back cover as the author's photo. And the bestselling novel became a reality.

The bestseller selection process has changed since then, but not much. One might think that total sales volume would be the only fair and accurate criterion for selection. Not so. The *New York Times*, for example, polls only a few pre-selected bookstores. Whatever titles sell the most copies in those specific stores become *New York Times* bestsellers. Titles that sell just as well or better in non-selected bookstores don't count.

Once a book gets on a bestseller list – any bestseller list, and by any means – sales everywhere become a self-fulfilling prophecy, much like a snowball that gathers more snow as it rolls downhill. The publisher dedicates great gobs of money for promotion, book reviewers add another two cents, booksellers feature the book on the counter or on a rack that faces the front door, and buyer awareness is enhanced by the book's visibility.

A book whose cover glares at shoppers as they enter the store will sell more copies than a book that is sequestered in the basement, in the back corner, on the bottom shelf, with only the lackluster spine showing, where a shopper must get down on his hands and knees to find it. A book's location has nothing to do with its quality or readability.

Scientology members took advantage of the bestseller selection process in order to promote their founder's fame (if not his already made fortune). L. Ron Hubbard was a fantasy author who created Dianetics in 1950. Dianetics purported to be a method of improving mental health. The system soon evolved into Scientology. Members protected the validity of the process with staunch religious fervor if not outright fanaticism.

When Hubbard returned to writing pulp fiction in the 1980's, faithful cult members staged a campaign strategy that was geared toward making him a best-selling novelist. Such a status could result in credibility for the man as well as for his so-called "church."

The Church of Scientology produced its pamphlets, brochures, and other promotional literature through its wholly-owned publishing company, Bridge Publications. As soon as they published *Battlefield Earth*, in 1982, they commenced an advertising blitz in all three media (paper, radio, and television). Concurrently, Scientology members and Bridge Publications employees descended upon bookstores in massive numbers. Using money from Scientology's multimillion dollar coffers, they bought every copy of *Battlefield Earth* that was on the shelves, and then asked for more. If none was available, they ordered them by the score.

It didn't take long for the Church of Scientology to be able to publicize its founder as a *New York Times* bestselling author. But it didn't end there. Hubbard pounded out ten more science fiction novels that became known as the Mission Earth series, or dekalogy. Utilizing the same strategy, all ten titles soon made the bestseller list. Then came three more titles that were published after Hubbard's demise.

The buyers could not be traced because they paid in cash. Thus there was no way to ascertain how many *different* individuals purchased the books, or how many buyers walked away with boxfuls. Then things really got bizarre.

Instead of printing new copies to meet the artificial demand, Scientology members and Bridge Publications employees returned their purchases to the warehouse for reprocessing. The next time a bookstore placed an order, it received copies that had already been sold. Some of these copies retained the original store's stamp. A bookseller received copies that carried another store's stamp, and sometimes they received copies that had their *own* store's stamp!

Eventually, this stratagem enabled the Church of Scientology to boast that their founder had written fourteen bestsellers in a row. Ironically, very few of those titles have actually been read. Mostly they have simply been recycled through the system.

How valid is the concept of "bestseller?" Like most statistics, book sales can be skewed any number of ways. Furthermore, shoppers can easily be tricked into buying books that they would not ordinarily purchase. Then, due to idiosyncrasies in human nature, nondiscriminating readers might promote the title accidentally by word of mouth, by saying that they read it, but without stating whether they enjoyed it. This is a psychological mechanism to prevent them from feeling that they were ripped off by an advertising con.

Meanwhile, titles that are more worthy to read are left to languish and gather dust. Never be afraid to say, "It may be a bestseller, but I've read better."

Who's on First?

Secondhand booksellers are not beyond falsely advertising their wares. The gimmick that galls me the most is the promotion of reprint editions as first editions. They do this all the time by advertising a reprint as "first edition thus." The unwary reader might not see or understand the word "thus," and will be led to believe that the book is a true first edition.

The definition of "first edition" is explicit: it is the first time that a written work is published in any form. There can never again be another first edition because, obviously, the next time the work is published it is "second."

When the word "thus" is appended to "first edition," it means that the advertised edition refers to publication in a different form (when the work was originally published in a magazine or newspaper) or by a different publisher (other than the publisher that originally published the work). Thus there are whole strings of "first edition thus" editions.

Take the space opera *Skylark of Valeron*, written by Edward E. Smith. It was first published as a serial in *Astounding Stories*, from May 1934 through February 1935. When Fantasy Press republished the novel in 1949, it could then be promoted as a "first book publication;" in other words, the first time the novel was published in book form (as opposed to magazine form). This gambit would mislead readers, who didn't know about the earlier publication, into believing that Smith had just written a new book (instead of one that was fifteen years old).

When Pyramid Books republished the novel in book form again, in 1963, it could be advertised as "first edition thus" because it was published by a different publishing house. When Panther Books republished it in 1975, it could be promoted as "first British edition." When Jove republished it in 1977, it could be promoted again as "first edition thus." The same goes for the 1980 Berkley Books edition. And so on and so on . . .

The way booksellers would have it, every time a book

is published by a different publisher, it becomes another "first edition thus." By this twisted reckoning, second editions almost never exist, thus allowing booksellers to advertise their wares with the catchall phrase "first edition."

Many publishers aid and abet this system by neglecting to provide a title's copyright history on the verso page. Without actually stating it, the absence of information can lead a new generation of readers into presuming that the book was newly written.

This is one more means of deception that is practiced by the publishing industry.

For what it's worth, second editions are far more rare than first editions. Every book has a first edition; only a few have a second edition.

Paper Dolls

Newspapers and magazines are influential media that can shape, misshape, or disshape (to create a nonce word) reality far more so than books.

In the 1990's, a survey determined that only 3% of the people polled had entered a bookstore in the previous year. Of that 3%, only 1% had purchased more than one book during the year in question.

Practically everyone reads newspapers and magazines, perhaps because a shorter attention span is required to read a piece or snippet in its entirety. Welcome to the world of sound bites and music video clips, whose fleeting scenes are so short and evanescent that the mind does not have time to process them before they disappear and the next one takes its place. Flicker imagery is all the rage. Concentration on a freeze-framed image might enable a viewer to discover the lack of content.

Be that as it may, I have had a long and sometimes frustrating association with the rags and the slicks, both as a writer and as a consultant. I had a penchant for writing in-depth feature articles because the length afforded me the opportunity to get into the meat of a story. Nowadays, feature articles are pretty much a thing of the past. The meat has been discarded for the marinade: flavor without substance. Editors seem to believe that people don't want their brains taxed with too many facts. Useful information is now stripped out of articles so that little is left but the gloss.

Ah, for the good old days, when an authentic piece of writing was appreciated.

Consulting Conundrum

Throughout the years it has been my custom to conduct primary research in archives, libraries, and museums that possess original contemporary documents. It was not uncommon for me to spend a week at a time in Washington, DC: mostly at the National Archives, but also at the Library of Congress, the Naval Historical Center, and the U.S. Coast Guard Historian's Office; and, immediately outside the District, at the Washington National Records Center and the office of the Judge Advocate General – depending upon the subject matter of my research.

Additionally, I have visited public and private libraries and museums from Nova Scotia to Florida, and in the States and Provinces that surround the Great Lakes. I have paid for these research trips out of my own pocket.

I estimate that by now I have spent more than a year and a half of accumulated days in various research facilities; two years if you count only official working days (261 days per year) and exclude weekends (104 days per year). I have also spent tens of thousands of dollars to procure photocopies of documents and reproductions of photographs. The wealth of material that I currently possess fills six four-drawer filing cabinets.

I incorporated this material into my magazine articles and later into my books. Long before I reached my present output of five textbooks and thirty-two history books, I became recognized as an expert on shipwrecks, scuba diving, and maritime related subjects.

This recognition was both good and bad. It was good in that it enabled me to find additional employment as a consultant for the publishing industry, television, documentary film producers, and the legal profession. It was bad in that some of these staid institutions expected me to work for free, so that they could earn money from my expertise, and from my years of data collection and from the money that I spent in the process.

By the 1990's, I was receiving as many as three phone calls per day from people who wanted access to my research materials, or who wanted to pick my brain over the phone about projects that they were working on (and getting paid for). Most of these people were newspaper reporters; a few were magazine staff writers; some were producers.

Not only was I spending up to two hours per day in consulting with writers who were getting paid for their work, but the constant disturbances were disrupting my writing schedule. This loss of personal productivity meant that I was earning less money. I had to put a stop to these costly annoyances and interruptions. I figured that if lawyers and film producers could pay for my time, so should everyone else. After all, museums and libraries charged fees for conducting research, as did private fulltime researchers.

I commenced business as a part-time professional consultant. This enabled me to get reimbursed for the time that I spent in conducting new research, and for providing the results of my previous research to those who were willing to pay for it. Although I began to earn more money, I found that most publishers and contract writers were too cheap to pay for my services.

Again this was good and bad. It was good in that their no-pay attitude freed more time for my own writing projects, thus enabling me to increase my income. It was bad because I learned a lot about how newspapers and so-called news magazines operated: unfortunate things that forever changed my outlook about the value of the content on the printed page that most people read because of its brevity and easy accessibility.

If only it were not so . . .

All the News That's *Free* to Print

Some of the conversations and email exchanges that followed my new business direction will prove revelatory.

I composed a fee schedule in which I specified my charges for various services. For consistency, I followed the same format as price forms that I collected from libraries and museums, which stipulated the prices that I had had to pay in the course of conducting my own research. Whenever a reporter wrote for information, I replied by sending him my fee schedule. If he called, I asked for an address so I could send my fee schedule to him. When I was traveling, my answering machine requested that the caller furnish a street or email address to which my fee schedule could be mailed or attached. It was all very professional, and way more professional than the responses I received.

Most reporters were outright arrogant on the phone when I told them that I charged a fee for consultations. They adopted the attitude that they had some God-given right to take up my professional time without offering compensation; that I was bound by the Constitution to give them the results of years of research for free; that reimbursement for my expenses was unheard of; and that I was obligated to return their calls and pay the long-distance charges. These pronouncements led to some lively arguments.

Many stressed or implored that they were not seeking a consultation but wanted merely to conduct an interview, and that no one charged money to be interviewed. My standard reply to this weasel approach was that the term they used to obtain information was irrelevant. "Interview" and "consultation" were interchangeable. I charged for my *time*, because I was the expert who had spent decades to obtain the information that they needed – and which they needed on the spur of the moment.

When one reporter berated me for withholding information pending promise of payment, I replied, "You're getting paid, and you don't know anything. I have all the answers, but you don't think their worth anything."

(Pretty much verbatim.)

After explaining to another reporter how many years it took me to track down his subject's history, I told him, "There's no information I have that you can't find for yourself, as long as you're willing to spend the time and effort to get it." (Or words to that effect.) He didn't want to expend either the time or the money or the effort to conduct his own research; he simply wanted to pick up the phone and have everything handed to him gratis.

To another reporter who objected fiercely to my fee schedule, I wrote, "If the only information you want is that which is free, you will likely get what you pay for." (Verbatim.)

And there's the rub.

Newspaper or Toilet Paper?

Time and time again reporters told me that newspapers either didn't pay for information or couldn't afford to. This was a verity that I confirmed by reading what they ended up writing without the advantage of my research or expertise. They didn't care whether an article was factual or not, as long as they could make the point that they wanted to make by quoting someone who was willing to give free advice, despite the fact that the person might not know what he was talking about.

Understand that I solicited none of these potential consultations. These reporters all contacted me because of my reputation in the media industry for knowledge and accuracy.

As I noted above, some reporters were so supercilious that they expected me to return their long-distance phone calls and, in essence, *pay* to give them free consultations.

One reporter was so frantic for information because of a Monday afternoon deadline that he called four times over the weekend. I was on a dive trip. Four times he heard my recorded message ask for an address or fax number to which my fee schedule could be sent. Four times he left despairing pleas to *please* call him as soon as I returned. Four times he failed to leave an email address or fax number. Finally, in a last minute panic, he called my business manager, Drew Maser, whose phone number was on my recorded message. He pleaded with Drew about his need to speak with me, but once again failed to provide an email address or fax number so that Drew could send my fee schedule.

I returned home late Sunday night. I listened to my messages first thing Monday morning. I didn't bother to return his call because he ignored my recorded request. He called me as soon as he got to his office, and explained the desperation of his need for certain information, which I assured him I could provide.

"But you never left an email address or fax number," I added.

"Did I miss a step?" he asked stupidly.

I managed to yank his email address and fax number out of him. I sent my fee schedule both ways. I never heard from him again. Apparently, his all-fired necessity for factual information vanished once he learned that he would have to pay for it.

Lest you get the wrong impression, you should understand how little this information would have cost each newspaper. My fee schedule is not exorbitant. For historical research I charge $75 per hour. (I charge more for legal work and television jobs.) I charge only for the number of minutes that I actually spend on a project (or on the phone). This breaks down to a dollar and twenty-five cents per minute. Thus a twelve minute phone job would cost $15. And this is for research that I had already done. All I charge for is the time that it takes me to pull folders out of my file drawers. The filing cabinets are centrally located near my desk. I can retrieve files while I am walking about my study on a cordless phone.

Voila! The job is done. The reporter does not have to drive or fly to the National Archives or to half a dozen other research facilities from which I originally obtained the documentation.

By way of contrast, here are some newspaper research rates that I happen to have on hand. The *Lincoln Star Journal* charges $60 per hour with a $15 minimum.

The *Tampa Tribune* charges $60 per hour with a $30 minimum. The *Arizona Republic* (and all other rags that are owned by Phoenix Newspapers) charges $100 per hour with a $25 minimum.

The Steamship Historical Society of America (where I have done extensive research throughout the years) charges $75 per hour with a *one hour* minimum. Full-time archive researchers charge between $30 and $50 per hour; they may spend hours on a project and never find what you are looking for.

In short, research is not free, and everyone has to pay for it – except for newspaper reporters who believe that they are high and mighty, and above everyone else. I wonder what their attitude is about paying consulting fees for medical advice, legal services, or car repair.

The absurdity of all this is compounded by this scenario: first I had to spend money to conduct the primary research. Newspapers then wanted the results of my efforts for free. Afterward, they would charge me and other researchers a fee to obtain the information that the newspapers had gotten freely from me. That makes a markup equal to infinity.

I have never declined to work for a reporter. I simply sent him my fee schedule and let him decline to hire me.

To the reporter who told me that he would mention my name in his article in lieu of payment, I replied, "I can't pay my mortgage by showing the bank an article with my name in it. They demand cash, and so do I." (Verbatim.)

Never – and I mean *never* – has a newspaper reporter agreed to pay for my services.

This reminds me of the apocryphal comment that was supposedly made by an early astronaut: "This rocket has a hundred thousand moving parts, every one of which was supplied by the lowest bidder." (Paraphrased.)

Similarly, all the news that reporters write was furnished by someone who agreed to work for nothing. What kind of quality can you expect from such a low-cost provider? Like I said, you get what you pay for.

Fact Checking

Not every mass-market publisher is so penny-pinching as the newspapers. I have consulted for book and magazine publishers who were dedicated to presenting only substantiated facts to their readers, and who were willing to pay for it. My consulting work in this regard was also intangibly rewarding by dint of the acceptance of my knowledge.

Encyclopedia Britannica allowed me to make additions and changes to entries that required minor adjustments. Authors such as Kevin McMurray included my input in books like *Deep Descent* and *Dark Descent.* Dozens of magazines published my articles about shipwrecks and technical diving.

Only once did I encounter an absurd situation in this regard. I wrote a piece for *Rodale's Scuba Diving* about wreck-diving off Virginia Beach, Virginia. They turned the tables on me by having a fact-checker call *me* to check on my sources. I found this ironic because I was usually the one who authenticated background data; never before had the facts in any of my articles been questioned.

A contretemps was created by the girl who posed as a fact-checker: a recent high school graduate and obvious airhead who knew nothing about research and documentation. She wanted to know what sources I used as a basis for the facts that comprised the mainstay of my article. I told her that I used only archival documents. That wasn't what she meant. She wanted to know what *published* references I used. I explained that I did not rely upon secondary source materials, because to do so might perpetuate erroneous or poorly researched material.

She did not understand the difference between primary and secondary research. I offered to send her copies of relevant documents that came straight from the National Archives. She wouldn't accept that. She had to know the titles of books and names of articles, plus their authors.

I began to understand the problem. She was thinking in terms of school term papers, which utilized only published material, and which included a bibliography of sources as proof that she had done her homework. The primary purpose of a term paper was to teach a student how to use a library, not to produce an original piece of work.

I told her that the information was published in *Shipwrecks of Virginia*. She found that acceptable – until she asked for the name of the author, and I told her that *I* had written the book. Now she said that she couldn't accept my own work as a source.

I had better ways to spend my time than by going ten rounds with an ingénue, and I was quickly losing my patience. I had already been paid for the article, so I said, "If you wish to withhold certain facts from your readers, feel free to do so." (Or words to that effect.)

"No," she protested. "I just need to have the name of a book." (More straightforward than her garbled explanation.)

So I made up a title and author. She was satisfied. My article was published as written.

The Disservice Award

Before I started to charge for my services, I suffered several foul encounters with reporters – encounters that soured me on the entire newsgathering process. Time after time they misquoted me, ascribed quotes that I never made, quoted me out of context, and so on.

My most egregious encounter was with one Theresa Foley. When she was writing a technical diving piece for the *New York Times*, she called me to ask how technical diving applied to the *Andrea Doria* – an ocean liner that lay south of Nantucket at a depth of 240 feet. She called me because I had written the book about diving on the *Andrea Doria*, as well as the book about technical diving. Almost in aside, she asked me how many divers had perished while diving on the *Andrea Doria*.

I was uncertain. I knew firsthand about the first three fatalities because I had recovered two of the bodies and had performed CPR and mouth-to-mouth resuscitation on another (unsuccessfully). But I was not present when the later fatalities occurred. I had heard about them through the diver's grapevine, but I did not know the actual number.

I thought that the number of fatal episodes in which I was not involved was between three and five. This equated to a total that was six at the minimum and eight at the maximum. This number was insufficient for Foley's need to establish the *Andrea Doria* as the most dangerous shipwreck in history. Despite my firm avowal, she ignored the facts because it wasn't what she wanted to hear. She wrote instead that more than sixty divers had died in the pursuit of their dreams to see the *Andrea Doria*. She even went so far as to claim that more people had died while diving on the wreck than had been killed in the collision and eventual sinking.

When I read the published article, I was aghast at Foley's grossly inflated body count. It was worse than that of an American general in Vietnam. Her exaggeration was the kind that was remembered and perpetuated. I wasted no time in attempting to set the record straight. First I confirmed the actual number of divers who breathed their last breath on the *Andrea Doria*: seven. Then I wrote to Foley and to the *New York Times*, and demanded a retraction. Foley deigned not to reply, and the *New York Times* refused to publish a retraction.

It doesn't look good for a newspaper to admit that it printed erroneous or misleading information. Even on the rare occasions when civic duty forces a newspaper to admit the error of its ways, it generally publishes the retraction of a first-page error on the last page in tiny print that is hard to find – serving the purpose if not the public. The *New York Times* chose to uphold its advertised standing rather than to admit to any wrongdoing.

My worst fears were realized when Peter Bennett copied Foley's outrageous misinformation in an article that he published a couple of months later in *Scientific American*. Bennett was the director of the Divers Alert Network – the very outfit that accumulated diver fatality statistics – so he should have known better. Once again

I acted promptly. Bennett grudgingly acknowledged the verity of my claim when I submitted documented proof, yet he refused to correct the fallacy in the *Alert Diver*: the quarterly journal of the Divers Alert Network, for which he wrote an editorial in every issue.

Likewise, *Scientific American* refused to publish a retraction.

If all this sounds like a cover-up to save reputations, so be it. The truth is that Foley knowingly lied, and no one else wanted to own up to the fact that they had been careless. They all wanted to protect their fragile public images. It was only through a long and arduous letter-writing campaign that I was able to stop the spread of this deadly urban legend.

What is the point of conferring with an expert if you are going to ignore his expertise? For that reason, I will not accept a consultation or interview without a signed contract which expressly forbids misquoting me, and which forbids quoting me out of context. I can't stop reporters from slewing the facts, but I can at least prevent them from quoting me as the authority from whom they obtained their distortion of the truth.

In the newspaper business, honest endeavor has since been subverted in the name of profit margins and circulation numbers. The primary purpose of the news media is not to tell the truth, the whole truth, and nothing but the truth, but to tell enough of the truth to sound believable to the readers and viewers, in order to sell newspapers and prime-time advertising.

Shot from a C(a)N(o)N

One time I received a request from CNN to appear on a television broadcast and talk about the historic significance of the Civil War ironclad *Monitor*. This came about because I had prevailed in a lawsuit against NOAA and secured the rights of Americans to visit the site, and because the U.S. Navy had just completed a major salvage operation on the wreck.

I submitted my standard fee schedule. A spokesperson duly informed me that CNN did not pay for television appearances. She expected me to take a day off of work, drive an hour and a half to the broadcast station, and give a live interview on camera. Instead, they got one of the Navy divers to appear. The interviewer asked him a series of questions to which he did not know the answers. He just kept repeating, "It was a great experience." (Or words to that effect.) They cut him off after two minutes of mindless repetition. That was all the coverage that the *Monitor* received from CNN.

I repeat: you get what you pay for.

Pabulum for the Public

As long as I've switched venues to television . . .

I was hired as a consultant for an episode of *Deep Sea Detectives*. Although I had never seen the show, director Jennifer Lorenz told me that before commencing work on *any* episode, they referred to my Popular Dive Guide Series as an historical reference source. Now they wanted me to appear on camera in an episode about the *Andrea Doria*, so I could describe the layout and condition of the wreck for the viewers.

This type of show is supposed to be a documentary. In reality, it is at best a docudrama: a dramatic presentation of a real-life incident. As I learned to my chagrin, *Deep Sea Detectives* didn't even meet the criteria of the latter category.

The incident that irked me the most occurred when the crew set up a shot on the bow of the boat. The actress was in position, the camera operator and lighting technician were ready to roll, the director was giving directions for the scene, and the hosts were discussing their dialogue. I was down below, staying out of the way.

Suddenly one of the hosts came to ask me a question about historical accuracy. He wanted to know how many women had dived on the *Andrea Doria*. I thought for a moment, then said, "At least a dozen or two." As I ran names and faces through my mind, I figured that there must be at least *three* dozen. A couple of minutes later I heard the host exclaim, "And Carrie Bisetti just became the thirteenth woman to dive on the *Andrea Doria*."

I dashed out of the cabin to correct them, but I was too late. The shot was already in the can and they had no intention of reshooting the scene. As it turned out, they didn't use the scene in the broadcast version. Instead, they used another scene for background, and did a voice-over of the host making the same declaration – *twice* – thus perpetuating a known error that could have been easily corrected in post-production.

I suppose it would not have been as sensational to claim that Bisetti was the thirty-seventh woman to dive on the *Andrea Doria*, but it would have been closer to the truth. In fact, after I brought this blatant inaccuracy to the attention of the world, the diving community took it upon itself to ascertain the exact number. It turned out that she was the fortieth such woman.

The *Andrea Doria* episode was rife with other mistakes, some of which were made out of stupidity, others that were made intentionally to glamorize the hosts. As I noted above, what is the purpose of hiring an expert if you are going to ignore his expertise? Instead of relying upon my knowledge and experience, they used my image as window-dressing to lend credibility to the show.

The misdirection of the *Andrea Doria* episode motivated me to watch a few other episodes in the series. In every episode that I watched, I found numerous mistakes, false assumptions, stupid allegations, historical blunders, multiple errors of omission, and overall sloppiness of presentation. I won't enumerate or annotate them here because I have already done so in a lengthy chapter in *Shadow Divers Exposed*, and in another chapter in my follow-up to *SDX*, *Shipwreck Heresies*. The two hosts were none other than the purveyors of falsehood in *Shadow Divers*.

According to the premise of *Deep Sea Detectives*, Chatterton and Kohler were supposed to solve a long-standing underwater mystery in every episode. The pattern that I observed was one in which the so-called detectives made a token trip to a targeted location, during which they made a couple of dives to establish their presence on the shipwreck for the viewers. They then miraculously "solved" a "mystery" that thousands of divers had supposedly been unable to solve over a span of many decades.

In reality, the "detectives" either created a mystery where none existed, or they took credit for solving a mystery that had already been solved years before by real investigators or experienced wreck-divers. Some trumped-up mysteries appeared to have been fabricated, then solved in post-production after a storyline was created around the meager underwater footage.

These deceptive techniques served to create mindless entertainment of dubious quality and doubtful educational value. Presenting such dross as true history is an insult to the intelligence of the viewing public.

On November 8, 2008, *Deep Sea Detectives* producer Vinnie Kralyevich frankly admitted to the audience in attendance at Metro West Dive Club's annual symposium that the show was largely contrived, both to appease television executives and to create viewer appeal. Kralyevich made no bones about the fictional intent and content of the series. Historical accuracy took a back seat to the business aspects of the show.

While I'm on the subject, I was almost involved in another Kralyevich project. Jeff Meltz, an associate producer at KPI (Kralyevich Production, Inc.), wanted me to provide the historical background of fifteen shipwrecks for an upcoming series about German U-boat depredations off the U.S. eastern seaboard. Since I wrote the book on the subject – *The Fuhrer's U-boats in American Waters* – everything he wanted was already in my files: the result of more than thirty-five years of primary research.

I agreed to do the job. He wanted photocopies of all my archival documentation of the subject vessels, U-boat deck logs, and so on; and he wanted photographic reproductions of all the vessel photographs that I had accumulated. If Meltz was going to hire me as an historical consultant for the series, I expected him to make an offer of payment for my time. Instead, he expected me to do all this work for free. He even expected me to pay for the photocopies and photographic reproductions.

I sent him my standard consulting contract, and never heard from him again. I suppose that authenticity was not a priority in the production of the series. Keep this in mind the next time you watch a television documentary. It is easy to fool viewers who have no previous knowledge of the subject that is presented.

I reiterate: you get what you pay for.

The Shape of Reality

The mass media does not shape reality; it shapes the human perception of reality.

Unfortunately, most people cannot see past the misshapen perceptions of subjectivity to accept genuine objectivity: the reality by which the Universe is constrained.

Thoughts are electrical impulses and chemical reactions in the brain. Those impulses and reactions do not interact with exterior objective reality. But they cause the person who is thinking those thoughts to act in certain ways, to behave in a certain manner.

Mankind as a species will find it difficult if not impossible to rise above his false perceptions as long as the media by which he obtains his information declines to comport itself responsibly. Every deviation from impartial truth – no matter how insignificant – leads people farther from reality and closer to a fantasy world in which truth is malleable and whimsical.

The Constitution of the United States guarantees freedom of speech, but with limits. Just as one is not free to create panic by yelling "Fire!" in a public place, the media should not be free to tell lies and partial truths. That freedom leads to damnation.

Section Six
Mobile Shams and Mockeries
or Absurdity in Motion

Going Postal

I still recall the perplexity I felt when I first entered a post office after starting my publishing business. I had an armful of packages that were the result of my pre-publication advertising campaign. The counter clerk asked me if I wanted insurance on the packages.

I was befuddled. I replied innocently, "Insurance for what?"

"To make sure the packages aren't lost or damaged," she replied.

My mind was atwirl and atwitter with possible responses. This was a post office, not a gambling casino. I was there to mail packages, not to buy lottery tickets. Buying postage was a business proposition, not a game of chance. When the postal service accepted mail, they were supposedly under contract to deliver – in more ways than one. So why should I need to ensure that they would do the job that I was paying them to do?

When I took my car to an auto dealer for maintenance or inspection, I expected them to guarantee their work. They didn't ask me to pay extra for protection in case they didn't do their job right. If they made a mistake or damaged my vehicle while making authorized repairs, they fixed the problem at their own expense.

When I purchased an electrical tool from a department store, they didn't try to sell me an insurance policy on the basis that the item might not function or be in one piece when I unsealed it from the packaging at home. If it didn't work, I could return it for a replacement or a refund.

If I hired someone to mow my lawn, he didn't preface the job with an indemnification offer in case he didn't cut the grass. He didn't even ask to be paid until the job was done to my satisfaction.

In other words, inherent in the cost of doing business was doing business right.

The United States Postal Service demanded payment in advance for a service that it would not promise to provide. In other words, they might deliver my packages – and then again, they might not; and if they delivered my packages, the contents might be in good condition when the package was opened – and then again, they might not. The Postal Service accepted no responsibility for the conduct or quality of its service. Take it or leave it.

I never heard of running a business as if it were a betting concession. I was interested in bookselling, not bookmaking. Nonetheless, I put my money on the counter as if I were staking a wager on a roulette wheel. As it turned out, I won nine times out of ten . . .

. . . which meant that I lost ten percent of my winnings. This is another way of saying that one out of every ten packages never reached its recipient.

The Great Unknown

Where did one in ten of my packages go? If they were taking up space in a dead letter office, the so-called office must be a mammoth-sized warehouse that was larger than the warehouse in which the Ark of the Covenant was stored after Indiana Jones unearthed it.

Although I may be tinged with paranoia, I am not suspicious enough to believe that the Postal Service targeted me personally. I think it is fair to assume that my losses were representative of the number of packages that went astray in transit.

According to the USPS annual report for 2010, they conveyed 658 million packages during the fiscal year. By simple extrapolation, this means that more than 65 *million* packages must *not* have been delivered. By the Postal Service's own admission, nearly 100 million items ended up in the dead letter "office" every year. This number includes mail of all classes.

Granted that some items were undeliverable because the addresses were invalid or illegible, with the same being true for return addresses, but that still leaves a lot of mail that didn't reach its destination. This is not a good track record by any standard business model. If a privately owned company failed to fulfill ten percent of its obligations – and kept the payment into the bargain – it would quickly go out of business for lack of patronage. It would also founder under the weight of lawsuits that would be filed against it for failure to provide its contracted service, for taking and keeping money under false pretenses, and for the loss of product that was neither delivered nor returned.

The government can get away with wholesale irresponsibility because, well, it's the government, and that's what governments do.

Mail Fraud

The loss of my packages was not the end of the matter. Because I operated in the private sector, and because I maintained a strict sense of honesty in my dealings, I had to make up the loss to my customers by sending them replacement books. Not only did I lose the cost of additional product, but I also had to pay the Postal Service again to deliver the goods that they didn't deliver the first time. Unlike the Postal Service, I did not charge my customers the second time around.

As if the loss of my product was not bad enough, the Postal Service refused to reimburse me for postage for the packages that were not delivered. They failed to provide delivery service, but kept the money anyway. This kind of activity constitutes fraud.

I filled out forms to have the packages traced, but nothing ever came of it.

Package loss was not the only problem I've had with the Postal Service. As my business grew, I began to sell books in bulk to retailers who then sold the books individually to their customers. Now I began to mail cartons that might contain as many as forty books.

On more than one occasion, the Postal Service duly delivered the cartons but minus some of the product.

This meant that somewhere along the line a postal employee opened the carton, removed some of the books, then resealed the carton and sent it on its way. This kind of activity constitutes theft. Mail theft is a federal offense.

Yet the Postal Service refused to pay for the stolen product if the package wasn't insured. I refer you back to the beginning of the chapter. Insurance was intended for accidental loss or damage, not for intentional theft by postal employees. Worse yet, the Postal Service refused to reimburse me for the postage.

The opening of a package to pinch its contents made me wonder about the single-copy packages that had supposedly been "lost." I have now concluded that none (or few) of my packages were ever actually lost. I have inferred that they were stolen by postal employees for the value of the contents. Here is the reason for my inference:

According to Postal Service protocol, if a piece of mail was undeliverable for any reason, it was sent to a "mail recovery center," (the latest buzzword for dead letter office, or dead parcel branch). There the packages were opened in an attempt to identify the rightful owner. In my case this would have been easy, because my name and address were printed on the back cover and copyright page of each and every book. Yet of the hundreds of books that "went missing" or mysteriously vanished, not a single one was ever returned to me.

I have filed numerous mail theft and mail fraud claims with the Postal Inspection Service, all of them *against* the Postal Service. I have never received a reply.

The Rising Cost of Insurance

I had to do something to curb Postal Service theft and gross mishandling. Retailers returned books that were damaged in transit, and I had to either replace them or issue a refund. So I started to insure packages when the value of the contents exceeded $50.

I did not insure single-copy packages because the combined postage and insurance charge exceeded the printing cost of the book. It was cheaper to lose the book than to insure it.

Take this example: I mailed a package that I insured for $100. The postage was $4.33; the insurance was $2.25. The insurance was more than 50% of the postage. Imagine, if you will, how much auto insurance would cost if you had to insure it for half the value of your vehicle.

On the other hand, I am now ahead of the game. I have collected more money from insurance claims than I have paid for insurance. Insurance income relates to profits because a lost, stolen, or damaged book is the same as a sale. In essence, I am now selling books to Postal Service employees, and the Postal Service is paying for them.

Over the years I have noticed a gradual increase in Postal Service insurance rates. At first I shrugged this off as the result of inflation, figuring that the increase was indexed the same as the increase in postage rates. But when I finally looked at the situation more closely, and compared the relative increases, it seemed to me that percentagewise, insurance rate increases exceeded postage rate increases.

In other words, instead of striving to improve service by losing fewer packages, damaging less product, and reducing postal employee theft by investigating claims and prosecuting thieves, the Postal Service employed the self-defeating system of raising the insurance rate. Inefficiency was rewarded, while the cost of that inefficiency was passed along to the customer.

The lack of incentive to work proficiently and show a profit is a problem that plagues all government-sponsored monopolies. The government increases taxes to hide its inadequacies. The Postal Service raises the postage rate to cover up its ineptitude. In this never-ending cycle, taxpayers and mail users are penalized for escalating incompetence.

If I tried to operate my business by increasing the cover price to mask wastefulness and disorganization, I would soon overcharge myself out of the market.

Guaranteed Delivery (or is it Deliverance?)

When I had to post some time-sensitive materials, I sent them by Priority Mail because delivery was guaranteed within two days. I should have known better than to trust Postal Service advertisements. The envelope was not delivered until five days later.

When I complained to the postmistress at the post office where I had mailed the envelope, she shrugged and said, "There's nothing I can do about it." (Or words in a similar vein.)

"But two-day delivery is supposed to be guaranteed. What good is a guarantee if you don't honor it?"

She offered neither excuse nor apology. Her attitude was, "Too bad. That's the way it is."

By comparison, Federal Express guarantees on-time delivery or your money back. The Postal Service offers no money-back guarantee. The postmistress would not refund my postage. Once again I paid the Post Office for service that I did not receive.

The Postal Service guarantee is nothing more than a promotional gimmick that constitutes false advertising. The Federal Trade Commission is supposed to enforce truth in advertising, but apparently they let the Postal Service flagrantly violate the law.

The End of the Cycle

As long as I'm harping on the Postal Service, I'd like to mention its stance against helping to save the environment.

Both as an individual and as a business person, I recycle packaging materials whenever possible: dunnage as well as boxes. I deplore companies that splatter their names and promotional literature over all six sides of a cardboard carton, making it difficult to reuse the carton for shipping purposes. I prefer cartons whose surfaces are blank.

A blank carton needs to be adorned with only an address label – or perhaps two labels: one for the addresser and one for the addressee. Postal workers can read these labels easily. The recipient can then tear off the label(s) and reuse the carton for outgoing product.

(In aside, one counter clerk complained that the address was hard to read. She suggested that I use larger labels. I pointed out that the address was typed on a typewriter, and that using a larger label would not increase the size of the type. She failed to get my point.)

Imagine my chagrin when I walked into a post office and saw a poster-sized announcement that they would no longer accept recycled cartons. In this age of environmental awareness, the Postal Service is among the few that support waste, one-time use, and throwaway products.

Ideally, I would like to see cardboard cartons replaced by nondescript hard plastic cartons that are resealable and reusable. Their extra strength and noncompressibility would not only protect the contents better than cardboard cartons, but their durability would assure a long lifespan despite Postal Service abuse and mishandling protocols.

Businesses and households would save their plasticartons (or plastons) and reship them. Households that accumulated too many plastons could drop off their extras at the post office or a local recycling facility, the same as people do now with other recyclables, so that households that needed them could collect the number and sizes of plastons that they needed.

But I don't think it will ever happen. Such efficiency would reduce profitmaking. Box manufacturers would undoubtedly lobby an antirecycling campaign. And businesses that were more concerned about imagery than quality would refrain from shipping product in plastons that were scuffed or scratched, and on which they could not plaster advertising. Such is the importance of appearance in America. Although some people may exclaim that it's what's inside that counts, many people can't see through external appearances to appreciate inner worth.

Unfriendly Skies

Everyone who travels consistently by air has horror

stories of delayed departures, canceled flights, missed connections, lost luggage, and so on. Except for misplaced baggage, the vast majority of these aerial complications is caused by inclement weather (snowstorms, high wind, and icing conditions being the most common) over which airlines have no control. No one is to blame because, when it comes to a contest of wills, Mother Nature generally wins – and generally for a good reason.

Another type of blameless situation occurred on a flight from Atlanta to Philadelphia. After the plane taxied along the runway, gathered speed for takeoff, and lifted into the air, I saw a massive amount of oil being purged from the starboard engine. I was appalled. My first thought was that planes shouldn't dump oil on the tarmac, not only because it was unsanitary, but because it would make the surface slick for the next plane that used the runway.

I was about to complain to the stewardess when the engine burst into flames. A huge ball of fire engulfed the nacelle. Then I realized that the oil dump was accidental: the result of a burst hose or connector. By this time the plane was circling to port and gaining altitude. The fire was quickly extinguished, I presume by shutting off the fuel supply. A few seconds later the pilot announced over the intercom, "We are experiencing technical difficulties and will be returning to the airfield." He used the same tone of voice that my grandmother used when she read a recipe. We must have been given priority clearance, because we kept right on circling and returned to the other end of the runway for a safe landing. I was the only passenger who observed the "technical difficulty."

Sometimes human error is at fault. On one flight from San Francisco to Chicago, for instance, the pilot announced that the plane did not have enough fuel to reach its destination. We were going to have to stop at an intermediate airport in order to refuel. I don't claim to be the most observant person in the world when it comes to starting my vehicle; I don't always look at the gas gauge after I crank up the engine. But I would think – I would *pray* – that a conscientious pilot or his ever-present copilot has a checklist on which such an observation is paramount.

When my van runs out of gas, it's an inconvenience. When an airplane runs out of fuel, it crashes. That is the quantum difference between driving and flying.

Not putting sufficient fuel in the tanks for the planned itinerary is more than a minor glitch. Filling stations for jet aircraft are less numerous than gas stations for cars and trucks.

In the event, the flight in my example above was fortuitous for some of the passengers because they were ticketed for the intermediate airport at which we landed for fuel. Their original flight plan called for them to change plans in Chicago and fly back (westward) to their final destination. They deplaned and their luggage was offloaded. For the rest of us the unscheduled stop was little more than a short time delay which fortunately did not cause anyone to miss his connection in Chicago. But the situation could have been disastrous.

This is only one example in which the human factor interfered with what was otherwise a smooth flight. I wish it were the only one.

Air Sick

Before commencing a long diatribe about inequities in the airline business, let me dispose of a few minor items that bother me (but may not bother you). The first is the flight attendant's opening statement about aircraft safety, which goes something like this: "In the event of a water landing . . . "

For jet aircraft there is no such thing as a water landing. Only amphibious planes can "land" on water. Any other type of plane that sets down on the water isn't landing; it's crashing.

The demonstration of donning life preservers is practically useless. It is given too fast for the average person to assimilate, much less remember in a state of stress or panic. I have reached under my seat any number of times. I haven't actually tried to release the seat the way I was told, but I never found any release mechanism or straps. The only way this demo would be of any value is to let each person disengage the life preserver and try it on, in order to become conversant with the placement of the straps and the means of securing them on his person.

On the other hand, I cannot help but applaud the flying waitress (euphemistically called a flight attendant) who demonstrated how to fasten a seatbelt to the accompaniment of a verbal description. Her comment afterward revealed a sense of humor that was not in keeping with airline protocol: "It works like any other seatbelt. If you don't know how to work it, you shouldn't be traveling unattended." (Or words to that effect.)

Lies, Falsehoods, and Outright Prevarications

Airline employees are forever telling passengers that such and such an act is prohibited by FAA regulations. While aircraft safety is the principal mandate of the Federal Aviation Administration, the FAA achieves its goal by regulating the conduct of airlines and, by extension, airline employees. It does not regulate passengers, over whom it has no authority.

One of the initial announcements that flight attendants make prior to departure is something like: "This is a nonsmoking flight. Smoking is not allowed in the cabin or lavatories. Tampering with, disabling, or destroying smoke detectors is against FAA regulations."

A review of FAA regulations reveals a quite different story. I quote: "Smoke detectors are intended to enhance detection by cabin occupants of hazardous fire conditions within lavatories. The trash receptacle is the critical ignition hazard potential in a lavatory because of its highly combustible contents which are susceptible to ignition by objects discarded by passengers. Detectors should provide warning commensurate with the ignition hazard early enough in the fire sequence to permit a timely response by a crewmember." (This must have been written by a college professor or Ph.D. candidate who was trying to impress his academic peers.)

Elsewhere it is stated: "Lavatory smoke detectors

may be included in the airplane minimum equipment list. Detectors are not specifically designated as 'backup' or 'supplemental' equipment items. A smoke detector is significant to cabin fire safety and should whenever practical be operative for flight. Since lavatory smoke detectors do not have an immediate or critical bearing on safety of flight, temporary inoperability of a detector would not warrant interruption of a flight schedule to return the aircraft to a repair station. A lavatory smoke detector should not remain inoperative indefinitely. Detectors should be checked frequently for proper operation; and if a detector is found inoperative, it should be repaired or replaced at the first practical opportunity, such as arrival of the aircraft at the first suitable facility. During interim scheduled flights, temporary loss of the detector might be offset by increased monitoring of the affected lavatory, or other compensating measures."

There is no mention of enforcement against passengers. The FAA is a regulatory agency, not a law enforcement agency.

I am not suggesting that passengers should tamper with, disable, or destroy lavatory smoke detectors; or that they should smoke in aircraft lavatories. I am declaring only that smoke detectors are not installed in aircraft lavatories to detect smokers in the act of smoking, and that the FAA does not consider the inoperability of lavatory smoke detectors to be a critical threat to aircraft safety, despite airline announcements to the contrary.

The Electronic Scam

Another airline scam is the one about "approved electronic devices." The chances that such a device might interfere with avionics are slim to none, and Slim left town. First of all, why must an electronic device be "approved" for flight? When you look into the matter, the electronic devices that are *not* approved are communication devices such as cell phones and Blackberries. Yet they operate on frequencies that are different from the frequencies on which aircraft communications, navigational instruments, guidance controls, and display systems operate.

Furthermore, the transmission wattage of personal electronic devices, whether they are approved or not, is so small that interference with avionics is unlikely if not impossible: a chimaera that is perpetuated by the airlines, not by the FAA (whose regulations the airlines credit). When was the last time your cell phone interfered with your radio or television reception? Or with the cell phone of someone standing next to you?

I submit that the reason the airlines do not want people talking on their cell phones during flight is because they want passengers to pay exorbitant charges ($5 per minute in some cases) for seat phones.

If a passenger ignored the warning and did use a personal cell phone, and was caught in the act of talking, what could the airlines do about it? Throw him off the plane? Fine him? Jail him afterward? None of the above. The threat is as empty as outer space.

I asked my friend Pete Piemonte about avionics interference. He is a corporate jet pilot with thirty years of commercial flying experience. He told me that on only one occasion has he experienced interference with avionics. That was when a passenger switched on an electronic device that caused a 20-degree deviation in the gyrocompass heading. After the device was switched off, the needle swung back to the correct course.

Pete investigated, and found that a bundle of control cables passed close to the seat where the person was sitting. But that happened when he first learned to fly, some thirty years ago. Technological improvements, better electrical insulation, modern construction techniques, and rerouting cables away from passenger seats have reduced this potential hazard to the near zero point. Furthermore, modern aircraft rely on GPS receivers and electronic tracking devices for navigational purposes, not compasses.

Pete speculated that if every passenger on a commercial aircraft used an electronic device simultaneously, it might – just *might* – cause a minor glitch in avionics. But he doubted it.

Flying Disunited

Consider this worst-case scenario. On a planned excursion to Mexico, I boarded a plane in Philadelphia for a flight to Washington Dulles International Airport, where I was scheduled to transfer to a plane for Cancun. The schedule called for a one-hour layover between the arrival of my plane in Dulles and the departure of the plane for Cancun. United Airlines operated both flights.

My Philly departure was delayed for forty-five minutes, first by a minor mechanical problem, then by traffic on the tarmac. Because of these delays, by the time my plane reached Dulles, another plane was occupying our assigned gate. All other United Airlines gates were also occupied. My plane was therefore redirected to an American Airlines gate.

United Airlines operated out of Concourse D. American Airlines operated out of Concourse A. Each of these concourses was isolated from the terminal and from each other – much like islands in a 12,000-acre lake. I couldn't run from one concourse to the other; I had to take a bus. The bus operated not on the immediacy of the passengers, like a taxi, but on a schedule. I ran to the bus platform, but then had to wait for the bus to arrive. After it arrived, I then had to wait for the bus's scheduled time of departure. The bus then weaved around airplanes that were either taxiing or docked, taking a circuitous route that was agonizing in its slothfulness.

As the bus finally pulled up to the Concourse D platform, I saw the boarding bridge being retracted from my Cancun plane at the adjacent gate. I ran off the bus as soon as the driver opened the doors. I made the fifty-yard dash to the gate in record time. The plane was sitting idle some forty feet from the window. Breathlessly I told the gate attendant that I had to get on that plane.

She responded by telling me that once the doors were closed, they could not be reopened because a delayed departure would incur a hefty fine from the FAA. This was a bold-faced lie! Yet I have been told this falsehood on more than one occasion.

The FAA couldn't care less whether or not a plane disengaged from its gate on time. Flight schedules were not maintained by the FAA, but by the airlines, and for their own benefit. Gates – indeed, entire concourses – were owned or leased by the airlines without FAA interest, approval, or intervention. The FAA imposes no fines or penalties for late departures. Airline policy was responsible for what the gate attendant blamed the FAA.

In addition to all of the above, what good does it do when a plane closes its doors or backs away from the gate when it doesn't take off? That action doesn't qualify as adherence to a schedule.

Whenever airlines want to evade responsibility for company policies, they invoke the FAA. Passengers believe what they are told because they don't know any better. FAA regulations sound more authoritative than company policies.

Three other people arrived behind me. Two women had been on my plane from Philly. One man was on the same bus from Concourse A. We all argued with the attendant to deploy the retractable bridge so that we could board. She kept shaking her head. She refused to call the pilot or anyone else in authority. She just kept insisting that the plane was not "allowed" to open its door once it was closed.

The plane did not move. It sat there for ten more minutes while we kept up a running quarrel with the gate attendant. She was adamant in her refusal to help. Eventually the plane backed away from the gate, turned, taxied to the runway, and then *idled in place for half an hour* before departing for Cancun without all of its passengers. The gate attendant then informed us that we were not the only ones to miss the flight. Several other people were on a connecting flight that was still in the air.

The plane arrived in Cancun more than fifteen minutes ahead of schedule.

The only advice that the gate attendant gave us was to go to the reservation desk and try to get on the next plane to Cancun – which, she informed us, was not scheduled to depart until the following day. Although she could have done this from her console, she walked away and left us in the lurch. We had to fend for ourselves.

Before proceeding farther with this manmade horror story, let me back up in order to present two other viewpoints that demonstrate the depths to which the airline stooped to proactively thwart amelioration of the circumstances.

The two women were part of a tour group that was vacationing in Cancun. They were friends with others in the group, all of whom lived in different parts of the country. This was their third trip to Cancun with the same group. As soon as the Philly plane landed, and "approved" electronic devices were permitted to be used, one of the women switched on her cell phone and called the group leader, who was sitting in the Cancun plane and who was waiting for the rest of the group to arrive. Passengers were still boarding.

When the stream of passengers stopped, the group leader informed a flight attendant that two of the group were on the ground and were on their way to the gate. The group leader asked the flight attendant to inform the pilot of their imminent arrival. The woman and the group leader kept the phone line open between them. By means of this running dialogue, they were able to provide the flight attendant with a continuous report of their progress. Thus the flight crew knew exactly when we reached the bus platform, when we boarded the bus, and when the bus left the platform.

At the same time, my group leader was in direct communication with the pilot. Marcie Bilinski was the organizer of our cave-diving trip. She and the rest of the group had departed from Boston. I was the only participant who was joining them en route. We were supposed to rendezvous at Dulles, fly together to Cancun, then rent a vehicle and drive an hour and a half south to the submerged drainage area known as the Riviera Maya.

Because Marcie flew with United Airlines so often for work, she was a high-mileage Gold Star member with special privileges. When the stream of passengers stopped, she informed a flight attendant that she needed to speak with the pilot. Marcie was permitted to enter the cockpit. She explained the situation to the pilot and copilot. By communicating via radio with company officials, they confirmed that my plane had departed late from Philly, but had already landed in Dulles.

Marcie pleaded with the pilot to postpone departure until I could reach the gate. Both the pilot and copilot said that they wanted to help but that they were instructed by a higher authority to close the door. Then without moving the plane, they idled forty feet from the window while they completed their preflight checks.

Marcie saw me through the huge picture window when I arrived at the gate. She watched as I argued with the gate attendant. She pointed me out to the pilot and copilot. Once again they communicated with the tower. Airline officials refused to give permission to open the door of the aircraft and to deploy the retractable bridge, or to let us board on a moving stairway. They ordered the plane to depart as soon as the flight crew completed their preflight checks. Marcie kept the pilot and copilot engaged in ardent conversation, trying to persuade them to let me board the plane – but to no avail. They said that they had to follow instructions; they did not have override authority.

To recapitulate: the flight crew, the air controllers, and company officials knew that the four of us had landed in Dulles and were within seconds of reaching the gate before the plane's doors were closed and the jetway was retracted. The gate attendant knew when we actually arrived. The plane idled forty feet from the window and sat in place for ten minutes while the pilot and copilot completed their preflight checks. Company officials instructed the plane to depart, with full knowledge that four passengers were standing at the gate. In effect, they ordered us to be left behind overnight. Then the plane sat on the tarmac for another thirty minutes.

At least three of us would have reached the gate on time if the Philly plane had docked at its pre-assigned gate (or any other gate in the United Airlines concourse) because that gate was right next to the gate of the Cancun plane. The docking deviation caused three of us to be late. The seats that we would have occupied remained empty.

I understand and accept complications that are caused by weather. Mankind is subservient to Mother Nature and acts of God. The absurdity of *this* situation is that it could have been avoided; or the issue could have been resolved had those in authority chosen to do so. Instead, company officials made a conscious decision to strand its passengers overnight. Not only did this decision lack ordinary compassion for the plight of the airline's customers, it was a decision that made no sense in terms of business and public relations. A little forbearance would have gone a long way toward ensuring that customer service was a company priority.

In the aftermath, the four of us were left to our own devices.

My personal position was particularly precarious because I didn't know where in Mexico I was going: not only did I not know the name of the hotel, I didn't even know what city it was in. I was depending on the organizer to lead the way after I joined the group. Marcie had arranged the car rental and accommodations. As a result of my separation and lack of knowledge, my anxiety level was high.

We four beleaguered travelers stuck together for mutual support. More than one hundred other displaced passengers were thronged in front of the United Airlines service desk. While the other three stood in line, I grabbed a red help phone and got in the reservation queue. I got help before the other three were halfway to the desk (less than half an hour later). I was able to get a seat on the following day's flight. I got seats for my erstwhile companions as well. I called them to me and gave their names to the reservation assistant. We were fortunate that seats were available on the next day's flight. Otherwise, we might have been stranded for days.

We were stuck in the airport overnight, so next we

descended upon a United Airlines help desk to see about our luggage and what sleeping accommodations could be made available to us. In less than short order we were told that our luggage had been placed in a secure holding facility from which it could not be retrieved. I didn't believe that our luggage couldn't be retrieved; I believed that no one wanted to bother to retrieve it. In either event, this left us without toilet articles, personal belongings, and a change of clothes.

(I always used to carry my toothbrush and toothpaste in my vest pocket, but I stopped doing so when toothpaste was banned as a carry-on item. More on that later.)

The only thing the help desk helpers would do for us was to make reservations at the airport hotel. The airline denied culpability for missing our flight. Therefore we would have to pay for our lodging . . . at more than $100 per room. The two women shared a room and split the cost. The man and I declined; we each went our separate ways.

My close friend Dave Bluett lived not too far from the airport, in Vienna. For the past twenty years, I had stayed at his house whenever I did research in Washington, DC. I didn't know his phone number and I didn't have my address book with me, but fortunately he was listed in the directory. And equally as fortunately, he had recently retired and was at home when I called. He picked me up and took me back to his house.

I called Marcie's cell phone. She was still in flight so she did not have her phone switched on. I left a message. She called me at Dave's house later that night, after her arrival in Mexico. The airline debacle caused the whole group to miss the first day's diving, because Marcie had to take the car and drive an hour and a half to Cancun to pick me up in the middle of the day.

You might think that I am ranting unjustly about a situation that can be viewed as an inconvenience. I agree that I am ranting, but I believe that my ranting is justified. This situation was not *just* an inconvenience; it was a *major* inconvenience. And it was one that was created intentionally by apathetic airline employees who could have ordered the doors opened and the jetway extended so that I and the other passengers could board. This action would not even have delayed the plane's departure, as the plane did not back away until ten minutes after our arrival at the gate.

The gate attendant was indifferent to my plight. The flight crew wanted to help but were stymied. The reservation desk assistant was exceedingly helpful. The help desk helpers were supportive and sympathetic, but were not authorized by airline protocol to extend free lodging for the night; nor could they personally get our luggage out of hock. We would have had to complain to the proper authority, but the help desk helpers didn't know who that authority was. The best they could suggest was to check with the people in baggage claim, or with someone above them in the corporate hierarchy.

The real culprits were the airline officials who blindly followed established airline policy instead of responding reasonably to the situation.

Green Barrettes and Special Farces

The situation above was not an isolated event. On a United Airlines flight from Philly to San Diego, I had a connecting flight in Denver. I had several hours between connections. I obtained the gate number from a corridor monitor, confirmed the departure place and time from the gate monitor, and sat down to read until boarding was announced.

A plane landed at my gate; not my plane. After the passengers deplaned, the crowd thinned as waiting passengers boarded a plane for a destination that was different from mine. I glanced at the gate monitor and saw that my plane was still on schedule. I read some more. The crowd thickened with the arrival of other passengers. When I next looked at the monitor, it showed that another flight preceded mine. I got anxious as my departure time approached, and people were called for this other flight. According to the monitor, my flight to San Diego had now been changed to a later time. In that case

I needed to alert my pickup that I would be arriving late.

The counter assistant assured me that my flight was still on time. "You must have read the monitor wrong."

I returned to my seat but I was not mollified. I could not read the monitor from where I was sitting. Boarding was announced for another flight. As people queued with their boarding passes, I knew that it was impossible for their plane to depart before mine was scheduled to arrive, deplane passengers, board passengers, and depart on time. My anxiety overcame the counter assistant's assurances. I walked to where I could read the monitor. The flight to San Diego was still on the board, but it was now scheduled to depart after the flight that was presently boarding.

A different assistant stood behind the counter. I explained my plight and flight to her.

She looked at the gate monitor. She told me that the flight that was showing was not my flight, but a later one. When she checked her computer, she found that my flight had been changed to a different gate. The plane was scheduled to depart in ten minutes.

I protested, "But I didn't hear any announcement."

She shrugged and gave me the new gate number. It was one gate away on the opposite side of the concourse: less than 100 feet. I ran. I dodged through the throng that shuffled along the middle of the corridor and made it to the other gate in about fifteen seconds. The gate attendant was swinging the door shut as I arrived.

"Hold it!" I shouted. "I have to get on that plane."

"It's too late, sir. Once the doors are closed we can't open them again." (Or words to that effect. The following dialogue is an approximate reconstruction.)

"But the plane is right there."

"I'm sorry sir." Despite her words of apology and apparent conciliation, she was openly hostile and antagonistic.

As I looked through the picture window I saw that the jetway was still pressed against the fuselage of the plane.

"The plane doesn't leave for ten more minutes." (By

this time it was actually nine minutes and fifty seconds till departure time.) "Tell them to open the door and let me on." (I meant the plane's door, not the gate's door.)

"We stop boarding ten minutes before departure."

I was insistent. "Tell them I'm here." I figured – or hoped – that if the flight crew knew that one of their passengers was standing at the gate, they would let me board.

"I'm sorry, sir. According to FAA regulations, we can't let anyone board after the doors are closed."

At that time I didn't know that she was lying about the regulations, but I argued vehemently nonetheless. We were still arguing as the jetway started to retract.

"But I was here on time. This plane was supposed to depart from Gate 23, not 24. There was no announcement about a gate change."

"It's your responsibility to watch the monitors."

Another assistant entered the gate from the jetway door.

I appealed to her. "I need to get on that plane."

"We aren't allowed to open the doors after they're closed."

Their falsehoods were consistent.

"Just call the plane and tell them to let me on."

By this time the jetway was fully retracted. I could see the pilot and co-pilot in the cockpit. They were still doing their pre-flight checks.

I kept arguing firmly but without raising my voice or using unsavory language. Neither one would pick up the phone to plead my case with someone in authority.

Assistant #1 continually shook her head and refused to make eye contact.

Assistant #2 didn't smile, but she worked the keyboard at the computer console. She told me that there was another plane departing for San Diego in a couple of hours. She turned over the computer to #1, "See if there are any seats on the next plane." Then she opened the gate door and entered the jetway.

The plane hadn't moved.

Assistant #1 was grim about taking orders. I had the

impression that she was subordinate to #2, because she did as she was told, albeit reluctantly and with a scowl.

At that moment two other passengers arrived breathless at the gate. One was silent but the other's volubility made up for both of them. Whereas I was angry, he was apoplectic. The talkative one was livid because he hadn't been called. He had been on standby since 8 o'clock that morning, when his plane had arrived too late for him to catch his connecting flight. It was now 4 o'clock in the afternoon. He had been bumped off four intervening flights because they were full. Now he was understandably desperate and irate.

His anger put more pressure on Assistant #1. She apologized without feeling but explained that there was nothing she could do. He left in a huff. The silent one remained.

The plane still hadn't moved.

Assistant #1 ascertained that the next scheduled flight departed in a couple of hours; it was the last one of the day.

"Put me on it," I said.

"You'll have to go to the reservation deck."

Now I was insistent. "You can do it from here. Do it."

She kept shaking her head but she ran her fingers over the keyboard. After a couple of minutes she said, "I can issue a ticket but the plane is full and there are twenty-three standbys. It's the last San Diego flight until tomorrow."

My heart sank. If there were so many standbys for San Diego, why hadn't the airline assigned one of them to my seat when I didn't show up at the gate on time? The situation was growing more absurd by leaps and bounds.

The printer started clacking as it printed a standby ticket. Unless twenty-four people failed to show up for the flight, I was going to be stranded in Denver overnight. Once again I was going to miss the first day's diving, because the boat left the marina at 8 o'clock the next morning. My luggage was already on the plane.

Assistant #1 took my original ticket from me, tore it

up, and handed me the new ticket. She was so flustered that she didn't speak except to give me the gate number. She never once made eye contact with me.

I didn't move. I was determined to stand there in full view of the flight crew until the plane departed. The quiet fellow stood right behind me.

By this time the plane's departure was overdue. And *still* it didn't move.

The jetway started to move toward the plane. Had my persistence paid off? Had the assistant called the flight crew or someone in authority? Had airline officials relented and resolved to let me have my seat? Had they decided to let standbys fill the plane? None of the above.

Assistant #2 emerged from the jetway. She explained that there was a mechanical problem in the cockpit, and that the jetway was being emplaced so that mechanics could board the plane to fix the problem. *But*, she would do what she could do to take advantage of this opportunity to get me on the plane.

She returned to the jetway. When she reappeared several minutes later, she said that the plane had three empty seats. *But*, the flight attendants didn't know if there was space available in the overhead bins for carry-on bags. If not, neither I nor the fellow standing behind me would be allowed to board. These particular seats didn't have seats in front of them for stowage underneath.

Surely, I suggested, at least one of the two hundred plus passengers would let me put my knapsack and computer bag under his seat. *But*, that was not allowed. I never learned why. A passenger is allowed to have only his own bag under the seat in front of him, not someone else's bag.

"Put them in with the checked luggage," I suggested. *But*, she said that "they" were not allowed to open the luggage compartment once it was closed. Again, I never learned why.

All these things of little or no consequence might keep me off the plane. The way it played out, persistence *did* pay off. Both of us were allowed to board – not because of standard airline procedure, but because of a malfunction that made it necessary for a mechanic to enter the plane. The flight attendants were overly accommodating and happy to have us aboard.

There was still one empty seat. No one bothered to call the guy who had been waiting for eight hours – or any of the other twenty-two standbys. Why not, I never ascertained. They just didn't bother. A lot of people were not going to reach their destination until the following day. They should have been more persistent and stood by the gate, because the airline was not persistent for them.

The mechanical problem was fixed in short order, and we were on our way into skies that were friendly, even if the airline was not.

The Airline Rulebook

There are rules, and there are rules, and there are rules for rules. No one seems to know the purpose of these rules. No one has the authority to break these rules. No one has the guts to bend these rules.

Airlines are run by rules whose origins are shrouded in mystery; rules that no one seems to understand, and that no one finds the least bit disturbing. Airline employees simply follow the rules blindly, unknowingly, uncaringly, unquestioningly, without wondering why they exist, and without recognizing that they might not apply in a specific situation.

These rules are obeyed as if they were laws of nature, like gravity. To an airline employee, breaking a rule is like stepping off a thousand-foot-high cliff.

Rules prevent people from thinking and from making intelligent decisions. When there is a rule for everything imaginable, what happens when the unimaginable occurs? A person is not allowed to board the plane, that's what. Because someone back in airline history lacked the imagination to conceive of a circumstance in which the overhead bins were full and someone might have to place his carry-on bag elsewhere.

Take, for example, the rule that you are not allowed

to hold anything in your hand during take-off. Is there a reason for this rule? Is this rule so important that a plane won't take off if a woman has her purse in her lap?

Perhaps once, long ago in the prehistory of commercial air travel, a passenger dropped an item that he was holding during take-off. Perhaps the item broke, or landed on his toe, or rolled into the aisle, where a stewardess could have tripped over it. So a rule was made to prevent it from ever happening again. Now that rule is inviolable.

Rules are supposed to be guidelines for rational thought, not loaded guns jammed against a person's temple. Rules cannot anticipate every circumstance in the universe. Yet airline employees follow company rules as if they were Commandments from God. When they are questioned about those rules, they blame the FAA: a catchall scapegoat that implements logical rules about aircraft safety, not company rules that are based on the presumption that strict adherence to departure schedules means closing the doors or retracting the jetway at the precise second that was printed on a timetable many months earlier, while a plane sits idle next to the gate as the last-minute safety checks are performed.

If it were true that the FAA issued hefty fines for late departures, the Administration must be a billionaire by now. More planes depart late – although usually by only a couple of minutes – than depart on time.

Nonce Rules

I think some rules are made up on the spot. After a backpacking trip to Glacier National Park, Cheryl Novak and I went to the airport in Kalispell, Montana, to catch our planes to our respective homes: hers in North Carolina, mine in Philadelphia. My flight left a couple of hours later than hers.

The Northwest Airlines counter clerk processed Cheryl's ticket, checked her backpack and suitcase, and directed her to her gate. When I handed him my ticket, he told me that it was too early for me to check in. On the contrary, passengers are always warned to check in early. This was the first and only time that I was told that I was *too* early. No amount of argument would sway him.

It's not as if there was a long line of passengers who had to be processed because of imminent departures. No one stood behind us. (Kalispell is a small airport, with no concourse and only half a dozen gates.)

For the next several hours, I had to drag my back-pack, suitcase, and carry-on knapsack everywhere I went: to the food court, the drinking fountain, the lavatory, and so on. It was a major hassle to lug all that weight around.

I wrote a stern letter of complaint to Northwest Airlines. Apparently my rhetoric struck a chord in officialdom, because they sent me an apology and a voucher for $100. I hope the counter clerk received a harsh reprimand.

No Tickee No Shirtee

My friend Emil Kraiser took his daughter on a ski trip to Colorado in the 1990's. They stayed at the family condominium. When it came time to go home, the daughter decided to stay for a few more days. Emil went to the airport by himself. When he checked in at the airport, he found that he had grabbed his daughter's ticket instead of his own. No matter, he thought: both tickets were written for the same flight; and anyway, he had paid for both of them.

It didn't matter to Emil, but it mattered to the airline. They refused to let him check in because the ticket he had was in his daughter's name.

What difference should this make, you might wonder? Any other ticket that you purchase anywhere in the world is transferable: bus tickets, theater tickets, concert tickets, amusement park tickets, movie tickets, tickets for sporting events, and so on. The only meaningful criterion is that the consumer should possess a prepaid ticket. So why shouldn't an airline ticket be just as valid?

As I have already demonstrated – and will do so

again in subsequent subsections – logic has little or nothing to do with airline operations.

Emil argued vehemently, but the airline stood their ground – and kept him on the ground as well. It didn't matter to the airline that he had proper identification. It didn't matter that he could prove that he had paid for both tickets. It didn't matter that his daughter had the same surname as his. What mattered was that the given name on the ticket was different from the given name on his identification card.

In order to get on the plane for which he already had a paid seat, he had to buy another ticket for the same seat! Because this ticket was purchased at the last minute, instead of months in advance, he had to pay an exorbitant price: more than double the original purchase price. Otherwise the airline would not have let him on the plane. He was not reimbursed for the ticket that he had purchased previously, and that he hadn't used.

This kind of rip-off isn't legal, and it certainly isn't ethical. I am aware of no law on the books that makes it unlawful for a passenger to use a ticket in another person's name. Nonetheless, the airlines maintain a policy that once a ticket is issued, it is cast in bronze. You can't sell it, you can't trade it, you can't give it away.

How did the system get this way? Why are the airlines permitted to operate beyond the law? Why doesn't some law enforcement agency investigate the matter? I wish I knew.

Saturday Night Live

A client hired me to fly to San Francisco for a consulting job. I had an unlimited expense account. I called U.S. Airways to purchase a plane ticket. The job was scheduled for Monday and Tuesday, so I figured on flying out of Philly on Sunday, returning on Wednesday

The airline operator gave me a choice of flight times. I picked one. Then she told me the cost: $1,596!

I was flabbergasted. That was way more than I was led to believe a transcontinental flight would cost. "Don't you have any cheaper flights?"

"Not on Sunday. But if you fly on Saturday the cost is $399."

It cost *four times* as much to fly on Sunday as it did to fly on Saturday, yet the distance was the same.

"Why does it cost so much to fly on Sunday?"

"Because you don't have a Saturday night stay-over." She said it matter-of-factly, as if she were telling a kindergarten class a well-known fact of nature, like, "The sun always rises in the east."

"What does that have to do with it?"

"If you stay over Saturday night, the rates are cheaper." Which said the same thing in a different way, without adding explanation. She made it sound as if a federal regulatory commission governed airfares that included Saturday night layovers as a travel inducement.

What did staying in a hotel on Saturday night have to do with airline rates? Although it seems nonsensical at first, a little cogitation reveals the twisted truth of the matter. Airfares were not reduced for weekend travel. On the contrary, they were artificially inflated as a way to rip off business travelers who didn't want to spend their precious weekend family time away from home, and whose fourfold fares were being paid for by rich corporations.

I have a policy of not being extravagant, even when I am working on an expense account. It took me only a moment to calculate that I could save the client money if I traveled on Saturday, paid an extra night's hotel fee, and charged my standard day rate for the extra day on the road. So that's what I did. The client saved a few dollars, I earned extra income, and U.S. Airways got paid what the flight was actually worth.

Congress has enacted laws against windfall profits and profiteering, but apparently they don't apply to airline companies.

Crossing the Double-Crosser

There are other ways to get around the Saturday night stay-over penalty, and avoid being cheated by crooked airlines. Consider this method that I could have employed in the situation above.

Instead of purchasing *one* round-trip ticket in accordance with my preferred flight plan of Sunday to Wednesday (which cost $1,596), I could have bought *two* round-trip tickets that cost $399 each: ticket #1 from Saturday to Wednesday, and ticket #2 from Sunday to Sunday. Each of these tickets incorporates a Saturday night stay-over: the previous Saturday night on ticket #1, and the following Saturday night on ticket #2. Total expenditure is $798, or half the cost of the single ticket without a Saturday night stay-over.

Blow off the Saturday departure on ticket #1 by not showing up at the airport to claim your seat. Depart on Sunday by using ticket #2. Return on Wednesday by using ticket #1. Blow off the Sunday return on ticket #2.

The airlines can't do a thing about it. Both tickets were paid in accordance with the airline price structure. Furthermore, the system is legal and doesn't violate any price gouging laws. Two empty seats are available for standbys (if the airline takes the initiative to call them).

A word of caution (okay, a couple of sentences): airlines have a habit of canceling return tickets when a passenger doesn't show up to claim his seat on the originating flight. You might ask how they can do that, when you paid for the seat and therefore have a legal claim to it. The answer is that airlines can do anything they want, as long as it doesn't violate any FAA regulations that they are so fond of quoting. Airlines operate above the law because the law doesn't stop them from doing so. (Remember how they victimized Emil Kraiser.)

The way to avoid cancellation of your return ticket is to call the airlines and explain that, although you missed the originating flight, you found alternative means of transportation to your destination, and still plan to return on your ticketed seat. Then they have to honor your ticket.

If you don't want the airlines to discover that you have dodged their Saturday night stay-over scam, buy your tickets from two competing airlines.

Unfair Airfare

Most of the time, a flight with connections costs less than a nonstop flight, even though the connections take you off course and increase the total mileage flown and the jet fuel burned, sometimes significantly. If you want to rack up frequent flyer miles, try taking the most circuitous route available; it might be cheaper, and you'll have more miles added to your account for free tickets.

What stake do airlines have in penalizing passengers who take the shortest and most fuel-economic route between two airports? I don't know. It doesn't make sense, but then hardly anything about airline price structures makes sense.

I can only note that there's almost always a difference in fares between nonstop flights and one-stop or multiple-stop flights, despite the fact that nonstop flights burn less jet fuel, and are more efficient to operate because the time that is required to land, deplane passengers, board new passengers, and take off again isn't doubled or tripled.

Cheryl Novak wanted to attend a conference in Kansas City. She planned to depart from Norfolk. She played around with airfares before purchasing a ticket. During the process, she discovered that a round-trip ticket cost more than three one-way tickets from Norfolk to Kansas City, thence to Indianapolis, thence back to Norfolk. This itinerary was not only cheaper, but afforded her the opportunity to visit long-time friends in Indianapolis, where she used to live. Go figure.

No Rhyme, No Reason, No Iambic Pentameter

As long as we're discussing whacky airfare structures, try this one on for size. Compare all the flights that go between two particular cities on the same airline. You'll notice that the fares differ throughout the day. A morning flight might cost more or less than an afternoon flight. Or, an evening flight might cost more or less than a morning flight.

The mileage is the same.

Additionally, the same flight at the same time might

cost more or less on different days of the week, and in different months of the year.

To put this into perspective, compare the price structure for transporting packages with the price structure for transporting people. The Postal Service and package delivery companies base their rates on the distance that the package must be transported. The reason for this – and I stress the word "reason" – is that it costs more to transport a package one thousand miles than it costs to transport the same package one hundred miles.

They don't charge for every individual mile because that would be too complicated to calculate. They lump distances into zones. Thus it costs more to ship a package from Zone 2 to Zone 4 than it costs to ship that same package to Zone 3, because Zone 3 is closer to Zone 2. This makes perfect sense.

Of course, there are aberrations that are unavoidable in light of the present state of technology. These aberrations occur close to the borders that separate the zones. If you ship a package from a point that is five miles east of a border, to a destination that is five miles west of the border, you pay a fee for crossing the artificial border; whereas you could ship that package several hundred miles eastward without crossing a border, and consequently pay a lower rate.

The same aberration is true for telephone calls, in which zones are designated as area codes. There are situations in which a caller incurs long-distance charges for calling his neighbor across the street. Logically, an area code has to change somewhere along a prescribed line of demarcation.

Viewed in the larger picture, these aberrations average out in the long run.

(In aside, I cannot help but mention a gross aberration with regard to the Postal Service. From the West Coast, one can mail a 4-pound package 2,500 miles westward or 2,500 miles eastward for $3.64. From the East Coast, the charge to mail that same package 2,500 miles westward is the same, but to mail it 2,500 miles eastward costs $38.65: more than ten times as much.)

So how are airfares determined? I have finally figured it out. They take a stack of cards and print a different fare on each card. They take a boxful of darts and
stamp a different flight number on each dart. Then they
fling the cards across a large room, and throw the darts
at the cards. When a dart pierces a card, the fare on the
card becomes the charge for the flight number on the
dart. They do this for every day of the year.

If this arbitrary selection process sounds like an aerial version of Pin-the-Tail-on-the-Donkey, so be it. But
now things get really bizarre without being facetious.

Two-Timing the Airlines

My son Michael and three of his friends wanted to
fly from Philly to Raleigh for a gaming convention. While
checking ticket fares online, they noticed that it was
cheaper to fly to Raleigh from Allentown than it was to
fly from Philly. Let me lay out the geography and logistics for readers who are unfamiliar with the area.

Allentown lies about 60 miles north of Philly. The
Philadelphia International Airport is not *in* Philly, but
southwest of Philly in neighboring Delaware County.
From where Mike lived in northeast Philly, the distance
to the Philly airport was 25 miles. The crosstown driving
time was at least 45 minutes if there wasn't any local
traffic, and if I-95 was running smoothly; but when
there were slowdowns on the Interstate or when local
traffic was heavy (during commuter time or when games
were being played at the downtown sports arenas), the
driving time could easily be an hour or more – sometimes much more.

Furthermore, checking-in at the busy Philly airport
was always a time-consuming process: the parking lots
were so far away that you had to take a bus from the
lots to the terminal; the lines at the ticket counter were
long; the security lines were longer; and you might have
to walk half a mile to reach your gate.

On the other hand, once you parked your car at the
Lehigh Valley International Airport in Allentown, it was
only a hop, skip, and a jump over the hurdles to the

gate. In other words, Although the drive to LVI was 35 miles farther than the drive to PIA, the house to gate time was shorter. Plus, the airfare was cheaper.

Mike and his friends carpooled to Allentown.

Not to give away the rest of story prematurely, let me quote some current fares instead of Mike's fares from several years ago. I will use San Francisco as a destination because the disparity is demonstrative.

At the time of this writing, the round-trip airfare on U. S. Airways flight #657 from Philly to San Francisco is $1,950. The round-trip airfare from Allentown to San Francisco is $994 – only a wee bit more than half!

It gets worse.

The way the crow flies, the distance from Allentown to San Francisco is about the same as the distance from Philly to San Francisco, because Allentown and Philly lie on nearly the same longitude, and San Francisco lies westward across the continent. (Technically, Allentown is a tail feather closer, but, as you will read in the next paragraph, that is irrelevant.) Given the same distance, you would expect the fares to be about the same.

Now comes the punch line. To fly from Allentown to San Francisco, you board U.S. Airways flight #4309 at LVI, fly to the Philly airport, and connect with flight #657 to San Francisco!

You read that correctly. You fly 60 miles farther in another plane, and connect with a flight that would have cost $956 more (nearly double what you paid) if you had originated on flight #657 instead of having connected with it from another airport.

In short, U.S. Airways flew a plane from Allentown to Philly just so they could charge those passengers half of what they charged passengers to fly direct from Philly. Or, to put it another way, the uninformed passengers who flew out of Philly were charged nearly double what the flight cost passengers who made a connecting flight from Allentown.

This kind of flight plan is beyond absurd. It qualifies as absurdity taken to the nth power. No wonder the airlines are in such desperate straits. Even my card and dart system couldn't produce results as idiotic as the airlines have produced by some incomprehensible means that defies all the laws of logic.

Weak-minded people are advised to avoid playing too much with online airfares, or you might find yourself buying a ticket to the funny farm.

But now things get even *more* bizarre.

Carving in the Middleman

You would think that after such a denouement, anything else that I could possibly write about airfares must be anticlimactic. You would be wrong.

In the old days, the only way to compare airfares and bargain for the lowest rate was to go to a travel agency or call each airline individually. Nowadays things are different. Travel agencies promote and sell all-inclusive vacation packages but seldom if ever are consulted only for travel by air without hotel, resort, or cruise line packages.

Airlines add a surcharge to the ticket price if you purchase your ticket direct from them, either by phone or at the airport. Currently the surcharge is at least $25. In this age of the Internet, airlines prefer passengers to book their own flights online. That way the airlines don't have to pay an employee to sell tickets.

In the subsection above I demonstrated how I used the U.S. Airways website to determine the cost and availability of flights to San Francisco from both Philly and Allentown. But you can also buy U.S. Airways tickets from other websites. The generic name for these alternative Internet vendors is "third party ticket discounters." They have descriptive website addresses such as Cheaptickets.com, Orbitz.com, Lowfares.com, Expedia.com, and Cheapoair.com. Likely there are others.

I searched these websites in order to compare their fare offerings with those of U.S. Airways. What I found was startling to say the least.

The Philly-to-San-Francisco ticket that U.S. Airways was selling for $1,950, I could buy from an online discounter for $1,275. That's about 35% off the U.S. Airways selling price, for a savings of $675.

The Allentown-to-San-Francisco ticket that U.S. Airways was selling for $994, I could buy for $756. That's about 24% off the U.S. Airways selling price, for a savings of $238.

If you compare the U.S. Airways Philly-to-San-Francisco fare of $1,950 with the online discounter Allentown-to-San-Francisco fare, the cumulative discount is about 61%, for a total savings of $1,194. You could fly round-trip to San Francisco two and a half times for the same amount of money; or fly once, and have enough left over to pay for meals, lodging, souvenirs, and a mortgage payment.

Lest I be misunderstood, the online discounter tickets were for the same seats, the same class, and the same flight numbers as the U.S. Airways tickets. The only difference was who you were buying your ticket from.

How is this possible, you may ask? I wanted to know, too, so I called U.S. Airways for an explanation. Hold onto your seat – and your ticket – for the answer.

"We can't compete with them. They buy tickets in bulk." (Pretty much the words she used.)

Granted that I am not a lettered economist, but I don't see how an airline cannot undersell a vendor to which the airline sold the tickets in the first place. The airline is the wholesaler; the online discounter is a retailer. Since America is a capitalistic society, we must presume that the online discounters are in business to make a profit, and not to undercut the airlines out of the goodness of their heart to their passengers, while losing their shirt in the process.

I would address this issue further, but by now I've lost my heart in San Francisco.

The Next-to-the-Last Fare Word
Not to beat a dead horse, but before I leave the subject of airfares, let me touch upon a few other irregularities in the airfare system – or rather, the air unfair

system – just so there will be no uncertainty about how ridiculous the system is.

This time I picked on the United Airlines website for my fares. I can fly from Philly to Washington Dulles for $474 (a distance of about 150 miles). Counting the time that it takes to drive to the airport, arrive early enough to park, check in, and go through security, then add flight time, I could reach the District of Columbia quicker by driving straight through. But that is neither here nor there.

Alternatively, I could fly out of Allentown and catch the same Philly flight for $416. Again, that is neither here nor there.

I can go even cheaper by flying from Philly to Boston (about 300 miles in the opposite direction) for $216, thence to Dulles (about 400 miles, passing over Philly in the process) for $178. That route is nearly five times the distance of the shortest route, and yields 700 frequent flyer miles at a total cost of $394 – a savings of $80 over the most direct route.

A straight line may be the shortest distance between two points, but it isn't necessarily the cheapest.

I've just decided to patent my card and dart invention.

The Last, Final, and Ultimate Fare Word – I Promise!

Once you've decided to travel by air, call the airline of your choice and inquire about ticket prices. The reservation clerk will quote fares for different flights that depart at various times. If the fares seem inordinately high, write down the information – fares, flight numbers, departure times, number of seats available, and so on – then say that you want to think it over.

Call again in half an hour. More than likely, the phone will be answered by a different clerk. Ask again for the exact information. You will be given different price quotes: some higher, some lower. There is no internal consistency within an airline. It's almost as if the clerks are making up the fares as they go along.

Keep calling until you get the best fare possible.

To Fly or Not to Fly, That is the Question

I can't help but mention the most recent innovation: a difference in the classification of tickets. Airlines now sell "non-refundable" tickets and "flexible" tickets.

A ticket that is "non-refundable" is one that is either used (by the person who is named on the ticket, of course) or lost. A "flexible" ticket is one that can be changed or canceled.

Actually, under most circumstances, both kinds of ticket can be changed, but there is a penalty for changing a "non-refundable" ticket. "Changed" means transferred to a different flight, a different time, or a different day. The current charge per change is $150 – which, incidentally, is more than the cost of some short-distance fares.

A "non-refundable" ticket cannot be canceled. Once you pay for the ticket, you have to use it to fly somewhere, sometime, someday.

But here's the rub. Using U.S. Airways figures from Philly to Seattle, a "non-refundable" round-trip ticket costs $492, whereas a "flexible" round-trip ticket costs $1,728 – about three and a half times as much.

Even if you missed both flights – the one from Philly and the one from Seattle – and paid the fee to reschedule for different flights, your total cost would be $492 plus $300, or $792. That's still less than half the cost of a "flexible" ticket, which has no penalties for changes.

If you don't get my point, you must work for the airlines.

Musical Seats

Buying a "non-refundable" ticket is no guarantee that your seat will be available when you arrive for your flight. "Non-refundable" applies to the passenger, not to the airline that issued the "unchangeable" ticket.

For one thing, the airline may have overbooked the flight. In pre-computer days I can understand this happenstance, but it is incomprehensible to me that it still occurs, and as often as it does. I can't count the number of times I have heard announcements asking for a volunteer to give up his seat because there weren't enough to go around for all the tickets that were sold for the flight.

One reason that passengers surge onto a plane as soon as the gate is open is because they are never quite certain that when they reach their assigned seat, it will be unoccupied. There's a hidden fear that they might find someone else sitting in it. When two passengers hold the same lottery number, the winner is usually the one who is already seated: possession is nine tenths of the law. In such a case, the plane won't take off until the situation is resolved.

A plane has a specified number of seats. Whenever a ticket is sold, a seat is deducted from those that are available. You can see this happen online. If you purchase a ticket and recheck availability, you'll see that the number of seats has diminished by one. Other times you'll try to buy the lowest-priced ticket that is advertised, and get a notification that the flight is sold out.

If you select a seat online, or call the airline to choose one for you, you will be told whether a certain window or aisle seat is available. If it's already taken, then you have to select a different seat. So how does it happen that sometimes two people are ticketed for the same seat? The airlines don't have an answer for this question, and neither do it. It just happens.

On the other hand, your "non-refundable" ticket won't be honored if the flight is canceled. A flight may be canceled because of weather, mechanical difficulties, flight crew problems, or, on occasion, because there aren't enough passengers to make it worthwhile for the airline to proceed with the flight.

In these cases, your "non-refundable" ticket suddenly becomes "flexible" by means of airline company fiat. The choice is theirs.

What's Good for the Goose . . .

Take a gander at this scenario. I just found a super cheap commuter flight from the Big Apple to Washington Dulles. The round-trip airfare is only $88.

But, the charge to take both my suitcases and bring them back is $120! That's right, folks. Space in the luggage compartment costs more than a seat; and my luggage doesn't weigh half as much as I do.

With an incongruity like that, is it any wonder that the airlines are flying topsy-turvy in this time of economic upheaval? It's cheaper to buy a seat for my luggage, but the airlines won't allow it. (Note that the *airlines* won't allow it, not the FAA.)

If I want to send an unaccompanied minor on this flight, there is an additional fee of $100 – each way.

If I don't want to child to be separated from his pet, there is another additional fee of $100 – each way. The pet must be small enough to stand and turn around in, but not protrude from, an approved carrying case that will fit under the seat in front.

And this is not counting $21 in taxes, security fees, airport surcharges, takeoff and landing fees, and so on. That's a bag of worms that I don't want to open. I'll let it go at doing the math for you: the hidden add-ons are 24% of the base fare. That's price gouging in anybody's book.

Kits, cats, sacks, and wives, what does it cost to go to St. Ives? It costs $629.

Unless the suitcases weigh more than 50 pounds. If the suitcases weigh 51 pounds each, there is an extra charge of $100 per suitcase, over and above the initial $120. Now it costs $829 to go to St. Ives.

Unless the suitcases weigh 71 pounds each. Then there's an extra additional charge of $200 per suitcase, over and above the initial $120. Now it costs $1,089 to go to St. Ives.

It breaks down this way: round-trip transportation costs $88 per person (plus $21 per ticket for taxes, fees, and surcharges), $200 more if the person is under age and alone, $200 more for a pet, and $520 for two 71-pound suitcases.

Although there is an excess baggage charge, there is no excess personage charge. A 300-pound man flies for the same fare as a 90-pound woman.

Looking at it another way, a 300-pound man can take that flight for $109 ($88 for the fare and $21 in surcharges), His luggage weighs less than half as much as his person, yet could cost nearly *six times* as much to transport. No wonder people are shipping their suitcases ahead of time via UPS.

Where's the taxi stand?

Shedding Excess Baggage

Speaking of baggage, I've experienced my share of irrational and ridiculous behavior at the ticket counter while checking in my bags. And I don't mean from the passengers.

One suitcase of a man checking in next to me exceeded the weight limit by two pounds. The ticketing agent threatened to charge him the excess baggage fee unless he rearranged his belongings. The man had to open both suitcases on the floor in front of the counter, remove two pounds stuff from the overweight suitcase, and cram the stuff into his underweight suitcase.

What was the purpose of shuffling his belongings? The total weight was unchanged. The luggage was not going to be weighed again, so only the ticketing agent would ever know that one suitcase was a smidgeon overweight. If the weight limit system were to be based on logic, the rule would read that the combined weight of both suitcases should not aggregate over 100 pounds. The distribution of that weight is irrelevant.

For that matter, the entire weight limit rule is illogical. The ability of a jet aircraft to take off is not constrained by a few overweight suitcases – not when you can have a cabin full of college football players instead of a group of senior women's auxiliary bridge players.

The only purpose of the weight limit on luggage is to fleece passengers without increasing ticket fares. It's a way to trick people into thinking that airline travel rates are low.

The airlines aren't the only ones to play tricks under the guise of rules. In order to avoid the embarrassment to which the man above was subjected, I've got a trick of my own that I've pulled on more than one occasion. First of all, I weigh my suitcases on a bathroom scale at home, and distribute their contents accordingly. The scales aren't all that accurate, so sometimes my suitcase might be over the limit on an airline scale. I purposely position the suitcase so that one end overhangs the platform. I watch the digital readout. If the weight exceeds fifty pounds, I tip up the suitcase with my toe until the readout is in the forties. Ticketing agents can't tell the difference between 49 pounds and 51 pounds when they lift the bag, so they aren't any the wiser as they carry the suitcase to the conveyor belt.

Another trick – one that works well only in winter – is to wear an overcoat with large baggy pockets, then fill those pockets with heavy items.

I always wear a knapsack that is filled to capacity as my carry-on bag.

If I'm going on a backpacking trip, I wear my heavy outdoor boots and clothing on the plane, and pack the lightweight stuff in my suitcase and backpack.

One time, when the ticketing agent saw my backpack, she asked if it held a backpacking stove and fuel container. I foolishly told her the truth. She asked me if there was fuel in the container. I said no; I carry the container empty when I travel by air. She made me dig the fuel container out of the pack so she could inspect it. She unscrewed the top and sniffed.

I knew that there were no gasoline fumes to smell because I always rinse the interior with fresh soapy water. She scowled and shook her head. She was looking for an excuse to disallow me to take the container. Such an action would effectively ruin my trip. She made the ticketing agents on either side of her sniff the container. I did a good job of rinsing it, because both of them said that they couldn't smell any residue. She continued to scowl, but she let me put the container back in the pack while she issued the baggage slip.

Ever since then, whenever a ticketing agents asks if I am carrying a backpacking stove or a fuel container, I answer "No." I also pack the fuel container in my suitcase, because they never think to look for it there.

If backpackers were not allowed to carry fuel containers on airplanes, most of them would quit flying. You can't rely on finding a place to buy a new fuel container at your destination, especially at night and on weekends. And who wants to throw away a perfectly good aluminum fuel bottle at the end of every trip? Not only that, but some backpacking stoves are self-contained: the fuel canister is built into the stove.

Another baggage trick that the airlines pull is claiming that, in accordance with FAA regulations – here we go again – you must accompany your luggage at all times. In other words, you must board the same plane that your luggage is on. It goes without saying that the FAA has no such regulation. The airlines use this ploy as an excuse to keep you from taking a flight that departs at a different time than the one that you are scheduled to take.

But they pull this excuse out of the baggage compartment only when *you* request a flight change. If the airlines forwards your luggage to your destination on a different flight, or accidentally sends it to the wrong destination, or forgets to put it on your plane and transports it on a later flight, then the fictitious FAA regulation doesn't apply, and the airline is careful not to mention it.

I wonder what would have happened on the Denver to San Diego flight that I was late for, if I had said (when they refused to let me board), "But my luggage is on that plane, and the FAA requires that I accompany it."

Baggage Claim

This phrase has two meanings in airline lingo: a place to collect your baggage at an airport, and an application for reimbursement for lost or stolen baggage.

On a recent Delta Air Lines flight, my backpack was not only rifled for its contents by a baggage handler, but it was sabotaged as well, perhaps because he didn't find any valuables. I was at the trailhead a hundred miles from civilization when I discovered that certain items were missing from my pack: my Swiss army knife, the tie-down cords for my tent, and the plastic spoon that was the only utensil I carried for eating freeze-dried meals. Worse yet, the pack's waist buckle was missing.

As every backpacker knows, you can't go on a five-day backpacking trip through rocky rugged country without an adjustable waist strap. The plastic buckle could not have fallen off; it was sown onto the strap; the loop was still stitched. Someone had to have smashed off the buckle with a hammer or some kind of solid metal implement.

Fortunately my camera bag had the same brand and same size buckle as my backpack. I cut the strap to remove the buckle, wove the backpack strap through the retainer, and left behind my camera bag; I stuffed my camera and lenses into my pack where they were not immediately accessible. I borrowed a knife and spoon throughout the trip, and did without the tent tie-downs.

Afterward, I sent a letter of complaint to Delta Air Lines. I received a form letter and a claim form. The only way that Delta would reimburse me for the stolen items was if I submitted a list of those items accompanied by a sales receipt for each item. I did not save years-old receipts for nondeductible items the way I saved them for tax deductible items.

The amount of money was negligible. The inconvenience was enormous. If I hadn't been able to jury-rig my equipment and borrow items that I needed, I would have had to return to civilization and lose a day off the trip.

I thought about submitting receipts for items that I *did* have, but that were not stolen, as a way of breaking even – but I decided that dishonesty was an airline affectation that I did not need to exacerbate.

Delta's way of avoiding responsibility for lost or stolen baggage is not in keeping with good company standards of fairness.

Airport Security . . .

. . . has become a big bone of contention in American air travel since the terrorist attacks on the Twin Towers and the Pentagon on September 11, 2001. The guarantee of commercial aircraft safety has become so onerous and expensive a task that a pundit might declare that it would be cheaper in the long run to sacrifice an airplane every now and again – in a form of aerial Russian roulette – rather than deal with the restrictions imposed by the Transportation Security Administration. The loss of the occasional plane is certainly cheaper than the cost of airport security – until you or your loved one is one of the passengers on a plane that is destroyed.

Anyone who has suffered the indignities and time delays of airport security checks might think it would be worthwhile to view an airline travel document as a lottery ticket, in which the winners reach their destination and the losers lose all. Such an attitude may sound attractive but it is an extremist point of view. As long as fanatics populate the world, we will have to deal with them and work with the TSA.

Life was simpler in the pre-9/11 days of airport security, when metal detectors and X-ray machines were not uncompromising barriers to swift and stress-free boarding. For his entire life, my friend Walt Daub never traveled anywhere without a penknife in his pocket. In 1988, when he and I and six fellow canoeists went on a wilderness canoe trip down the Nahanni River in the Northwest Territories, a luggage inspector relieved him of his knife, put it into a plastic bag, and gave it to the pilot, who returned it to Walt at the end of the flight. You'll never see that happen again.

While passing through Canadian customs, another baggage inspector did not recognize all the metal objects that showed up on the X-ray screen as Bob Lindquist's daypack passed through the machine. The inspector asked him to unzip the pack. He did. The inspector rummaged through his belongings, making a show of dissatisfaction at various metallic objects, then reluctantly passed him through.

Bob pointed to me and said in a loud voice, "That's nothing. He's got an ammo box in his pack."

At that moment my pack passed under the X-ray

scanner. Clearly outlined on the viewing monitor was a large rectangular object that looked suspiciously like an ammunition box. Two armed guards put their hands on their pistols and moved toward me with hostile intent. The inspector instructed me to unzip my pack. I did so, and removed the olive drab ammo box from where it had been nestled among my spare clothes. The tension mounted when I wasted no time and commenced to unsnap the locking mechanism. The guards' arms tensed.

Only an idiot would carry ammo in an ammo box if he didn't want it known that he was carrying ammo. The waterproof box contained my camera, lenses, and film. I had to prove that the camera was functional and did not contain a firing mechanism; I had to remove the lens so they could peer inside the camera body; I had to demonstrate that one could look through the telephoto zoom lens and see an image out the other end; and I had to show that each film canister did indeed contain film.

I always have trouble on long-distance dive trips because I carry two underwater strobes that are the size of footballs. Inspectors never recognize them for what they are. But as soon as I point out the flash tube assembly, it clicks in their minds: it's like a regular strobe only bigger.

A Foggy Smile for the Camera

Speaking of film, I should like to point out that many TSA employees are not as knowledgeable or well-informed as they should be.

Once when I was putting my luggage on a conveyor belt that passed through an X-ray machine, a TSA agent saw the camera that was hanging around my neck, and asked casually if I had any film in my suitcase. I told him that I did, so as to avoid the hassle of avoiding the carry-on scanner. He informed me that the radiation that was used for checked baggage was far more intense than the radiation that was used for carry-on bags. He suggested that I remove the film from my suitcase. I did.

(In all my air travel, he was the only one to mention how destructive the checked-baggage scanners were.)

TSA agents at the security checkpoint assured me that film whose ISO rating was 400 or less would not be affected by the X-ray machine that irradiated carry-on bags. Only faster film might be affected. They were only partially correct.

After I found that a roll of processed film was fogged, and the pictures on it were ruined, I backtracked my travel itinerary and correlated it with the batches of film that I took on each photo shoot. I learned something that the TSA should have known and warned me about. Either the TSA didn't know this about irradiating film, or they chose to keep the information concealed from passengers in order to keep up the pace of the security lines: sacrificing integrity for celerity.

I learned that the X-ray effect was cumulative.

While it may be true that one pass through an X-ray machine would not adversely affect slow-speed film, several passes would degrade it, and several more would ruin it.

Let's say that I went on a trip with a batch of film. On a domestic flight, my film was X-rayed twice: once out and once back. On an overseas flight, my film was X-rayed four times: once upon departure, once upon arrival and passage through foreign customs, once upon departure for home, and once again through American customs.

The film that I didn't use I took on my next trip.

On a research trip, my film had to pass an X-ray examination every time I entered the National Archives. Some days I passed in and out of the Archives three to four times. If the trip was several days in length, my film got irradiated many times over.

Everyone knows that hospital technicians wear lead aprons, and leave the room and hide behind a lead shield every time they X-ray a patient. They do this not because a single X-ray is harmful, but because they know that the effects of irradiation are cumulative. The same goes for film.

After learning this fact the hard way, never again did I permit my film to pass through an airport X-ray machine. I requested – or demanded when TSA personnel tried to talk me out of it – that my film be examined manually. This was a long and laborious procedure.

I generally went on a photo shoot with a couple dozen rolls of film of different speeds for different lighting conditions. A TSA agent had to open each canister, drop out the roll, examine it, reinsert the roll into the canister, and secure the lid: a time-consuming process at best, but a necessary process in order to protect my film from radiation damage.

One agent opened only those canisters that I had previously removed from the cardboard box. He told me that he didn't have to examine canisters that were sealed in their original boxes. The next time I flew, I took only film that I had not removed from the manufacturer's cardboard box. A different agent – at the same airport – opened every cardboard box.

Not only is there no consistency of examination from one airport to another, there is no consistency within the same airport. Each TSA agent conducted the examination differently.

Security Quirks

Nowadays, passing airport security can be more like enduring a full invasive medical exam complete with colonoscopy but lacking anesthesia. These security checks are supposed to be thorough – but how thorough are they, really? And how absurd are they? Let's examine airport security with the same depth of commitment that airport security employs when they examine passengers.

My friend Jim Murtha belongs to the same electrical union that I belonged to: Local #98. He told me that when a new concourse was under construction at the Philly airport, the workers cut a hole through the fence that separated the employees parking lot from the terminal so they wouldn't have to walk around the airport and go through security checkpoints.

The interior doors that connected the new concourse to the terminal were fitted with key pads that required a pass number to open. The workers scrawled the pass number on the lintel so they didn't have to get a guard to let them through every time they needed to enter or exit the terminal.

Workers were forever carrying toolboxes and cartons of material and supplies into the terminal. These boxes and cartons were not inspected because they were in the hands of construction workers. It doesn't take much imagination to dress like a construction worker.

When I worked as an electrician, I proved that I could go anywhere in an office building completely unopposed. Secretaries and office workers looked up when I entered an office, assumed that I was a maintenance worker, and went about their business, figuring that I had a right to be there. I did, but that's beside the point. My tool pouch was a universal passkey.

On Your Mettle

I hardly know where to begin when it comes to illustrating absurdities in the security check system. Let's start with metal.

The alarm sounded as I walked through the metal detector. A TSA security agent asked me to step aside so he could brush me with a wand. He got a signal return from my hip area. I showed him that I had removed my belt buckle. I had nothing in my pockets. Yet every time he passed the wand along my left hip, it detected the presence of metal.

I stuck my hand inside my pocket. There was nothing there. Finally I turned the pocket inside out. In the pocket lint I found the pull tab from aspirin tablet.

The agent pursed his lips and nodded. "These instruments are extremely sensitive. Nothing gets by them." (Or words to that effect.)

If that were true, I pondered, why weren't the detectors triggered by the fillings in my teeth, the frames of my eyeglasses, or my pants' zipper? I'm still pondering.

Another time I was returning from a dive trip to Grenada. In my carry-on pack I carried my underwater camera housing, my regulators, and my decompression computers; they were breakable and, altogether, were worth about $10,000. My two suitcases held 95 pounds of dive gear and 5 pounds of clothing.

I passed through security without a hitch. I was called to the baggage room because of a question about my suitcases. To enter the baggage room, I had to pass my knapsack through another X-ray machine, and walk through another metal detector. The security agent asked me to open my suitcase and identify a long cylindrical object that showed on the X-ray monitor. I did as he asked, and identified the auxiliary scuba tank from which I had removed the valve. (Smugglers used to put dope in such tanks and pressurize them.)

My person and my luggage went through two security check points in Miami: first through customs, then through airport security. By studying his X-ray monitor, the customs agent correctly identified the scuba tank and a large seashell, but found nothing else to question.

I didn't realize my mistake until I unpacked my luggage at home. I had forgotten to remove the dive knife that was strapped to my regulator instrument cluster!

The irony of these two incidents is that security personnel detected an aluminum pull tab that measured one-quarter inch in diameter, but four times in a row failed to detect a very sharp stainless steel knife. I had access to that knife during flight, because I kept the pack on the floor in front of my feet.

Even more ironic, on a 2002 flight from Sydney, Australia to Espiritu Santo, on an Air Vanuatu flight that was operating under the auspices of Qantas, the inflight meal was a complete steak dinner with all the fixings. Every passenger on the plane was issued a steel steak knife with a sharp point and a serrated edge. Had I tried to smuggle that very same knife onto the plane, I would still be trying to explain myself from behind prison bars.

Not to pile irony on top of irony (or ironmongery, as the case may be), take a look at the number of concourse restaurants that serve meals with steel cutlery. You will be amazed. Who needs to smuggle a knife when it's easier to steal one after passing through security?

Silly Restrictions

Maybe I don't hang out with the right kind of people, but I don't know anyone who is afraid of a nail file or cuticle scissors. Yet I have had both of these items confiscated. They weren't given to the pilot for safekeeping, either, to be returned after the flight. They were kept.

Oh, sure, I was given the option of mailing them to my destination, but TSA didn't provide postage stamps or packaging materials. I would have had to get out of line, take a bus back to the parking lot, drive first to an office supply store and then to a post office, and then drive back to the airport. How ridiculous. A wise guy might declare that the TSA is more synonymous with overkill than a terrorist. Perhaps "excessive" is a better word under the circumstances.

I witnessed a raging argument between a TSA security agent and a young mother who was feeding her baby from a bottle as she was passing through the security checkpoint. Seems that the baby was hungry, but the security agent found that the milk bottle was too large to meet security requirements. I would think that if the baby could drink the formula without any harmful effect, the milky liquid was not likely to be explosive. But that would be me.

Many women now carry plastic knitting needles instead of metal ones, because the plastic needles don't show up on X-ray scanners. Has it occurred to anyone that a plastic needle can be just as deadly as a metal one, when thrust into the brain through the ear or eye?

I've seen women merrily knitting away with plastic needles, both at the gate and on the plane, but the TSA does nothing about it. Who are they kidding?

Also banned in carry-on luggage are shoes with gel inserts. I have Dr. Scholl's gel insoles in all my footwear – jogging shoes, hiking boots, and dress shoes – because they provide extra cushioning and comfortable arch support. According to the TSA list of banned items, I can't carry these shoes in my daypack, but I can wear them on my feet. Who's kidding whom? Are they afraid that a terrorist is going to stink someone to death?

Not with a Bang, but a Whimper

Sometimes I carry a pair of water bottles in my day-pack. Either they are already empty, or I empty them before reaching the security checkpoint. Afterward I refill them from a drinking fountain or a lavatory spigot. Then I add powdered, sugar-free Tang to make a refreshing drink to imbibe during the flight.

Liquids and gels must be carried in containers that have a capacity of no more than 3.4 fluid ounces. This size was chosen to limit the blast radius of chemical explosives by not permitting more than 3.4 fluid ounces of an explosive to be mixed.

A passenger's aggregate of such containers must fit in a one-quart clear plastic bag. The number of chemical containers was chosen to limit the amount of explosive material that a solitary terrorist could carry onboard.

I can't be the only person to think how easy it would be for a *group* of terrorists to combine their quota of chemical explosives, and mix them in an empty water bottle.

Who does the TSA believe they are placating by enforcing such meaningless restrictions?

Federal Phantasms

I have friends who hold Top Secret security clearances, or higher – such as Sensitive Compartmented Information. They have stories to tell that boggle the mind. Most of the stories I have never heard because they are highly classified. They don't tell me, and I don't ask. I curb my curiosity with the knowledge that they won't reveal state secrets anyway, and my insistence would only strain our friendship. And if they did mention something accidentally that I was not supposed to hear, it could compromise their job or level of clearance.

I cannot give out their names for reasons of security – *their* security. But I *can* tell travel tales that are non-classified, as long as I protect their anonymity. I will combine these people in the nom de plume of a single character and use the masculine pronoun. Let's call "him" Derf (Fred spelled backward).

As a federal government courier, Derf was transporting a sealed briefcase that was filled with sensitive documents. He had official paperwork that authorized him to transport the briefcase, and that sanctioned its passing through airport security without being unlocked or examined in any way, including metal detection and X-radiation. He also had photo ID's from the DOD, the FBI, and the CIA. But Derf still had to remove his shoes and walk through a metal detector. It stands to reason that if Derf had wanted to destroy a plane, he would have hidden explosives in the briefcase and not in his shoes or elsewhere on his person.

Another Derf was on the way to a tradeshow. He was carrying a collapsible banner that was too long to fit in his suitcase. This nine-foot-long banner consisted of three metal rods that folded down to three feet. This was not a problem as far as TSA was concerned, so he passed through security without a hitch. He returned home that night, then flew out of the same airport the very next day. This time a different TSA supervisor was on duty. She would not permit Derf to take the banner on the plane, claiming that it could be used as a weapon.

The TSA took away an eyeglass repair kit that one Derf had in his briefcase. This was the kind of kit that they sell in supermarkets and pharmacies; it was the size of a stubby pencil, and consisted of three itty-bitty screws and a tiny screwdriver, for replacing lost screws in the temple. They claimed that the kit was dangerous. Note that they didn't just take the tiny screwdriver and let him keep the screws; they took the plastic tube and all its contents. After passing through security, he was able to purchase an identical kit from a concourse vendor.

One female Derf wore a leather hairband through the security checkpoint. They took away her pencil, but said nothing about the long metal rod that held the hairband in place. The rod was the length of the pencil, and the points were much sharper.

Time is of the Essence

Sometimes the lines at airline check-in counters are extraordinarily long. People are checked in on a first-come-first-served basis. This system is fair under most circumstances, but not when departures are imminent. A lot of people miss their flights because there is no mechanism for serving passengers whose planes are preparing for takeoff.

There are times when people need to be taken on a priority basis, even if it means jumping to the head of the line. But this isn't allowed. Travelers are forced to wait their turn no matter how urgent their needs.

We can be thankful that hospitals don't operate this way.

United Airlines has emplaced a rule that passengers must check their baggage more than three-quarters of an hour prior to departure time. Otherwise they will not be allowed to check in.

A Derf of my acquaintance arrived at the airport nearly two hours before his plane was scheduled to depart. He spent more than an hour in a slowly moving line. When he reached the self-check-in console and tried to process his ticket, the machine refused to issue a boarding pass because he had a suitcase to check, and only 44 minutes remained before the scheduled departure time.

Heavens to Murgatroyd – he was one minute late! Not late for departure, but late for checking in a suitcase. United could not blame this one on the FAA.

Anxiously he explained his plight to a nearby attendant, expecting human intervention in the programmed response from the computer. The attendant refused to help, claiming that adherence to the rules was absolutely paramount. An argument ensued. He may as well have been arguing with the computer. The attendant shook her head and reiterated endlessly that the rule could not be broken.

Derf had to take a later flight and miss a high-level security meeting.

Section Seven
Sacred Subjects
or Touching the Untouchables

Forbidden Topics

There are certain subjects that people are loathe to discuss because of the possible repercussions against their reputation. I think that I have demonstrated sufficiently that I bar no holds, and that I have no compunction against putting my rational self on the line. When I call 'em as I see 'em, I do so with logic and reason that oppose senseless sentiment and emotion. I've taken flak for this in the past, and I'm likely to take more flak in the future. So be it.

There are absurdities even in those institutions that are considered sacrosanct. An absurdity is absurd no matter who is offended by having the absurdity pointed out to him.

The State of the Union

When I applied for the apprenticeship program at Local Union #98, the International Brotherhood of Electrical Workers had a simple and straightforward process for determining eligibility. Applicants were required to take an aptitude test.

Electricity is dangerous. Electrocution is an occupational hazard. Electrical work consists of a wide variety of disciplines, from highly technical electronic control work to bending pipe to pulling wires to connecting high-voltage distribution panels to reading wiring diagrams to splicing wires to hooking up motors to installing services with "hot" cables to . . . well, you get the point.

The apprentice program is four-years in length. The hands-on part of electrical work is learned through on-the-job training. The theory of electricity and its technical applications are learned in the classroom. The classroom studies are intensive. A great deal of time is spent on the science of electricity and mathematical calculations. Apprentices are also taught how to treat victims of electrocution: cardiopulmonary resuscitation, artificial respiration by mouth-to-mouth, and other life-saving methods.

The number of new apprentices was determined by attrition of the previous year: as union members retired, moved away, or died.

The union wanted only the brightest and best-educated applicants because, if an electrician made a mistake on the job, it could result in the injury or death of a coworker. Therefore, apprentices were chosen by their test scores, from the top toward the bottom. If the union wanted to hire twenty-eight apprentices to fill one classroom, they accepted the applicants who achieved the twenty-eight highest test scores: from number one to number twenty-eight. This method ensured the finest quality in union electricians.

The government threw a kink into this perfectly logical system when it enforced the hiring of minorities in occupations that did not meet the newly established ratio. Minority applicants did not always qualify for the electrical union because they failed to meet the academic standards. As a result, the percentage of electrical union minority workers was below the government par.

In order to rectify the disparity, the next batch of apprentices was required by law to contain a certain number of minorities. Of the fifty-eight apprentices in my graduating class, seven were minorities. The only way to get those seven minorities into the union was to deny membership to seven applicants who were better qualified. In the event, more than fifty better-qualified applicants had to be skipped over before the highest-scoring minority was reached. I don't know how many applicants were skipped over in order to reach the seventh minority applicant.

The union did not discriminate against minorities. It simply accepted the cream of the crop of applicants. The federal edict imposed reverse discrimination, by discriminating against people who possessed intelligence and education, because these smart individuals did not have the right color skin or the correct ethnic background. Furthermore, minority apprentices could not be flunked out of the apprentice program no matter how poor their grades.

This free ride for minorities resulted in unqualified electricians, and in the downgrading of the union intellectual pool. The minorities in my classroom constantly interrupted the classwork because they did not understand the science and could not do basic math. Some were high school dropouts. Teaching came to a grinding halt while the instructor explained to the minorities what the rest of the class readily understood.

I've shared a foxhole with minorities, and I was glad that they were in there with me to protect my back. The most dangerous deep dives of my career I shared with a minority; my life was entrusted to him and to his expertise. Many of my friends and acquaintances have been minorities. I have nothing against minorities who have earned their place in society by means of study and hard work. What I deplore is discrimination that has bureaucratic approval.

Every occupation entails some form of discrimination. The electrical union discriminates against dim-witted applicants. Movie producers discriminate against aspirants who can't act. Theatrical agents discriminate against hopefuls who can't sing or dance. Research and development companies discriminate against claimants who do not have college degrees in the sciences that they are researching and developing. Computer companies discriminate against people who have no background in computer technology. School systems discriminate against would-be teachers who have not earned bona fide teaching degrees. Auto repair shops discriminate against contenders who cannot fix engines or adjust brakes properly. Civilian offices discriminate against secretaries who can't type or take dictation. And so on, and so on . . .

Do you enjoy watching movies whose actors can't make expressive faces? Would you watch a show whose players can't hold a tune or keep in step? Do you want unqualified scientists recommending drugs for your child's medical condition? Would you be happy with a computer that didn't work because the designers were inept? Do you want your children taught by teachers whose primary qualification for the job was being a minority? Do you want your car repaired by someone who doesn't know what he is doing? Would you want a secretary who couldn't do basic secretarial work? Do you want your house wired by someone whose slipshod work might result in burning down your domicile? Do you want to undergo surgery by a doctor who got into medical school only because a quota had to be met?

Ask yourself these questions when the subject next arises with respect to guaranteed employment for people who can't do the job for which they were hired, while those who *can* do the job are collecting unemployment compensation. When you hire incompetent workers, the work they do will be substandard.

If minorities want good-paying positions in America's workforce, they should have to work for that position the same as non-minorities do. They should accept the public education that is offered to them. They should learn to speak and write the English language well, because accurate communication is important, and English is the national language of the United States.

Minorities are not deprived of public education. In many cases they refuse to accept it. They should be made to accept responsibility for that refusal.

The Union of Discontent

Anyone who has read *The Jungle* by Upton Sinclair knows what the world was like before the advent of unions. My paternal grandfather was laid off from his job with the railroad after nineteen and a half years of faithful service, so that the company wouldn't have to pay retirement benefits. Unions put an end to sweat shops, low wages, long hours, and shameful exploitation of workers by unscrupulous employers, in addition to setting standards of pay and fair treatment for non-union shops.

But unionism is a double-edged sword whose blade cuts both ways. Unions can be as corrupt as the companies whose policies they seek to temper. In the 1970's, the balance of power between contractors and unions swung like a pendulum out of control to the side of the unions, corrupting an inherently imperfect organization which operated beyond the pale of checks and balances that form the cornerstone of any democratic system.

A common union affectation in its opposition to the supervisory power that was wielded by contractors was the sanctimonious attitude of the membership with respect to perceived grievances. Unions stood up for members under the theory that they were innocent members of the family. No matter what the circumstances, the contractor was always wrong. The epitome of this attitude occurred when police investigators arrested a handful of union members who destroyed hundreds of thousands of dollars' worth of property belonging to a non-union contractor. The local unions established a defense fund by increasing dues and by withholding money from our pay, with full knowledge that the accused members were guilty of committing the crime. The rationale was that a strong legal defense was for the good of the union.

I objected strongly to supporting the defense of acknowledged criminals. If they did something wrong, they should pay for it. The willful destruction of property stretched far beyond the presumption of upholding solidarity. My standpoint aroused disapproval from fellow workers who sided with the accused simply because they belonged to a union, as if membership bequeathed God-given rights to which other citizens were not entitled.

In my experience, unionism is nearly always fanatical.

An Insider's View

I dealt with other union inequities on a daily and more personal basis. The stereotypic blue collar worker is perceived as a person who guzzles coffee, gawks at girls, curses with regularity, and makes too much money. It's true that construction workers are well paid, and with good reason. Jobs are seasonal with unemployment common when cold weather sets in. The work can be harsh under outdoor conditions of extreme heat in summer and subfreezing temperatures in winter. And the work is dangerous.

This latter condition is often overlooked by white collar workers whose severest injury on the job might be a paper cut. Construction sites are full of hazards. Minor injuries abound, major accidents occur, death sometimes eventuates. I once had all the skin burned off both hands by hot tar that slopped through an air vent in the roof.

During the construction of one skyscraper there were five fatalities in the eighteen months that I spent on the job: a stone mason fell off the side of the building when a marble slab slipped from the clutches of a crane and fell through the roof of the cab, crushing the operator; one carpenter was catapulted out of the side of the building (before the walls were erected) when the scaffold on which he was standing collapsed; another carpenter fell down an elevator shaft when he tried to walk off with a sheet of plywood that covered the opening; I don't remember how the fifth one died.

An electrician was electrocuted when he grabbed a high-voltage bus bar that was mistakenly energized. His heart stopped and he was stuck to the copper bus by reflexive muscle action, but his partner kicked the ladder out from under him, administered CPR and mouth-to-mouth resuscitation, and brought him back to life. These accidents were deeply regretted, but no one thought the number was unduly high.

The truth of the matter is that most construction workers are conscientious, highly skilled, and honest – but they don't get their share of publicity. Furthermore, the paranoia rampant in union ideology plays upon a person's innate weaknesses and subordinates his ability to overrule ingrained allegiance. Bad influence is difficult to overcome without uncommon strength of character.

I worked with some men who stumbled over an hour's work in a day only because it was unavoidable. Yet when a contractor fired such a sluggard, the union took the side of the member despite the evidence against him. If unions had a mechanism for getting rid of idlers who give unions a bad name, a greater purpose would be served.

Instead, the union keeps recycling members despite their overt reputations as trouble-makers and non-producers. Such a member would be sent to a job site; the foreman would recognize the member, would know right away that he wasn't going to work, would give him the requisite two-hour payment for show-up wages, and send him back to the union hall. Some workers collected as many as four show-up checks in a single day: full pay for the day. The union had good cause to kick these members out of the union, but never did.

I knew for sure that our union was in trouble was when one of the worst loafers was elected as a business agent.

Union Slowdowns

Electricians had to buy their own hand tools (an expense that is not required of office workers). I was nearly crucified when I showed up with a spiral ratchet screwdriver. This ingenious hand-operated tool both tightened and loosened screws by pushing down on the top of the handle instead of twisting the handle. Rotation was imparted to the screw head by means of spiral-cut grooves in the shaft. I could tighten a screw in one second flat with one or two pushes; whereas it took many seconds and a great deal of exertion on the wrist to turn a solid-shaft screwdriver manually. The union disallowed the use of this tool because it was too fast and efficient.

Contractors furnished powder-actuated tools. Although this tool was called a "gun," because it fired a .22 caliber cartridge to actuate a piston which propelled a fastener into concrete, it would discharge the blank round only when the muzzle was pressed hard enough against the concrete to push back the slider that otherwise prevented the firing pin from striking the primer. You couldn't point it at someone and shoot him with a pointed fastener.

When installing conduit or electrical metallic tubing on a concrete surface, we "shot" fasteners into the concrete in order to secure the clamps. During the first year of my apprenticeship, I was shooting away one day as the shop steward watched my evident expertise with the gun, and the rapidity with which I laid EMT. He called a meeting with the foreman and my pusher (a sub-foreman in charge of a gang of workers, not a drug lord). In order to retard my productivity, they contended that apprentices were not allowed to use powder-actuated tools.

Prior to joining the union, I was a weapons specialist in the Army infantry. I qualified as expert in all light arms from the Colt-45 automatic pistol, the M-14 semi-automatic rifle, the M-16 automatic rifle, the M-60 machine gun, hand grenades, and the M-79 grenade launcher, to the light anti-tank weapon (the modern version of the bazooka). In training and in combat, I had probably fired more rounds than everyone else on the job put together. You can understand how absurd their proclamation sounded to someone with my level of experience – especially as I had never fired any weapon as *small* as .22 caliber. Furthermore, I was fresh from the battlefields of Vietnam, while none of the trio had even served in the military, much less in combat.

They took the gun away from me. For the rest of that job, I had to use a hammer and star drill to gouge circular holes in the concrete, then use expansion bolts to secure the clamps. This process was physically exhausting and took many minutes instead of several seconds.

On another job, the foreman threatened to fire me because he said that my productivity made the other workers look bad by comparison.

Yet when I became a foreman, I found that a hard-work policy can become infectious, resulting in greater satisfaction among the employees and more work accomplished for the contractor. The latter equates to larger profits, which does more to further the cause of unionism than complaining about picayune matters.

Unhealed Wounds

According to union diatribe, non-union workers were "scabs" who took work away from the union. Try as I might, I was too blind to see any distinctions between union workers and non-union workers. All had families to support, mortgages to pay, children to educate, and community obligations to observe. My failure to distinguish one from the other led to arguments in which I defended the rights of non-union workers to earn a living and provide financial security for their families.

I reasoned that there was a discrepancy in the notion that non-union workers took away jobs. There were only a certain number of jobs to go around, and no matter who got those jobs, the same number of workers were employed. In the big picture there was no loss of work. In actuality, the distribution of work was uneven and discriminatory.

Instead of campaigning against non-union workers, I suggested, why not bring them into the fold and let them join? Then "they" would be "we": one big happy family working together toward a more equitable lifestyle for all. If this sounds socialistic, the concept is no more socialistic than the doctrine behind unionism. The majority of non-union workers would have jumped at the opportunity to join. The main reason they didn't already belong was because the unions wouldn't admit them.

I found no sympathetic ears among my fellow members. They all believed that the door to the local union hall should be closed behind them in order to protect the status quo. Thus unionism in practice was not the same as unionism in theory. In practice, unions urged inequality: disadvantaging certain individuals to sustain the advantages of the select.

The union philosophy was not one of sharing the wealth, but of protecting the wealth by preventing others from sharing in it.

Union Make-Work Projects

This insufferable mindset reached idiotic proportions in an instance when fluorescent ceiling fixtures were delivered to a job from a factory that had pre-wired the tube assemblies complete with a five-foot armored cable extension that was ready for splicing into a junction box. The union held that the cable extension took work away from electricians on the job. (In the past, the flexible steel sheath was cut from a 100-foot coil and was installed on site; wires were then cut and pulled through the cable.) The union forced the issue by having a worker undo the internal splice, pull out the wires, hacksaw two inches off the steel cable to simulate the time it took to cut it off the coil, then reinstall the wires and splice a new connection – on every one of thousands of ceiling fixtures. And the contractor had to pay wages for this absurdity!

Another time, a tractor-trailer arrived at the job site to deliver electrical supplies. The trucker was intent on doing his job quickly and professionally, so he could get back on the road. He had half the truck unloaded before someone discovered what he was doing. The shop steward not only made him stop unloading the truck, but made him reload the material that he had already unloaded.

According to union rules, truckers were only allowed to place boxes on the tailgate. Electricians then put the boxes on the ground because it was "their" work.

Arguments between shop stewards of different trades erupted all the time on big jobs. Unions were obsessive about which work was theirs. There's no such thing as interdisciplinary cooperation among union construction workers. If a box of electrical material was in the way of tile setter, he wasn't allowed to move it aside; he had to go find an electrician to move it for him. If a plumber stacked pipe where a partition was supposed to go, a carpenter had to get a union plumber to move the pipe. And so on ad infinitum, ad nauseam.

The watchword on union jobs was rivalry. The watchword on nonunion jobs was teamwork.

IBEW Pension Fraud

I prefaced these subsections about unions by noting that in nonunion days, when employers held the upper hand, my grandfather was laid off six months prior to the time at which he could claim retirement benefits from the railroad.

For ten years I paid union dues and had money withheld from my pay for my pension plan. Despite this tenure, when I reached the age of retirement and applied to the International Brotherhood of Electrical Workers for benefits, they refused to acknowledge my vested pension. They also refused to return the money that I had paid into the pension plan.

As a dues-paying union member, I fared no better than my nonunion grandfather.

Disunion

In addition to my inside views of union operations, I have also had views from outside the union. When I retired from the electrical union, I started a career as a freelance author, underwater photographer, and lecturer. I was hired to lecture at a technical diving conference that was being held at the Moscone Center in San Francisco.

Union laborers jealously guarded their jobs. If any vendors attempted to bring in their own booths and materials, they were stopped at the door. Moving anything inside the building was union work. A lot of tables and booths had to be moved into position, but there were only so many laborers to do the work. Vendors were frustrated by delays that lasted several hours.

I experienced the epitome of this "moving" attitude when I set my projector on a table that was provided as a projection stand. Because the image was slightly larger than the screen, I moved the table about six inches closer. A union laborer happened to be hovering at the auditorium doorway. He rushed across the room and angrily announced that if I wanted the table moved, I had to call for a laborer to do it. I was not allowed to move the table myself.

This led to an argument. I moved the table again right in front of his eyes. He threatened to get the shop steward to shut down the whole symposium. I called his bluff by telling him to "go ahead and do it." (In actuality, I used a two-word phrase in which the word "off" was preceded by a four-letter epithet.) He stormed out of the auditorium. I proceeded with my presentation. The shop steward never appeared.

The technical diving conference became an annual event. They never again held the conference in San Francisco; and, I was given to understand, many other conference holders avoided San Francisco like the plague, because of the same counter-productive union radicalism that I experienced. In the long run it was the unions that lost out, because no one wanted to put up with them. Conference holders moved to other cities.

Rules of Order

It is important to keep in mind that "rules" are neither "laws" nor "regulations."

Rules cannot be enforced by the police, by district attorneys, by judges, by juries, or by Congressional mandates. No one will serve time for failure to follow rules. There may be consequences for disobeying rules, but generally only for those individuals who belong to the organization that promulgates them, and only if those individuals wish to maintain their membership.

Likewise, union rules are private guidelines or procedures which are not enforceable by the justice system. Union members can be disciplined by the union for breaking union rules, but such disciplines cannot be enforced upon people who don't belong to the union.

If a union member commits some grievous offense against the union, he can be kicked out of the union. But he cannot be prosecuted in court.

The union could not do anything to me for moving a table at the Moscone Center. They could have lodged a complaint against the conference committee, who then could have tried to intimidate me into cooperating with the union: for example, by threatening not to invite me to lecture at future conferences. But no one could fine me, jail me, or have the police expel me for my effrontery at not going along with an obviously absurd situation.

The union could have picketed the Moscone Center. That would have been advantageous to the conference vendors because they would no longer have to deal with the union; they could then move all their own equipment and tables.

It is illegal for pickets to physically prevent anyone from crossing a picket line. Pickets may intimidate people by their presence, but it is unlawful for pickets to make vocal threats or threatening gestures. Vendors, presenters, and attendees could have crossed the line with impunity from union interference.

Intimidation works only against people who allow themselves to be intimidated.

The Snapshot Rule

The rule that irks me the most is the one that forbids photography in public and private institutions such as museums and art galleries. Many times I have asked for an explanation of the rule. No one has ever been able to give me one. Staff members merely parrot what they were told to say: "Photography is not allowed." (Or "not permitted.")

When I've asked to see the printed text in the rulebook, it couldn't be provided. After many years of asking this question, I've come to the conclusion that there *is* no rulebook; or, if there is, it does not contain any explicit text that forbids photography.

The rule against photography appears to be one that is commonly accepted for no other reason than the fact that it is commonly accepted. Someone made it up one time, and it caught on among museum staffers the way a catchphrase catches on among the public at large.

Nor is there any rationale for a "no photography" rule. No staffer has even given the matter any serious thought; they merely accept it as a given, like the phases of the moon, because "that's the way it is." This moronic attitude is passed on from senior staff members to junior staff members so that the entire staff is infected with a bunch of nonsensical rules whose origin is unknown.

This kind of "staff infection" pervades museums and galleries like the bacterial infection that it simulates. This manmade infection is untreatable and self-perpetuating. It started sometime in the distant past, and spread like a disease that cannot be eradicated.

There is nothing illegal about taking pictures in a museum or gallery. Security guards cannot arrest you, nor can they confiscate your film or delete digital files from your camera. Under extreme provocation they may call the police. Your best defense is to stay calm and not make a scene – and quietly take your pictures. Staff members or security guards may try to intimidate you into vacating the premises, using the pretext that breaking a museum rule is synonymous with breaking the law. Argue quietly but firmly and maintain your position. After you've made your point, and gotten all your pictures, you may concede to leave the building – but only after your admission fee is refunded. Otherwise, stand your ground.

Even if police respond to a call, there is nothing they can do to you. You can freely admit that you were taking pictures. The police are empowered to enforce the law and maintain the peace. Because you have broken no laws and are acting peaceably, he will be in a quandary about how best to resolve a situation that the museum has created. You should act politely and reasonably. Let the museum people get angry and lose control.

Imagine a staffer shouting to the police, "He was taking pictures!"

On more than one occasion I have been accosted by museum staffers because I was caught taking pictures. (I wasn't trying to hide the fact.) When they recited the museum mantra ("Photography is not permitted."), I simply shrugged, said "I know," and walked away. None has ever called a security guard. I was never thrown out of a museum for taking pictures. The rule is unenforceable unless a pusillanimous patron lets himself be bullied into submission.

Rule of Thumb

In the preceding subsection, I did not mean to imply that you should break rules just for the fun of it. You shouldn't lean against display cases because you might break the glass. You shouldn't touch paintings because you might damage a priceless work of art. And you shouldn't do things that are socially unacceptable.

I am not advocating anarchy. I am merely suggesting that you don't allow yourself to be treated like a sheep.

Most rules are based on reason. For example: don't step across the white line while a bus is in motion because you will block the driver's view. Don't jump to the head of the line because it violates the system of order. Don't eat or drink in a library because you might spill food or water on a valuable book.

On one hot summer day in a New Jersey beach restaurant, the manager would not seat me because I was wearing a sleeveless T-shirt. The situation was awkward because my friends were shown to a table while I was held back at the door. This put me on the spot.

Two women who were standing behind me thought that they were going to be turned away too, because they were wearing sleeveless blouses, but the manager seated them without comment.

Naturally I asked why he let them eat but not me. He explained that New Jersey health codes did not permit patrons to exhibit underarm hair. I understood, but I told him that I didn't have another shirt with me. He provided me with a loaner that he kept on hand for just such an occasion. I returned it after the meal.

Many rules have been around for so long that no one bothers to question them. People obey them because they are told to do so. Men are not allowed to carry small knapsacks into a museum; yet women are allowed to carry large handbags. Taxpayers are not allowed to enter a school building unless he is a student there or has an appointment, despite the fact that his taxes support the maintenance of the building. Stockholders are not allowed to enter the premises of companies in which they own stock.

Sometimes, rules are made up on the spot in order to browbeat visitors or exercise authority over them. This occurs mostly in government offices, such as when a clerk tells you to stand on a certain spot and gets angry if you move away from that spot.

My point is not to disobey rules for the purpose of making trouble, but to question rules that seem arbitrary and capricious. Then act rationally and appropriately.

Destitution Bound

There is so much talk about the war on poverty that one might believe that a truce is in the offing. Nothing could be farther from the truth (or from a truce).

I make this statement bluntly: poverty will never end. Never, ever. This war is one that cannot be won.

To elaborate, poverty will never end because people won't let it end. The "people" in this case constitute two disparate groups at opposite ends of the spectrum: those who wish to end poverty, and those who wish to maintain it.

To word it differently, the so-called "people" are infected with a bipolar disorder in which the mainstream of society lives well at one pole, while a few poor folks survive as best they can at the contrasting pole. These two groups of people constantly work against each other; neither is willing to yield.

There is not even solidarity among mainstream patrons who judge the standards of poverty and attempt to make amends for societal disparities. A commonplace sign of the times is one that proclaims severely: "No shoes. No shirt. No service."

This means that a needy person who can't afford footwear or upper body raiment is denied the right to obtain the very attire that he must possess before he can acquire those items: a classic paradox in logic or catch-22 (with appreciation to Joseph Heller for coining the term if not for inventing the concept).

If you gave your pocket change to an undernourished child who was barefoot, he would not be allowed to enter a store to buy the basic sustenance that he needed to satisfy his hunger.

On the other hand, if you gave cash to properly clothed adults, some of them would waste the money on everything *but* food while their families starved. So why give them anything?

The sad truth of the matter is that most poor people are poor because they choose to be.

Hear me out before you brand me as the worst bastion of heresy.

Renters Disease

One of my earliest jobs as an electrician was doing renovation work on a low-cost housing project. With respect to housing, "low-cost" referred to the rental rate that was charged to the tenants, but equated to high cost for the government agency that subsidized construction and/or maintenance of the project.

Due to the establishment of stricter building codes, the Department of Housing and Urban Development (HUD) required specific modifications to be made to existing living quarters that were occupied by low-income tenants. For the most part these modifications consisted of installing additional electrical outlets in apartment buildings.

It is interesting to note that high-cost apartment complexes were not affected by these code changes because those structures were not under the authority of HUD. Thus low-income tenants received advantages that high-income tenants did not.

My workmate on this job was Roger Heist. Fishing wires through walls entailed time and expense that were not within the budget. Instead, we installed surface-mounted raceways and outlet boxes called Wiremold.

Every day we had to enter occupied apartments and work around tenants who never seemed to be gone for work. I was awestruck as I watched one woman empty her trashcan by opening the window of her second-floor apartment, and dumping the contents into the alley. Old trash in the alley was piled more than five feet high. Out of sight, out of mind . . .

One family had a dog that was tied to the kitchen table by means of a yard-long length of rope. Day after day the dog defecated within its sphere of travel. The excretions had not been picked up for weeks. Dozens of stinking turds lay scattered under the kitchen table. The children kicked them aside when they sat down to eat. No one bothered to pick them up.

In another kitchen, we had to move the electric range in order to install a dedicated outlet on the wall behind it. Cooking grease was splattered so thick on the linoleum that the legs of the range were cemented to the floor. Neither of us could break the range free from its coagulated bondage. Only by shoving in tandem did we manage to rip the legs out of the solidified grease. Then the range got away from us; it slid across the floor like a skater on ice, until it crashed against the opposite wall. A horde of cockroaches exploded in all directions after the roof of their home ceased to cover them.

I stuck the end of my rule in the indentations that were created by the vacated legs. The grease measured more than a quarter inch thick.

One apartment stank so bad that neither of us could breathe in it. My nose and throat constricted when I tried to inhale. The slightest whiff of air made me gag. We did the job by taking turns at breath holding: one of us would take a deep breath, dash into the apartment, work until he needed to breathe, then escape into the hallway to gasp in some semi-fresh air; the other would do the same while the first one was catching his breath. It took twice as long to screw Wiremold to the wall, pull conductors through the raceway, make splices, and connect wires to the receptacle, but that was the only way we could get the job done. Meanwhile, the lone woman who occupied the apartment sat indifferently in a chair in the living room.

Squalor was not confined to quarters. The hallways were littered with refuse. The plaster walls were gouged with holes. Broken glass was sprinkled on the floor because tenants had shattered the fixtures to steal the light bulbs. The fire escapes were used as trash dumps, making it difficult to walk up and down the stairs.

The laundry room was a disaster area. Most of the machines didn't work because tenants had torn them apart to steal coins from the collector box, or because they had ripped the tubing out of the wall to sell the copper for its scrap value. I didn't see any rats, but their droppings lay thick behind the machines.

One tradesman caught a couple engaged in stand-up sex in the stairwell. They didn't pause or glance in his direction as he passed them on the landing.

These people didn't *have* to live the way they lived; they *chose* to live that way.

Making Do

I was appalled by the difference between the low-income (or no-income) populace of suburban Philadelphia and the peasants I met in Vietnam.

The villages and hamlets had no running water, no electricity, no heat or air conditioning, no appliances, no motorized conveyances, and no artificial means of communication. The people lived in thatched-roof huts with bamboo walls. Their furnishings were handmade. Their clothing was sparse. They had no money. They appeared to my ingenuous eyes to be poor . . . until I later saw what poor meant in America.

Vietnamese peasants were primitive, not poor. They possessed a keen strength of character. All except the smallest toddlers worked in the rice paddies every day, all day. Water buffalo grazed outside the village perimeter. Pig sties were positioned among surrounding hooches. Chickens ran freely throughout the hamlets.

Yet every village was immaculate. There was no such thing as litter. Mamasans regularly swept the dirt floors of the hooches. The dirt passageways that separated the hooches from each other were without cigarette butts, scraps of paper, or chicken poop. Men and women squatted on the ground without complaint, while children sat quietly at their sides.

Vietnamese indigents were more cultured and better mannered than their Philadelphia counterparts. They were clean, hard-working people. The City of Brotherly Love would be better off with their tired, poor, huddled masses than the ones the city was saddled with.

If the taxpayers only knew how their hard-earned dollars were being misspent.

The Housing Project Debacle

Urban renewal projects with low-cost housing have been in existence for more than half a century. Most of these projects have long since been demolished: first by the people who lived in them; then, when the buildings became uninhabitable and not worth the cost of repairs, by demolition crews.

The most famous of these projects was Pruitt-Igoe, in St. Louis, Missouri. This massive complex consisted of thirty-three 11-story buildings that contained 2,870 units. Construction was completed in 1956 at a cost of more than $55 million. The tenants were so destructive that the entire complex had to be torn down after only twenty years of use. Footage of the collapsing buildings was used in the no-dialogue visualization movie *Koyaanisqatsi*.

That should have been the swan song for low-cost housing projects, but supposedly smart people in government didn't take heed from this fiasco.

At its prime level of occupancy, the Cabrini-Green project in Chicago, Illinois housed more than 15,000 impoverished people. Tenants slowly wrecked the apartments until the buildings had to be imploded with dynamite because they were unsafe to occupy. Similar projects in other large cities met identical fates. Yet the government keeps building them at the taxpayers' expense, so that non-taxpayers can destroy them.

The Difference and Indifference of Being Poor

You would think by now that the do-gooders in the country would have learned the lesson that there are two kinds of poor people. I call them the "good poor" and the "bad poor."

The good poor are unfortunate folks who are temporarily out of work, or have low-paying jobs, or suffer from impaired mental capacity. Despite these handicaps, they are honest people who want to raise their families as best they can with what they have.

The bad poor are ingrates, deadbeats, and criminal types who avoid honest work, who steal or destroy public property, who prey upon innocent people, who take advantage of a system that was designed to assist the good poor, or all of the above.

The difference between the two kinds of poor is "attitude." The good poor have a positive attitude toward life, while the bad poor have a negative attitude. Poorhouse advocates either don't understand this difference or they refuse to accept it. They lump paupers together as if all of them were downtrodden by an unsympathetic society. In trying to be fair to everyone, irrespective of their tendencies for good or evil, they further the interests of the bad poor who undermine the respectable intent of the system, and who ultimately destroy it through their felonious activities. The good poor – those underprivileged people who deserve the support of society – lose out as victims of collateral damage. Worse, they end up being castigated by the masses because they are tarred with the same brush that blackened the bad poor.

There is a solution to the problem of helping the deserving poor, but it will take courage to implement the necessary changes.

Disqualifying the Bad Poor

Whether you like it or not, the first thing you need to understand and accept is the reality that there will always be poor people. Always. There are several reasons for this.

Some people choose to be poor. Although these people are poor by choice, I don't mean to imply that they have made a conscious decision to be paupers. Rather, they have chosen to do everything in their power to escape from honest employment. Because they don't *want* to work for a living, they have elected to be poor by default.

Shirkers include career petty criminals who are incompetent at their preferred vocation; corrupt women who pick motherhood as an occupation so they can live off the proceeds of their children, whether it be from multiple child support or from government subsidy; and arrogant individuals who believe that they shouldn't have to work because the world owes them a living. These parasites wouldn't accept work if you gave it to them; they want handouts, not jobs. They are the nonproducing dregs of society.

These are harsh words, I know; but they are true words. I don't feel sorry for any of these lowlifes. They deserve to be as destitute of material wealth as they already are of basic morality.

Some people are poor because they are low-functioning. This category includes individuals who, through no fault of their own, were born without the mental capacity to comprehend the intricacies of high-paying jobs. They are relegated to low-paying jobs that do not require much thought: jobs that can be learned by rote and repetition. Not only can these people be good at those jobs, but they are glad to have them. Furthermore, they are not discontent with their station in life. Because of their impairment, they can hardly conceive of a better way of life: a kind of blindness that works in their favor. They appreciate a helping hand.

Then there are those who are mentally deficient: from the underdeveloped to the severely retarded. They are to be pitied for their lack of intellectual inheritance. They may be able to hold menial jobs with some supervision. They are satisfied with their lot because they lack the comprehension to desire anything more.

Now comes the tough part: convincing society to separate the good from the bad, in order to provide for the good and exclude the bad, and to isolate the bad so they can't harm the good segments of society. If this means building big prison camps, let it be. This is cheaper in the long run because it replaces the cost of construction and demolition of subsidized housing projects and apartment complexes.

Poor people should have to qualify for government subsidies and low-cost housing. Right now, the only qualification is poverty. If different criteria were applied – say, lack of a criminal record and a willingness to accept work – the good poor could receive more benefits because the benefits that are available would not have to be shared with criminals and undeserving loafers.

Another way to reduce poverty is to increase the minimum wage. Employers would compensate for the decrease in profit margin by increasing the retail price of their products, thereby spreading the additional production cost throughout society as a whole.

An alternative way for the poor to accrue monetary benefits is to pair those benefits with working hours. Instead of giving away money in the form of free subsidies that do not differentiate the good from the bad, job holders could earn credits for every hour worked. Credits could then be turned in for food stamps, which have acceptable spending constraints.

All these methods together can replace the present welfare system, and put malingerers where they belong: in jail or out in the cold.

The stumbling block to overcome is convincing do-gooders and politicians that welfare reform supersedes their personal agendas. Guilt-ridden do-gooders suffer from the mistaken belief that bestowing enough money on poor people will raise them out of poverty. Politicians historically pass legislation that is geared toward their reelection, by advocating bills that sway the largest contingent of benefit recipients to vote for them.

They don't accept the fact that poverty is a state of mind.

Raising the Bar

As I noted above, poverty can never be abolished – and for more reasons than those that I have already cited.

If you look back into history, you can readily see that the most poverty-stricken individual today is richer than the richest person who lived a mere two centuries ago. I am talking in terms of living standards that most people take for granted.

At the time of the War of 1812, America was largely an agricultural society. Most of the population lived on farms, in log cabins that did not have electric lights, central heat, air conditioning, fire alarms, smoke detectors, sprinkler systems, labor-saving appliances, insulated walls, hardwood floors, wall-to-wall carpets, telephones, radios, televisions, DVD players, and numerous other amenities that are nowadays considered standard.

In those days many children went barefoot until they reached their teens. Women did not have brassieres or tampons. Men did without silk shirts, creased trousers, and velour sweaters. No one had cotton swabs, dental floss, aspirin tablets, ballpoint pens, microwave ovens, automobiles, health insurance, or thousands of other items and commodities that are commonplace in the twenty-first century.

Come to think of it, America in the eighteen hundreds sounds much like Vietnam today. Americans didn't complain then, and Vietnamese don't complain now. Complaints come from modern Americans who bemoan the things that they don't have but aren't willing to acquire if it takes hard work; or any work.

Poverty can never be abolished because society keeps redefining the term. Yesterday's luxuries are today's necessities. Today's luxuries will become tomorrow's necessities.

There can never be a perfectly homogenized society. There will always be some people who are not as smart as others; some who are physically weaker than others; some who have less initiative than others; some who can't dunk a basketball as well as others; and some who just don't give a damn.

Section Eight
The Insanity Clause
or Santa Lost His Way

Hodgepodge 101

In this final chapter I will get the ball rolling by introducing a wide array of absurdities and unexplainable doings that I have encountered at various times throughout my life. There is no rhyme or reason to the arrangement, any more than there is rhyme or reason to the non-quantifiable situations that are portrayed. Perhaps disorder is appropriate.

The Dual Key Dilemma

Ever since I first learned to drive a car, I have wondered why they came with two keys: one key to unlock the doors and trunk, and a different key to turn the ignition. The door key had a square finger grip; the ignition key had a round finger grip. Having two similar keys meant that you always had to look at each key in order to determine its function.

I have asked about this a hundred times and have never gotten a satisfactory answer. No one seems to know. I have questioned auto dealers, auto mechanics, used car salesmen, and key makers. Mostly they just shrugged and grinned.

The only one to even hazard a guess was a salesman at a Chevy dealership. He suggested – without much conviction – that if you lost your door key and an unscrupulous person found it, and if that person knew to what car it belonged, he could open the door and ransack the interior but he could not start the engine and steal the car. This explanation was spacious at best.

The corollary to this speculation is that if you lost your ignition key and an unscrupulous person found it, he couldn't steal the car because he couldn't open the door. I submit that this is not an insurmountable problem for any unscrupulous person who possessed a brick or a jack handle.

In either case, I never met anyone who kept the two keys on different key rings. They always kept both keys together on the same key ring. It goes without saying that you can't lose one key without losing the other.

Be that as it may, I always found two keys a burden – just another chunk of metal to cram into my leather key case. I was ecstatic when I bought a new Chevy van that came with a single key to operate all four doors plus the ignition . . . until I learned the peculiarities of the key. To my chagrin, the key unlocked the driver door by turning clockwise, it unlocked the passenger door by turning counterclockwise, it unlocked the side door by turning clockwise, and it unlocked the rear door by turning counterclockwise. The key switched on the ignition by turning it clockwise. I had to live with this idiotic lock design for the next ten years.

The situation worsened when I bought a Ford van. Not only did I have the same clockwise and counterclockwise problem, but the lone key's finger grip was encased in molded plastic so thick that I couldn't snap my key-case cover over it. To make matters worse, the remote device for the electronic door lock was twice the size of the key.

This is a clear case of absurdity becoming more absurd – or, if I might coin a comparative word, becoming absurder. I would also like to coin the superlative word absurdest, except that such a word implies that there is a limit to human absurdity, which I think is absurd.

Hooray for the Handicapped

I could never understand the reasoning behind the award of handicaps to golfers and bowlers who were less skilled in the sport than winning professionals. The way the handicap system works, a player is given points to make his average score equivalent to that of a player who has a higher average score. In other words, it puts all the players on the same playing field.

In theory, this gives a less-skilled player a better chance to win against a more-skilled player. In reality, it reduces the more-skilled player to playing against himself. In order for the more-skilled player to win, he no longer has to get a higher score than his less-skilled opponent; he has to get a score that is higher than his own average score.

In other words, the more-skilled player is penalized for his greater skill. In competition, there is no longer any difference between a more-skilled player and a less-skilled player. They are all "average" players.

In Perspective

If the educational system adopted this practice, A students would have two grades taken away from their grade point average; B students would have one grade taken away; D students would be given a grade; and E students would be given two grades. Everyone would graduate with a C, the same as the average student in the middle of the bell curve.

There would be no students at the top of their class, and no students at the bottom of their class. This arrangement would represent a true classless society.

Hitting Below the Belt

Wearing seatbelts used to be a choice that intelligent people made for themselves. Somewhere along the line, the American government decided that it had to take that choice away from its citizens, on the supposition that its citizens weren't smart enough to wear seatbelts on their own responsibility. The government passed a law that made wearing seatbelts mandatory, subject to a fine for noncompliance.

This law – like many other do-good laws – took away an inalienable right that was guaranteed by the Constitution of the United States. An identical parallel is the helmet law for motorcyclists.

I would not be surprised to learn that seatbelt advocates, lobbyists, and political proponents were heavily invested in the auto industry, which stood to profit the most by such a law. But that is only speculation on my part.

State and federal representatives who sided with the passage of the law stood to gain by garnering votes at election time, because a strong stand on safety would show how much they cared about the health and welfare of their constituents.

Be that as it may, the seatbelt law does not apply to everyone. There are exclusions. Absurd exclusions. And absurder exclusions.

Absurd: drivers and passengers on mass transit vehicles do not have to wear seatbelts. Indeed, seatbelts are not even provided on taxis, buses, trams, trains, trolleys, or streetcars. An intelligent person who wants to protect himself in the event of a crash is unable to do so.

Absurder: seatbelts are not provided on school buses, either. Children, society's most valued commodity, are totally unprotected in the event of a bus crash. With all the hoopla about protecting children – from neighborhood watches to strict child pornography laws – it is absurd that a mother and her children must obey the seatbelt law when she drives the kids to the bus stop, then sees them merrily on their way through high-speed traffic without seatbelts.

Mail-order Conundrum

I don't know how many times I've seen catalogues and mail-order advertisements that are accompanied by this caveat: Allow six to eight weeks for delivery. It must be thousands. I've always wondered why a company should take so long to send a product. The implied rationale is that the U.S. Postal Service is responsible for the time delay. Not true.

In general, USPS can deliver a first class envelope anywhere in the contiguous forty-eight States in three to four days. It (or they) can deliver a parcel post package in a week to ten days. Thus the total time for which the USPS is responsible is two weeks at most. I have confirmed this timeline in two ways: my check has always been cashed less than a week after I mailed it, and the postmark proved when the package was delivered to the Post Office.

By simple subtraction, the company must spend four to six weeks in processing an order. Why so long? The second implied rationale is that the company is backlogged because it is besieged with orders. However, the fallacy in this rationale is: How can a company *always* be backlogged the same amount of time?

To put it another way, how can a company *start* with a backlog? There can't be a backlog when the very first order is placed. A backlog must increase gradually as more and more orders are received. Yet the delivery time never changes: it never gets longer; it never gets shorter. The company always takes a month to a month and a half to process an order. So what is actually happening to an order while it is being "processed?"

If you were hoping that I was going to furnish an answer to this conundrum, you will be sadly disappointed. One of the frustrating aspects of absurdities is that often they can't be explained. They just are.

My best guess is that an order simply sits idle while the company rakes in money.

One might suppose that a responsible company that got behind in handling orders would hire extra help until there was no more backlog. But this never happens. It appears that taking orders has priority over fulfilling obligations. The customers in this case always come last.

Who's on First?

One of a shopper's most frustrating pastimes is standing in line to get service, to pay for purchases, to obtain information, and so on. Sometimes the lines are long because "they" (the store or company or government agency) did not hire enough clerks. Other times there are not enough cash registers to handle a temporary load.

One time I was in a particularly long line that was moving slowly. Every time the line moved ahead by one person, the woman behind me shoved her shopping cart against my butt and ankles. I am not by nature an aggressive or hostile person, but after she bumped me for the third time, my patience was exhausted. These bumps were no mere accidents. I turned around and shoved the cart hard against her fat belly. I said angrily, "Stop bumping me with your cart, Lady."

Instead of apologizing, she stammered, "But someone will get in front of you," implying that anyone who got in front of me, got in front of her.

I spoke in a voice that was calm but firm. "No one will get in front of me. The order is determined by my position in line, not by how much space separates me from the person in front of me. Now keep your distance."

She grimaced, but did as she was told. Afterward, to irk her and to prove my point, I intentionally left a large space between me and the person in front of me – large enough to fit a person and a shopping cart.

The shopping line shuffle proceeded without interference.

What I find particularly annoying is not shopping line pushers – who are few and far between – as much as phone line jumpers. How many times have you stood patiently in line, or sat in front of someone's desk, only to have the clerk or office worker postpone your business in order to answer the telephone, and then keep you in abeyance while he engaged in a long conversation with the caller?

The sad truth is that telephone calls take precedence over people in the flesh. One time I got so frustrated by the number of phone call interruptions that I went home and called the department in whose line I had been standing. I got immediate assistance. Of course, this scheme works only when you are in line to ask for information.

Even this scheme is not foolproof. While a phone call takes precedence over someone in person, a second phone call takes precedence over the first phone call. Nowadays, with the proliferation of Call Waiting, the first phone call is put on hold while the clerk deals with the second phone call.

As it is written in the *Bible*, "The first shall be last and the last shall be first." How did the disciples know that, two thousand years ago?

The Monopoly Muddle

President Teddy Roosevelt made history and friends, as well as corporate enemies, when he instituted federal antitrust laws that sought to disband conglomerates that were fixing prices and monopolizing business. The original trustbuster would be appalled to learn that a century later the American government was actively supporting monopolies under different guises.

Government-sanctioned monopolies and federal price-fixing gambits are so entrenched in American society that people take them for granted, failing to recognize them for what they are, despite the impact they make on everyday life.

After I started my publishing business, I received regular promotions from Pitney Bowes. They were in the business of manufacturing franking machines, or postage meters. The basic machine or meter consists of a scale, a calculator, and a printer. You placed an envelope or package on the scale, selected the postage class, and printed a metered stamp. Advertisements extolled the convenience of not wasting time in the post office, and of saving money by not putting excess postage on bulky envelopes.

It sounded like a worthwhile long-term capital investment, but there was a catch. You couldn't purchase the machine; you could only rent it. After some basic figuring, I calculated that the rental fee was way more than I could ever hope to save on postage. Convenience was a problematical virtue.

Pitney Bowes made no money on the sale of postage; there was no mark up. They earned their income on the rental of the machine. No matter how much or how little you used the machine, Pitney Bowes had a guaranteed profit. Only Pitney Bowes and three other companies were licensed by the government to own the machines.

How did they get a gig like that? What Article or

Amendment empowered the government to choose which companies could make a guaranteed profit by monopolizing the postage meter business? Why wasn't this business conducted by the U.S. Postal Service, which had to perform the delivery service for which the postage was purchased?

I don't know.

Notice how sleekly and insidiously the government avoided referring to the franking machine rental business as a monopoly. Instead, these companies were "licensed" by the government to perform a service, for which they received a comfortable income.

In addition to "licensing," another euphemism for a government-sanctioned monopoly is "concession." For example, the National Park Service chooses which concessionaires may operate gift shops and snack bars within Park boundaries. These concessionaires possess preferred vendor status to the absolute exclusion of non-sanctioned vendors (who operate outside Park jurisdiction, and who offer less expensive goods and services).

These government approved companies oppose free enterprise.

A Trashy Situation

Other monopolies are tolerated as long as they are owned and operated by the government. A case in point is the collection of trash in Philadelphia. Cost increases grew to such an extent that a private contractor offered to assume the collection of Philadelphia's trash for half the amount that taxpayers were already spending – and calculated that he could still make a sizeable profit by means of more efficient operation. He even offered to buy the city's trash trucks as part of the bargain.

The city commissioners turned him down cold. As their reason, they cited the loss of jobs of city employees. This rationale was typical bureaucratic thinking. The loss of city jobs would have been exactly offset by the jobs that would have been made available when the private contractor hired new workers.

Bureaucrats! Can't live with them, can't kill them.

It Works When It Works . . .

On occasion I've had trouble with my credit cards. Most difficulties were easily resolved. For example, on one road trip I nearly ran out of gasoline in a shore resort where the prices were jacked up beyond all reason. I bought just enough fuel to enable me to drive another fifty miles, where I knew the prices were more reasonable. When I tried to buy cheap gas an hour later, the tank went dry after pumping less than a gallon. I drove for another couple of miles, found a gas station that had anticipated weekend traffic, and filled up.

When I tried to use my credit card several days later, it was declined. I called Discover to ascertain the reason. It turned out that their computer system was programmed to automatically put a hold on an account when certain usage criteria were met. Three gas station purchases within an hour triggered an alarm because it simulated the usage of a stolen card.

The Discover representative was apologetic, but I assured him that I was not annoyed in the least. After all, the protection was for my benefit.

Another time, I went shopping on an Internet used-book consortium. I placed items in my shopping cart until I was ready to check out. A dozen booksellers were paid at one fell swoop. Within hours I started to receive email acknowledgments from fast-acting store owners. The next morning, however, I started to receive cancellation orders from slow-acting vendors, who claimed that my credit card had been declined. I called Discover. The rep explained that although I made a single payment to Abebooks.com, the consortium did not process the transactions; instead, each vendor acted individually. The computer shut down my account after the first few transactions because of the quick multiple usage trigger. The rep reopened my account, and placed an override on the computer for temporary abeyance of the multiple usage trigger. I reordered the books without further difficulty.

On yet another occasion, I was on a road trip when my credit card was declined. I called Discover. Once again the computer had closed my account because of short-term multiple usage. Only this time I was not responsible for triggering the default. My credit card had been counterfeited. I was in South Carolina when the counterfeit card was used to make purchases in Louisiana. This time the account remained closed. The rep assured me that I was not responsible for the unauthorized transactions, and that my account would be reinstituted with a different account number. A new card would be sent to my home overnight. I could not access my new account until I authenticated receipt of the replacement card.

I did not plan to return home for several weeks. So I switched to my Visa account. Only then did I learn that the card had expired, and the replacement card had been either stolen or lost in the mail. They promised to send another card with a new account number to my home.

This left me in the middle of a trip without a functioning credit card: a difficult situation for a traveler in modern day society. I muddled through, but determined upon my return to obtain another backup.

. . . Except When It Doesn't

I currently receive at least one pre-approved credit card offer every week. I submitted the next application that was delivered in my mail. Several weeks later, my application was declined without explanation. Next I submitted two pre-approved online offers; both were declined. I submitted half a dozen more during the following year. Every one – even though it was pre-approved – was declined without explanation. I concluded that the pre-approval announcement was a promotional scheme (or scam).

Unlike most Americans, I had no debts. My mortgage was paid off. I did not have a vehicle loan. My credit cards and utilities were paid automatically every month by electronic transfer from my savings account; I had never missed a payment. My financial situation was clearly in the "no risk" category. Little wonder that I was always pre-approved. So why were my applications declined?

I was still pondering this strangeness when I decided to move to the mountains. I found a house that I liked, and made an offer that was accepted at once. Realtor Al Francino hooked me up with a mortgage company called Countrywide. Renee Wyant, Countrywide's broker, calculated my earnings and pre-qualified me for the mortgage. When she checked my credit score, she found that my credit rating exceeded 800. This placed me among the top 13 percentile of Americans, meaning to creditors that I occupied the least risky category.

But, despite the fact that I was putting down more than 25% of the purchase price on the mountain house, and earned sufficient income to meet the computed monthly mortgage payments, she found a quirk that kept Countrywide from approving the loan.

I was deceased.

It was news to me. I was still breathing. My pulse was normal. I ate low-fat foods on a regular basis. I drank enough liquids to keep myself properly hydrated. I jogged two or three times a week. I made public appearances. And what's more, I paid my bills on time. Nor did I sleep in a coffin.

Night of the Living Dead

I was a consumer, but not a consumer of human flesh or blood.

My presumptuous decease led to a number of comical conversations between Renee and me. After she read my Internet bio, she commented that I was pretty active for a dead person. I retorted, "You should have seen how active I was before I died."

The problem stemmed from a credit card account that MasterCard had cancelled for lack of use. The credit score form consisted of a series of check boxes. As a reason for cancellation they had checked the wrong box, and sent me off this mortal coil (in an economic sense).

Equifax, Experian, and TransUnion all had me listed as dearly departed. Yet they also showed that for five straight years after my exaggerated demise, I continued to pay my credit card bills on a monthly routine – something that dead people are not in the habit of doing. Nor do zombies, vampires, or other undead monsters act responsibly in financial matters.

This misapplication of my livelihood explained why my credit card applications were denied despite a perfect track record and imbursement history. But it left unexplained why no one ever noticed the disparity between my passing and my paying. Don't potential creditors – who are living and breathing and supposedly intelligent human beings – ever examine the credit reports and correlate them with the scores? Apparently not.

Flight of the Phoenix

Death hadn't slowed me down in the least, or impaired my ability to think. I called MasterCard and explained that I had risen from the grave only to learn that newly sought creditors entertained grave doubts about my fiscal responsibilities. Although my voice on the phone proclaimed my current animation, they saw in their records that I was indeed being carried as one of the late lamented. Two kind ladies commiserated with my situation. I didn't have any difficulty in convincing them of my liveliness.

They were eager to help correct an obvious clerical error. In order to update their records, however, the company required some form of proof other than an anonymous voice on the telephone. I faxed them a copy of my driver's license slash photo identification, which had been issued after my premature burial. They quickly put me back into the land of the living.

Resurrection Deferred

The mortgage company subsequently approved the application for which I had already been pre-qualified. But one debacle led directly to another.

The day before settlement, first Al the realtor and then Renee the broker called to tell me that the mortgage company had changed its mind and refused to make the loan. Renee's supervisor had "re-run the numbers" (recalculated my earnings) and now ascertained that I did *not* make enough money to fit their ever-tightening formula of income versus outlay. My annual income was short by $250!

The realtor went ballistic. He shouted, "I spend that much in a weekend." How could they turn me down for such a miniscule amount?

The broker was nonplussed and apologetic, but unable to effect any change because her supervisor's authority superseded her own. She tried to come up with some kind of plan that would meet the bank's requirements and satisfy the supervisor's objections.

The realtor and the broker stood to lose their commissions, and I stood to lose a retreat that I wanted very badly.

The Fax of Life

I didn't like having my fate in someone else's hands. I took the immediate initiative to call my own bank (Wachovia) and make an appointment with the local mortgage consultant. Julie Davies worked my numbers and pre-qualified my application. Two days later I had another mortgage commitment. Settlement was rescheduled . . .

. . . but there was one more hitch in my gitalong. Wachovia approved the mortgage, but when I left my Philly house for the office of the lawyer who had done the title search and who was handling the settlement (Anthony Roberti), the bank had not yet sent the commitment papers to him. Not until thirty minutes before the scheduled time of settlement did the bank fax the paperwork to his office. He barely had time to finalize the settlement sheet and make photocopies for the seller and me to sign.

How did bankers conduct business before the invention of the fax machine? Pony Express?

After the settlement, Renee, the Countrywide broker, learned that her supervisor had made a mistake in reworking my earnings. She had accidentally left out a sizeable portion of my income. I received no apology from either the supervisor or her bank. I threatened to sue, but I didn't. I claimed a chargeback with my credit card company, to recover the amount I had paid for the mortgage application. Countrywide did not refute it.

Boob Tube Anomalies

When pay television was first announced, it was promoted as an alternative to broadcast television because their movies and shows did not have commercials. Cable companies relied on viewing fees for profits. Now viewers could watch television without annoying interruptions. This created a minor problem for viewers because they no longer had gaps between shows to go to the bathroom; they learned to live with it.

As cable and satellite companies continued to grow in popularity, they gradually introduced commercial advertisements as a way to augment their earnings. Now people had time to go to the bathroom.

But, now pay TV viewers were not only inundated with long commercial advertisements, they were *paying* to watch them.

The Veblen Effect . . .

. . . is an anomaly that is not likely to go away any time soon. In 1899, University of Chicago professor of economics Thorstein Veblen published a book entitled *The Theory of the Leisure Class*. This now-classic volume espoused the manner in which rich folks prominently and wastefully exhibited their wealth as a means of establishing recognizable status. Veblen coined the phrase "conspicuous consumption" to describe this extravagant expenditure of gross income (or gross expenditure of extravagant income).

Nowadays, the best way to display conspicuous consumption is to purchase items that are identified by their exorbitant price tags. Manufacturers have been quick to take advantage of this quirk of human nature – "keeping up with the Joneses" – by creating merchandise with classy but empty-headed appeal. These overrated products have come to be known as Veblen goods.

Take an ordinary pair of dungarees, price them double or triple what they are worth, advertise them as designer jeans, and voila! – you have produced a Veblen good. These jeans are no better than any other pair of dungarees – they are not made of better materials and they won't wear longer – yet people pay for them through the nose: not because they represent a good value for the money, but because they cost so much.

Want to make those dungarees even more attractive? Drag them behind a car in order to age them artificially, tear them apart at the knees to simulate long and common usage, and voila! – now you have faked a pair of poor farmer's dungarees that are all the rage.

The great contradiction in these Veblenesque products is that increasing the price serves to increase the demand. People pay for "show" value instead of actual worth. The purpose of purchasing extortionate dungarees is to prove to the Joneses how much money you can afford to spend on frivolities – assuming, of course, that the Joneses share your attitude, and prize frivolous spending as much as you do.

Luxury candies fall into the same category. If you want to impress someone with how much you are willing to spend on a gift, you can give her a box of Whitman's chocolates at $10 per pound, Russell Stover chocolates at $33 per pound, or Godiva chocolates at $45 per pound. Godiva chocolates are no more scrumptious than Whitman's (in my opinion). The extraordinary price is what sells the more expensive product, not the flavor or consistency. High-priced chocolates literally melt your money in your hand as well as in her mouth.

Fine wines don't tease the palate much more than low-cost brands. Flashy cars must still obey legal speed limits. Real diamonds don't glitter much more than artificial diamonds or exquisitely poured and cut glass, and are largely indistinguishable from the lower grade commodities unless you examine their facets under a loop. In fact, many women who own tremendously expensive jewelry wear paste in public because they are afraid of theft. It the fake jewels can fool everyone but the experts, what's the point of buying the real stuff?

All these items and more qualify as Veblen goods. Given the penchant that Americans have for false imagery, buying nothing for something is probably a permanent phenomenon.

The Appliance of Insurance, and Vice Versa (with Emphasis on Vice)

Manufacturers have found a new way to make money over and above the sale of their products. It's called "extended service warranty." In the old days, I refused to buy appliances that came with only a 90-day guarantee. If the manufacturer didn't believe that their washer or dryer would last most than three months without breaking down, who was I to disagree?

Today most appliances and electronic gadgets come with one-year guarantees. This sounds reasonable, but make sure you read the fine print. My new furnace came with a five-year warranty, but when it broke down after two years of mild use, I had to pay a service call charge of $85 to replace a warranteed part. (I was not charged for the $50 part.) Comfortmaker, the manufacturer of the furnace, did not reimburse me for the service call.

Make sure that parts *and* labor are included in any guarantee.

That being said, how good of a deal is an extended service warranty for both parts and labor? It depends on the product, the repair cost of the product, the replacement cost of the product, the cost ratio and duration of the extended service warrantee, and the integrity and capability of the warranty provider.

Rocket science it's not, but let me throw some examples at you to make it easier for you to understand what you might be up against, and why I've reached the conclusion that I will advocate at the end of the subsection below, entitled "The Self Service Plan."

The first gimmick you'll encounter is carefully worded misinformation about the length of the extended service warrantee. Take this typical example: "You'll be protected for three full years for only $150." Fast talk and simple math might lead you to believe that the cost that you must pay up front and in full equals $50 per year. Not bad. But when you think it through, you'll realize that the first year is already guaranteed for free. The extension on the original warrantee is two *additional* years, or three altogether, not three additional years. This means that you'll be paying $75 per year for those extra two years. Not so good.

The real fallacy with respect to large household appliances (washers, dryers, refrigerators, dishwashers, trash compactors, and water heaters) is that defects are likely to manifest themselves in the first year of usage, when the manufacturer's original warranty is still in effect. Aside from working the kinks out of the system, appliances are unlikely to break down in the second or third year from ordinary usage. Most manufacturers won't extend their warrantees beyond three years because there's no profit in it, as that is when breakdowns are likely to occur from normal wear and tear.

In the long run, it's better for the consumer to gamble without an extended service warrantee, especially in light of my alternative strategy. (See below.)

Nowadays there's a bandwagon rush to offer extended service warrantees for practically every product that has moving parts or electronic components, and even some that don't. In most cases, these plans pay off in little more than peace of mind, and sometimes not even that. Salesmanship is based on the premise that consumers find comfort in the belief that their product won't cost them any more money than what they have already paid. Like most beliefs, this one is not supported by any form of proof, and often delivers only a false sense of security.

Two possible exceptions to my stricture against extended service warrantees are for vehicles and computers. I wrote "possible" because much depends upon the correlations that I noted six paragraphs above.

Driving Miss Daisy Crazy

Take a Ford van whose sticker price is $36,000 and for which the extended service plan costs $2,000 for six years or 100,000 miles, whichever comes first. The cost ratio is 5.5%; that is, the cost of the extension package is 5.5% of the cost of the vehicle. Two thousand dollars is a lot of money to lay out on a gamble that you might not recoup, but not as much as you think when you consider what the package includes, and its potential for saving you money over the lifetime of the vehicle.

The bumper-to-bumper package covers everything from soup to nuts and bolts, except for certain spelled-out components that are maintenance items. Some exclusions are tires, brake pads, muffler, light bulbs, and wiper blades (but the wiper motor is *not* excluded). Except for the exhaust system, these exclusions are relatively inexpensive items. The *in*clusions are the expensive items: engine, transmission, drive train, universal joints, and emergency roadside assistance.

Because so many mechanisms are difficult to reach, and a lot of time may spent on disassembling and reassembling unaffected hoses, wires, and components, labor is generally more expensive than parts. The average repair bill today is in the neighborhood of $500. A transmission job can easily cost $4,000 to $5,000.

So maybe – just maybe – an extended service plan for your vehicle is worthwhile. It's up to you to apply a formula that weighs cost against usage. If you're a little old lady from Pasadena who uses her car to drive to the market once a week, you're wasting your money. If you habitually travel cross-country to out-of-the-way places, it might be worth its weight in gold.

If you never have a major problem, take joy in the fact that you weren't stranded for a week in Lower Jebip while your transmission was overhauled.

HAL 9000 and Beyond

In the 1970's, when Texas Instruments started marketing handheld calculators, I rushed to the store to buy one. The retail price was $110. They were selling so fast that they were sold out by the time I got to the store. The clerk told me that more units were on order, and should be available the following week. A week later I returned to the store. Not only were the units in stock, but the price had dropped to $100. I was shocked. Usually the price goes up when a product is in demand.

The price continued to drop over the next several years, like a falling stock: $10 here, $20 there. In the 1980's, rapid advances in microchip technology drove calculator prices down to $10. Eventually, office superstores were giving them away for free just for making a purchase. I got a couple that were the dimensions of a thick credit card, and that fit in my wallet.

A similar transformation occurred with laptop computers. The physical dimensions were constrained by an ergonomic keyboard and a screen with a comfortable viewing size, but the price dropped dramatically as memories got larger and speed got faster. My first computer cost $6,000; my last cost $500. For one-twelfth the cost, I now have a computer that is more than a thousand times better with regard to memory and speed. It's also more dependable.

Computers can be touchy, unreliable, and expensive to repair. They can go caput at any moment, as well as time and time again. They're great when they work, frustrating when they don't. And if you don't know this already, then you're from another planet.

When I switched on my Dell computer in the morning, I never knew if it was going to start up properly. I had so much trouble with it that I would have been on a first name basis with the techies if there hadn't been so many of them spread around the world, and if I could have understood their thick foreign accents. They were smart; just indecipherable. In any case, the problems were not with the hardware but with the inferior Microsoft operating system: Windows ME. Dell got stuck with having to fix a bad product that was furnished by a subcontractor that didn't accept the liability of its shortcomings.

When my hard drive went up in smoke (literally),

Dell shipped me a new computer by Federal Express.

Next I upgraded to Toshiba, both with and without an extended service plan. In case #1, I paid $1,000 for a laptop that I bought from Circuit City. The store offered to extend the one-year warranty for two more years, for an additional cost of $200; or $100 per year, at a cost ratio of 20% of the purchase price. I bought the total package only because Toshiba didn't advertise on the box that it offered the same deal for less money. Not until I uncrated the computer at home did I learn the error of my ways.

The software suffered several minor glitches that required technical support that was provided over the telephone. The average time per session that I was put on hold was thirty minutes to an hour. The techies were not all that conversant with my make and model. They tried different operations until one of them fixed the problem. The average trial-and-error session lasted from twenty to thirty minutes.

One time I had a glitch that the techie couldn't fix. He had me go through a dozen routines; none of them worked. Finally he threw in the towel and told me to call Toshiba's technical support team. I could do that, but because I bought my service plan from Circuit City, Toshiba required prepayment of $25 per session before they would agree to provide support.

I learned to live with the problem but that wasn't the point. I had paid for a service that Circuit City couldn't furnish. I wrote a nasty letter to the company and demanded my money back for the extended service warranty. They pointblank refused.

The lesson I learned was to buy a service package direct from the manufacturer, not from an aftermarket outfit that lacked honesty, expertise, and dependable response time.

Another thing to keep in mind is that stores go out of business. When that happens, your service plan is terminated. It makes more sense to buy a service contract from a big-name manufacturer who understands the product and who is likely to be around for a while.

When I bought my next Toshiba laptop, I figured on buying the extended service warranty direct from Toshiba. According to the application form in the box, a two-year extension on the one-year guarantee cost $400, or $200 per year. Since I paid $500 for the computer, the cost ratio was an outrageous 80%.

This is equivalent to paying $28,800 for an extended service warranty on that $36,000 van that I used as an example in the previous subsection.

I decided to gamble on the quality of the product, justifying my decision like this: manufacturing defects were likely to appear during the first year of operation, while the computer was under its original warrantee. If I had a minor problem after the initial year, I could probably get it fixed via Toshiba technical support for an acceptable amount of money: $25 for telephone software support, or somewhat more if I had to return the unit to an authorized repair center for hardware support.

Even if the computer became a total loss, I was already $400 ahead of the game. I could buy a brand new computer for only $100 more than I had saved by not purchasing the sucker plan. And the new computer would be faster and have more memory than the old one.

I'm keeping my fingers crossed.

Cold Spell

The Philadelphia Gas Works currently charges $99 for its annual parts and labor plan for a natural gas furnace. According to their advertisement, customers "enjoy savings from costly repair bills and peace of mind knowing that reliable service is right around the corner." With this plan, PGW guarantees that "a trained, professional technician will provide service" on the same day if you call before noon, or no later than the next day if you call after noon.

I paid for this plan for 36 years. Granted that 36 years ago PGW didn't charge $99 per year, but the cost factor was the same in proportion to the average annual income of the time. Viewed from a different perspective, today's charge is pro-rated in accordance with the inflation index. What this means is that over the course of 36 years, I paid PGW the equivalent of $3,564 in today's dollars.

During the time that I paid for protection, the furnace operated flawlessly and didn't need a bit of attention. When it finally broke down, I confidently called the Philadelphia Gas Works maintenance plan hotline to report the problem. That was when I learned the cold-hearted truth about the value of PGW's parts and labor plan.

It might have been true that reliable service was right around the corner. What the ads neglected to mention was that the service wasn't around *my* corner. The telephone dispatcher duly informed me that I couldn't expect to receive any service for at least two weeks. In the event, three weeks passed before a maintenance worker put in an appearance. During all that time my house was totally without heat.

The worker spent all of two minutes in looking over my furnace. Then he announced that it couldn't be fixed.

I said, "You have to fix it. I have the maintenance plan."

He told me that they didn't stock parts for my furnace any more. It was too old. The furnace would have to be replaced, but replacement wasn't covered by the parts and service plan. He closed the gas valve and left.

PGW did not install furnaces. I had to buy a new furnace and have it installed by an independent contractor, at a cost of $1,850. (I received estimates as high as $2,200.) In other words, I paid PGW nearly twice the cost of a new furnace, for a protection plan that provided nothing more than a false sense of security.

Had I not paid PGW for a worthless maintenance plan for all those years, and banked the money instead, I could have paid for the new furnace with the money I saved, and gone on a free Caribbean vacation while the furnace was being installed.

The Self Service Plan

The moral of all these horror stories is that extended service warranties or parts and labor plans are usually not worth the investment on an individual basis, and are certainly a waste of money when taken together in aggregate.

They often expire without being needed. The purchase price might not be cost effective with respect to the actual cost of repair or replacement of the unit. When you do need service or repair, you might learn that the warrantor is incompetent and can't or won't do the job. You might find your warranty voided altogether by a clearly unscrupulous warrantor that promotes exaggerated service that they have no intention of providing.

Extended service plans are big money makers for the warrantors. If there were no profit in it, warrantors wouldn't try to sell you the package. But if you follow my advice, you can be fully protected for extended service, parts, and labor, and save some money in the long run. Much money. Not only the money that you will save by not purchasing such plans, but the huge profits that those plans would otherwise earn for the warrantors.

The service plan that I advocate is global in nature. It covers all your appliances in one fell swoop. It pays on demand. It pays in full. It not only saves money; it earns money. And it relieves you of the frustration of dealing with disreputable warrantors time and time again. That is true peace of mind.

Start by opening a dedicated savings account at the bank of your choice. Whenever you buy a product for which you wish to have an extended service plan, deposit into this account the money that you would have paid to the warrantor. The account will grow quickly, not only from funds that you add periodically, but from interest that accrues on the balance. Before you know it, you will have enough dough to service all your baking needs.

Whenever an appliance needs service or replacement, pay for it from money in this account. The leftover money will continue to earn interest. If the account grows too large, invest some of the money in certificates of deposit or some other high-yield interest-bearing instrument.

Begin your personal warranty plan today, and enjoy service with a smile.

Miscellaneous Imponderable Notions

My cell phone service is provided by U.S. Cellular. For a flat monthly rate, my service plan includes 750 so-called "free" minutes per month. Although these minutes are advertise as free, they are not: they are built into the price structure of the service plan. On the other hand, toll free calls – calls that are not billed to the caller on a land line service plan, such as 800 numbers and 866 numbers – are billed to me at an additional charge of 25 cents per minute. Why are long distance toll calls free, while toll free calls are not?

My utilities and credit cards are paid automatically via electronic funds transfer; yet all the companies include a return payment envelope with my monthly statement.

The government has legalized price-fixing, but only when the government is fixing the price. It has fixed utility prices under the euphemism of "regulating" prices. Unlike other production companies, utility companies must apply to a government utility commission for permission to raise their rates (and thereby increase the profits for their shareholders). To get around these government regulations, utilities add "adjustments" to their base rate and usage fees.

The Philadelphia Gas Works charged me what they called a "weather normalization adjustment" because I didn't use as much gas as they wanted me to use. Thus I was penalized for my conservative usage of natural gas for home heating purposes.

The Philadelphia Water Revenue Bureau took a different tack. In addition to the standard service and usage charges, they added a fee for "billing and collecting costs." Of my monthly bill of $48.76, $9.21 (or 19%

of the total) constituted "billing and collecting costs." My bill would have been $39.55 without the adjustment. The city's population exceeds 1.5 million residents; you do the math to calculate how much money this adjustment brought into water department coffers – *per month!* My bill was paid automatically by electronic funds transfer from my savings account; this entailed zero billing and collecting cost.

On the other hand, if the government determines that a company has earned too much money on its investments, it penalizes the company by imposing a "windfall profit tax."

My Whirlpool dishwasher is fitted with two racks or baskets that are made of steel which is coated with baked enamel. The vertical separation posts are corroding and falling off like a dog's undercoat in spring. Everything else is functional: the housing, the door panel and lock, the valves, the sensors, the microprocessor controls, the digital displays, the electric motor, the pump mechanism, the heating element, and the wash and rinse cycles. When I sought to purchase replacement baskets from the manufacturer, I found that they cost more than a brand new dishwasher!

The value of diamonds is artificially inflated by diamond consortiums. They control the common perception of rarity by stockpiling diamonds instead of releasing them for public consumption. Billions of dollars' worth of diamonds are stored in warehouses, yet the government does nothing to halt a policy that is clearly fraudulent. To make matters worse, mining companies keep digging for more diamonds to stockpile.

Restaurants are allowed to deceive diners by charging market prices for scallops and crab meat, when in fact they are serving shark slices that are made circular by means of a cookie cutter, and Pacific pollack that is flavored with crab juice.

No matter how you phrase it, a sanitary engineer is still a trash collector, a graphic novel is still a comic book, and a person with a severe mental disorder is still crazy.

AMENDMENT
Living with Absurdities

False Impressions

Not every apparent absurdity is as absurd as it seems; or even absurd at all.

I have heard people complain about the high cost of movies that are sold for home viewing on digital video discs (alias digital versatile discs). The list price of blank DVD's depends upon the purchase quantity. They are not sold singly. The current price for five-pack is about $10, or $2 each; for a ten-pack: $12 or $1.20 each; for a twenty-five-pack: $23 or 92 cents each; for a fifty-pack: $27 or 54 cents each; for a one-hundred-pack: $50 or 50 cents each.

If you can buy blank DVD's in bulk for half a buck, people are wont to say, what gives movie companies the right to charge as much as $50 for one movie on diskette? It appears to be a mark-up of 10,000%.

The answer is simple but often overlooked by short-sighted buyers: you're not paying just for the cost of the diskette and the time that it takes to copy the digital file, but for the millions of dollars that it cost to produce the movie. Nowadays, it might cost upwards of $50 million to make a motion picture. The production cost is then amortized in the sale of DVD's. Added to these costs are the costs of packaging, promotion, and distribution.

No one can ever predict how movie goers will react to a particular motion picture. Some critically acclaimed movies never earn a profit because they don't do well at the box office and because DVD sales are low. Yet a cheap slasher film might make a fortune.

Fifty percent of the ticket price goes to the theater that shows the flick. And 40% to 50% of the gross receipts for DVD sales goes to the retailer. If you think that movies on DVD are overpriced, you have the option not to purchase.

Dumb Plastic

DVD's are kept in paper sleeves or plastic cases in order to protect them from damage. While I was pricing DVD's, I also priced plastic protective cases. They can be purchased in lots of 100 for 35 cents each. The smallest lot available is a package of 10, in which the protective cases cost 42 cents each. This means that a chunk of dumb plastic – a kind of plastic that is simply poured into a mold and doesn't "do" anything – costs nearly as much as the highly sophisticated technical plastic disc that is designed to store high-grade optical media in digital format!

Cardboard mailers cost $1.40 each in packages of four, or 35 cents each. Go figure.

A Prescription for Success

I have also heard people complain about the high cost of prescription medicines. Although it may be inappropriate to repeat what I wrote about DVD's – you have the option not to purchase – the situation is similar in that people fail to take into account the *total* cost of production.

I've seen statistics which claim that the percentage mark-up on the active ingredients in brand-name drugs is in the thousands, or tens of thousands. As everyone knows – or should know – statistics can be skewed to reach preferred but erroneous conclusions.

For example, I once did a survey of diver fatalities on the wreck of the *Andrea Doria*. I found that every fatality occurred during the month of July. Someone who didn't know any better might conclude that July was a bad month for diving on the wreck. When you look at the big picture, however, you see that optimum weather conditions for that area of the ocean run from the last week of June to the first week of August.

Very few trips were scheduled for June because of low water temperatures. Almost no trips were scheduled for August because it was hurricane season. As a result, nearly every trip was scheduled for July. This explained why all the fatalities occurred during that month.

The statistics for drugs was skewed in similar fashion. The mark-up ratio was based only on the production cost of active ingredients in relation to the final retail price, with no other costs factored into the equation. Deliberately ignored were the associated costs of combining the pinch of active ingredient with a sizeable inactive substrate, of compressing and forming the ingredients into the shape of a tablet, of the machinery that was necessary to insert the tablets into individual tamper-proof metal foil wrappers, of packing the foil wrappers inside plastic or cardboard containers, of distributing the containers to pharmacies nationwide, of promoting the product through doctors and newspapers and magazines and television, of the standard mark-up that contributes to the pharmacy's profit margin, and, most expensive of all, of the research and development of the active ingredient.

Pharmaceutical companies may invest tens of millions of dollars and years of laboratory research in the discovery and testing of a single drug, only to learn that the medication is ineffective or has so many side effects as to be useless for human consumption. The whole investment then gets written off as a loss.

When a new medication is discovered to be helpful in the treatment of a condition or disease, the company must then prove its safety and efficacy to the Food and Drug Administration – no small hurdle and an expensive one to boot.

After an FDA-approved medicine goes on the market, mass production can begin and the active ingredient can be manufactured for a miniscule amount. All the monetary steps that precede the medicine's appearance on the pharmacy shelf must be taken into account in order to determine the true mark-up.

On the other hand, the public *is* mislead when pills are advertised as having "extra strength" when in fact the active ingredient is not stronger; there is just more of it: perhaps 500 milligrams instead of 325 milligrams. Three "regular strength" pills just about equal two socalled "extra strength" pills.

Advertising Side Effects

What I do find absurd is television advertising of brand name pharmaceuticals. In many cases, more time is spent on describing adverse side effects than is spent on describing the curative features of the drug.

These cautionary warnings have been made necessary by the rash of ludicrous lawsuits that have resulted when a consumer experienced a minor side effect about which he wasn't apprised. But that's another story . . . for another book. Or books.

Read the rest of this Amendment.

By Way of Explanation

When I initially laid out the book that you hold in your hands, I intended it to consist of three connective parts: The Absurdity Principle, The Ludicrous Lawsuit Syndrome, and The Irrationality Factor.

As I noted in the Preamble, I have suffered from this principle, syndrome, and factor all my life – and always against my will. I have also fought these facets of human nature whenever possible. The present volume can be taken as another form of protest against absurdity, ludicrosity, and irrationality.

When I assembled the notes that I had been collecting for 15 years – 25 typewritten pages of subject titles, and three folders stuffed with cutouts and printouts – I began to see the immensity of the task that I had assigned to myself. I started writing. By the time I had completed half of Part One, I knew that everything that I wanted to write would not fit in a single book-length volume. I either had to delete an enormous amount of material, or I had to improvise. I improvised.

One book thus became three books, each consisting of one of the original Parts. These books are now subtitled "Common Nonsense in Modern Society," "Madcap Inequities in the Legal Process or Tipping the Scales of Justice," and "Discourses in Human Folly."

My improvisation has created some categorical inconsistencies in that some subject matter from either book could just as well satisfy the parameters in one of the companion volumes. This means that my placement of certain topics might seem somewhat arbitrary. I acknowledge this paradoxical condition of overlapping subject matter.

Peel and Repeal

Even three books do not have enough space to contain all the absurdities, ludicrosities, and irrationalities that are part and parcel of modern American society. I suspect that an entire series could be written about ludicrous lawsuits alone, and without being repetitive. Perhaps if I have enough energy, and receive sufficient feedback, I will expand the trilogy to a series. But that is not my intention at this time.

Furthermore, the reader should note that I have written mainly about situations in which I was personally involved, or at least had first-hand knowledge. It boggles my mind to try to imagine how many other situations must exist of which I am totally unaware. I am only one person, relating situations from one life's experiences. If you multiply my personal experiences by the population of the United States, the product will give you some idea of the sheer number of absurdities that must be occurring every day, every hour, every minute.

For now, though, I would like to recapitulate a few of the salient features in the present volume, in order to emphasize their inequities.

It will come as no surprise that I feel great enmity toward the National Oceanic and Atmospheric Administration. Many of NOAA's agencies do great things, such as producing nautical charts, forecasting marine weather, emplacing navigational buoys, and so on. But some NOAA agencies are totally out of control, the National Marine Sanctuary Program being a prime example. This Program is an abomination of the way government agencies are supposed to operate.

The Administration has known this for more than 25 years, yet no one has taken the initiative to hold the agency accountable to the American people, and to ameliorate an intolerable situation. The Program cannot be salvaged. It must be abolished.

In the same light, the Marine Mammal Protection Act must be repealed so that American citizens may have access to their docks and boats without fear of prosecution. It is bad enough that the framers of the Act did not anticipate the negative ramifications in the wording of the Act, and how that wording could be turned against honest people; it is worse that no one in authority has the sense or sensibility to see the harm that the Act is doing, and to do something constructive to remove that harm. The latter is more absurd than the Act itself.

As long as I am on the subject of repeal, I cannot help but mention the Abandoned Shipwreck Act and the other Acts that were passed by a single individual, the disreputable Robert Byrd. Nor can I refrain from mentioning all the riders that he and fellow representatives attached by means of stealth and misrepresentation. These unethical actions are not in keeping with the democratic principle, because the American people did not have a say in their passage.

I submit that Congress should repeal every rider that was ever attached to a bill, in order to give the people and their representatives the opportunity to vote against those riders.

I submit that Congress should repeal every bill that were passed without majority consent. By majority, I mean the way the Constitution intended "majority" to mean: the majority of all representatives, not just those representatives who waited until midnight when the chamber was empty so that could cheat the American people of their voting rights.

It may never happen. It will *probably* never happen. But that doesn't mean that it *can't* happen, if enough people unify their efforts to *make* it happen.

Absurdities – all absurdities – must be eradicated from the face of the Earth, and underground if necessary, else modern society will find itself overwhelmed by their cumulative nonsense, and mankind will go the way of the dinosaur and the dodo.

The Popular Dive Guide Series
Shipwrecks of Massachusetts: North
Shipwrecks of Massachusetts: South
Shipwrecks of Rhode Island and Connecticut
Shipwrecks of New York
Shipwrecks of New Jersey (1988)
Shipwrecks of New Jersey: North
Shipwrecks of New Jersey: Central
Shipwrecks of New Jersey: South
Shipwrecks of Delaware and Maryland (1990 Edition)
Shipwrecks of Delaware and Maryland (2002 Edition)
Shipwrecks of Virginia
Shipwrecks of North Carolina: from the Diamond Shoals North
Shipwrecks of North Carolina: from Hatteras Inlet South
Shipwrecks of South Carolina and Georgia

Shipwreck and Nautical History
Andrea Doria: Dive to an Era
Deep, Dark, and Dangerous: Adventures and Reflections on the Andrea Doria
Great Lakes Shipwrecks: a Photographic Odyssey
The Fuhrer's U-boats in American Waters
Ironclad Legacy: Battles of the USS Monitor
The Kaiser's U-boats in American Waters
The Lusitania Controversies: Atrocity of War and a Wreck-Diving History (Book One)
The Lusitania Controversies: Dangerous Descents into Shipwrecks and Law (Book Two)
The Nautical Cyclopedia
Shadow Divers Exposed: the Real Saga of the U-869
Shipwreck Heresies
The Shipwreck Research Handbook
Shipwreck Sagas
Stolen Heritage: the Grand Theft of the Hamilton and Scourge
Track of the Gray Wolf
USS San Diego: the Last Armored Cruiser
Wreck Diving Adventures

Visit the GGP website for availability of titles:
http://www.ggentile.com

Dive Training
Primary Wreck Diving Guide
Advanced Wreck Diving Guide
The Advanced Wreck Diving Handbook
The Technical Diving Handbook
Ultimate Wreck Diving Guide

Nonfiction
The Absurdity Principle
Wilderness Canoeing

Science Fiction
A Different Universe
A Different Dimension
A Different Continuum
Entropy (a novel of conceptual breakthrough)
A Journey to the Center of the Earth
The Mold
Return to Mars
Silent Autumn
Subaqueous
The Time Dragons Trilogy
        A Time for Dragons
        Dragons Past
        No Future for Dragons

Sci-Fi Action/Adventure Novels
Memory Lane
Mind Set
The Peking Papers

Supernatural Horror Novel
The Lurking: Curse of the Jersey Devil

Vietnam Novel
Lonely Conflict

Videotape or DVD
The Battle for the USS Monitor